PCs
FOR
DUMMIES®
WINDOWS® 7 EDITION

by Dan Gookin

WILEY

Wiley Publishing, Inc.

PCs For Dummies®, Windows® 7 Edition

Published by
Wiley Publishing, Inc.
111 River Street
Hoboken, NJ 07030-5774

www.wiley.com

Copyright © 2010 by Wiley Publishing, Inc., Indianapolis, Indiana

Published by Wiley Publishing, Inc., Indianapolis, Indiana

Published simultaneously in Canada

For general information on our other products and services, please contact our Customer Care Department within the U.S. at 877-762-2974, outside the U.S. at 317-572-3993, or fax 317-572-4002.

For technical support, please visit www.wiley.com/techsupport.

Wiley also publishes its books in a variety of electronic formats. Some content that appears in print may not be available in electronic books.

Library of Congress Control Number: 2009937837

ISBN: 978-0-470-46542-4

Manufactured in the United States of America

10 9 8 7 6 5 4 3 2 1

WILEY

About the Author

Dan Gookin has been writing about technology for over 20 years. He combines his love of writing with his gizmo fascination to create books that are informative and entertaining and not boring. Having written more than 115 titles with 12 million copies in print translated into more than 30 languages, Dan can attest that his method of crafting computer tomes seems to work.

Perhaps his most famous title is the original *DOS For Dummies,* published in 1991. It became the world's fastest-selling computer book, at one time moving more copies per week than the *New York Times* number-one best seller (though as a reference, his book couldn't be listed on the *NYT* Best Seller list). That book spawned the entire line of *For Dummies* books, which remains a publishing phenomenon to this day.

Dan's most popular titles include *Word For Dummies*, *Laptops For Dummies*, and *Troubleshooting Your PC For Dummies*. He also maintains the vast and helpful Web page www.wambooli.com.

Dan holds a degree in communications/visual arts from the University of California, San Diego. He lives in the Pacific Northwest, where he enjoys spending time with his sons and playing video games inside while they watch the gentle woods of Idaho.

Publisher's Acknowledgments

We're proud of this book; please send us your comments through our online registration form located at `http://dummies.custhelp.com`. For other comments, please contact our Customer Care Department within the U.S. at 877-762-2974, outside the U.S. at 317-572-3993, or fax 317-572-4002.

Some of the people who helped bring this book to market include the following:

Acquisitions and Editorial

Senior Project Editor: Mark Enochs

Acquisitions Editors: Katie Mohr, Tiffany Ma

Copy Editor: Rebecca Whitney

Technical Editor: James F. Kelly

Editorial Manager: Leah Cameron

Editorial Assistant: Amanda Graham

Sr. Editorial Assistant: Cherie Case

Cartoons: Rich Tennant
(`www.the5thwave.com`)

Composition Services

Project Coordinator: Lynsey Stanford

Layout and Graphics: Ana Carrillo, Ashley Chamberlain, Timothy C. Detrick, Christine Williams

Proofreader: Shannon Ramsey

Indexer: Potomac Indexing, LLC

Publishing and Editorial for Technology Dummies

    Richard Swadley, Vice President and Executive Group Publisher

    Andy Cummings, Vice President and Publisher

    Mary Bednarek, Executive Acquisitions Director

    Mary C. Corder, Editorial Director

Publishing for Consumer Dummies

    Diane Graves Steele, Vice President and Publisher

Composition Services

    Debbie Stailey, Director of Composition Services

Contents at a Glance

Table of Contents

Introduction

Say hello to the nearly all-new 12th edition of *PCs For Dummies!*

This book was written just for you, someone who doesn't want to turn into a computer nerd or fall in love with computers or technology. No, this book was written because something complex and mysterious, like a computer, can make a smart person like you feel like a dummy.

Computers are now commodity items, tossed into a big-box store along with the toaster ovens and plasma TVs. The PC is a commodity, yet it's not any easier to use than it was a decade ago. The cheerful person in the store can't help you. There's no computer manual. And that toll-free phone number they gave you connects you with a foreigner who reads you a script in heavily accented English. Obviously, a book like this one is more than needed — it's a necessity.

This book helps restore your confidence by explaining how computers work in a manner that's simple, easy to understand, and, often, entertaining. Between this book's yellow-and-black covers, you'll find quick, helpful information about using your computer. This book uses friendly and human — and often irreverent — terms. Nothing is sacred here, and you'll find no painful jargon or condescending tone. You and your needs are the focus.

The result is that, after reading this book, the computer, while still a technological marvel, will no longer intimidate you.

What's New in This Edition?

There have been one dozen editions of this book, and you're lucky enough to be holding in your hands the most recent, best edition. As is my tradition, I thoroughly update each edition of this book, adding information on new technology, removing obsolete stuff, and giving the text a gentle massage to keep the material light and fresh.

Specifically, this book has been updated to cover the Windows 7 operating system. Additionally, you'll also find these new topics:

- The latest information on the new computer designs, including the popular One PC

- The latest on expansion options, including eSATA, plus tips on adding external storage to your PC

- Updated and complete information on media cards, which provide the latest in removable storage for your computer

- New information on computer security, which jibes well with the new Action Center in Windows 7

- Lots of new material about your online life, including social networking sites and sharing photos and video on the Internet

- Information on setting up your PC for your children, including ways to limit their computing time and restrict access to games and other software

- The Cheat Sheet, which once appeared just inside this book's front cover, is now available online: www.dummies.com/cheatsheet/pcs.

- General up-to-date and current information on all aspects of PC technology, hardware, and software — tidbits too numerous to mention here

As in years past, I present all the information in this book in a sane, soothing, and gentle tone that calms even the most panicked computerphobe.

Where to Start

This book is a reference. You can start reading at any point. Use the index or table of contents to see what interests you. After you read the information, feel free to close the book and perform whatever task you need; there's no need to read any further.

Each of this book's 31 chapters covers a specific aspect of the computer — turning it on, using a printer, using software, or heaving the computer out a window in the best possible manner, for example. Each chapter is divided into self-contained nuggets of information — sections — all relating to the major theme of the chapter. Sample sections you may find include

- Turn the darn thing off
- Using the Internet to set the clock
- Eject a media card or thumb drive
- Stopping a printer run amok

 ✔ Downloading a program

 ✔ Burning a DVD from recorded TV

 ✔ Dealing with a cyberbully

You don't have to memorize anything in this book. Nothing about a computer is memorable. Each section is designed so that you can read the information quickly, digest what you have read, and then put down the book and get on with using the computer. If anything technical crops up, you're alerted to its presence so that you can cleanly avoid it.

Conventions Used in This Book

Menu items, links, and other controls on the screen are written using initial cap text. So if the option is named "Turn off the computer," you see Turn Off the Computer (without quotes or commas) shown in this book, whether it appears that way onscreen or not.

Whenever I describe a message or information on the screen, it looks like this:

```
This is a message onscreen.
```

If you have to type something, it looks like this:

Type me

You type the text *Type me* as shown. You're told when and whether to press the Enter key. You're also told whether to type a period; periods end sentences written in English, but not always when you type text on a computer.

Windows menu commands are shown like this:

Choose File⇨Exit.

This line directs you to choose the File menu and then choose the Exit command.

Key combinations you may have to type are shown like this:

Ctrl+S

This line says to press and hold the Ctrl (Control) key, type an *S,* and then release the Ctrl key. It works the same as pressing Shift+S on the keyboard produces an uppercase *S.* Same deal, different shift key.

What You Don't Need to Read

It's a given that computers are technical, but you can avoid reading the technical stuff. To assist you, I've put some of the more obnoxious technical stuff into sidebars clearly marked as technical information. Read that information at your own peril. Often, it's just a complex explanation of stuff already discussed in the chapter. Reading that information only tells you something substantial about your computer, which is not my goal here.

Foolish Assumptions

I make some admittedly foolish assumptions about you: You have a computer, and you use it somehow to do something. You use a PC (or are planning on it) and will use Windows as that computer's operating system.

This book was written directly to support Windows 7. Even so, notes in the text apply to Windows Vista. I even tossed in some stuff about Windows XP when I was feeling rather saucy.

Windows comes in different flavors, such as Ultimate, Business, and Home versions. Differences between them are noted in the text.

When this book refers to Windows without a specific edition or version, the information applies generically to both Windows 7 and Windows Vista.

This book refers to the menu that appears when you click or activate the Start button as the *Start button menu.* The All Programs menu on the Start panel is referred to as *All Programs,* though it may say only *Programs.*

Icons Used in This Book

This icon alerts you to needless technical information — drivel I added because even though I can't help but unleash the nerd in me, I can successfully flag that type of material. Feel free to skip over anything tagged with this little picture.

This icon usually indicates helpful advice or an insight that makes using the computer interesting. For example, when you're setting fire to the computer, be sure to wear protective goggles.

This icon indicates something to remember, like turning off the iron before you leave the house or not trimming your nose hairs with a butane lighter.

This icon indicates that you need to be careful with the information that's presented; usually, it's a reminder for you not to do something.

Getting in Touch with the Author

My e-mail address is listed here in case you want to send me a note:

```
dgookin@wambooli.com
```

Yes, that's my address, and I respond to every e-mail message. Note that I reply to short, to-the-point messages quickly. Long messages may take more time for me to reply to. Plus, I cannot troubleshoot or fix your PC. Remember that you paid others for their technical support, and you should use their services.

You can also visit my Web site, which is chock-full of helpful support pages, bonus information, games, and fun:

```
http://www.wambooli.com
```

Where to Go from Here

With this book in hand, you're now ready to go out and conquer your PC. Start by looking through the table of contents or the index. Find a topic and turn to the page indicated, and you're ready to go. Also, feel free to write in this book, fill in the blanks, dog-ear the pages, and do anything that would make a librarian blanch. Enjoy.

Part I
Hello, PC!

The 5th Wave   By Rich Tennant

"I think the cursor's not moving, Mr. Dundt, because you're using the chalk board eraser instead of a mouse."

In this part . . .

*I*t's been called a fast idiot, the ultimate solution for which there was no problem, a toy, Satan's spawn, a godsend, *Time* magazine's Machine of the Year 1982, and perhaps the most miraculous gadget ever invented. I'm speaking, of course, about the personal computer, the PC.

Loathe it or love it, the PC is now a part of everyday life, a gizmo as common as a desk lamp and with more uses than a Swiss Army knife. Whether you already have a PC or are looking to buy one in the near future, use this part of the book to bone up on basic computer stuff.

Chapter 1

Your Computer Won't Explode

*I*f you're a fan of science fiction television or film, you're probably quite familiar with the concept of the exploding computer. Sparks, smoke, flying debris — it all appears to be a common function of computers in the future. Sure, they could just beep and display error messages when they die or are thwarted by Captain Kirk's irrefutable logic, but where's the fun in that?

My point is to relax. Computers are not evil, and they're not out to get you. In fact, you probably want to get the most out of your PC investment because you've heard about all the wonderful things a computer can do. The key to building a productive, long-term relationship with such technology is to understand the computer. You don't need to have Einstein's IQ to do that. You just need to read and enjoy the easy, helpful information in this chapter.

Clear Computer Concepts

A computer is the simplest of devices. It joins a long line of new technologies that originally might have appeared frightening but in the end turned out to be entirely useful.

For example, a coffee pot combines dangerous, scalding water with a legal stimulant to provide you with a delicious beverage. A lawn mower whirls sharp blades of metal around yet safely keeps the grass short. A microwave oven uses lethal beams of energy to cook food. And, the TV remote helps you gain valuable fat cells, vital to keeping you alive through lean times, by preventing you from walking the short distance to your television set. Truly, you have nothing to fear from modern technology after you understand it.

At its most basic level, the computer is a gadget that receives input, does something with that input, and then produces output. Figure 1-1 cheerfully illustrates this concept.

Figure 1-1:
What a
computer
does at its
simplest
level.

The act of receiving input, modifying it, and then producing output is incredibly simple, but at the same time it's bursting with enormous potential. That's why the computer is capable of doing so many things.

The "input goes into computer and produces output" equation is the foundation of these three basic computer concepts:

- I/O
- Processing
- Storage

The following sections expand on these notions, distilling for you what you could have learned in a computer science class, had you bothered to take one. Or, if you did take a course in computer science, the following sections explain what you missed while you were sleeping.

I/O

All computers are obsessed over the letters *I* and *O*. It's *IO* as in "I owe," not as in Io, the third-largest moon of Jupiter.

IO stands for input and output. It's commonly written as I/O, which are the two things a computer does best. In fact, I/O is pretty much the *only* thing a computer does. Consider this popular nursery song:

> *Old MacDonald had a Dell*
>
> *E-E-E I/O*

You get this whole I/O concept down and you've tackled the essence of what a computer is and what it can do.

- ✔ The devices connected to your computer are divided into input and output camps. It has input gizmos and doodads and output doodads and gizmos.

- ✔ The computer receives information from *input* devices. The keyboard and mouse are two input devices, as are scanners and digital cameras. They all send information to the computer.

- ✔ The computer sends information to output devices. *Output* is anything the computer produces. The stuff displayed on the monitor is output, sound is output, and the pages the computer prints are output. The monitor, speakers, and printer are all output gizmos and doodads.

- ✔ Some devices can do both input and output. Imagine! The computer's storage system is considered both an input device and an output device. A gizmo known as a modem sends *and* receives information. (See Chapter 14 for information on what a modem is and why you should care.)

- ✔ Ed McMahon didn't say "I/O" on the old *Tonight Show*. He said "High-ho!"

Processing

What the computer does between input and output is *processing*. It's what happens to the input to make the output significant. Otherwise, the computer would simply be a tube and computer science would be renamed Plumbing.

Processing can be as simple as doubling a number. Or, it can be as complex as converting a series of ones and zeros into a symphony or a full-length motion picture. The key to the computer's success is that the processing takes place quickly. Also, the computer doesn't mind doing the processing, especially on repetitive tasks that would normally drive a human being bonkers.

- ✔ Processing is handled inside the computer by a gizmo known as (logically enough) a processor.
- ✔ See Chapter 6 for more information on the processor.
- ✔ By itself, the processor doesn't know what to do with input. No, the processor relies on instructions to tell it what to do. Those instructions are referred to as *software*. The topic of software is covered later in this chapter.

Storage

The final part of the basic computer equation is storage. Storage is necessary because the processor needs a place to perform its magic — a scratch pad for mad doodles, if you will.

Computer storage comes in two forms: temporary and long-term.

Temporary storage is supplied as *memory*, or *RAM*. Memory is where the processor does its work, where programs run, and where information is stored while it's being worked on. RAM is the microprocessor's playground, its workshop, its den.

Long-term storage in a modern computer is provided by storage media. *Storage media* includes hard drives, flash drives, media cards, optical discs, and CDs and DVDs. Long-term storage allows information to be saved and recalled for later use — like putting clothes in a closet or all your junk in a storage unit. It's the place where things go when the microprocessor isn't directly working on them — but from where stuff can be retrieved later, if necessary.

- ✔ If you were a computer, your temporary storage would be your memory. So when someone tells you their phone number, that information is processed and temporarily stored in your head. Long-term storage is similar to a pad of paper: You write down a phone number on a pad of paper so that you can use it later.
- ✔ All computers need storage.
- ✔ RAM is an acronym for *random access memory*. It's often just called memory.
- ✔ The most popular form of long-term storage is the computer's hard drive.

- ✔ The computers on the Apollo moon missions had lots of storage, for their day. The reason was so that the astronauts wouldn't have to manually input the programs the computer needed to run. Even so, a lot more typing and programming were going on in the capsule than you would imagine.

Hardware and Software

Like many great teams throughout history — Abbot and Costello, steak and potatoes, death and taxes — a computer system is a blend of two different things. Those two things are hardware and software.

Hardware is the physical part of a computer — anything you can touch and anything you can see. The computer console, the monitor, the keyboard, the mouse — that physical stuff is hardware.

Software is the brain of the computer. Software tells the hardware what to do.

In a way, it helps to think of hardware and software as a symphony orchestra. For hardware, you have the musicians and their instruments. Their software is the music. As with a computer, the music (software) tells the musicians and their instruments (hardware) what to do.

Without software, hardware just sits around and looks pretty. It can't do anything because it has no instructions and nothing telling it what to do next. And, like a symphony orchestra without music, that can be an expensive waste of time (especially at union scale).

To make the computer system work, software must be in charge. In fact, it's software that determines your computer's personality and potential.

- ✔ If you can throw it out a window, it's hardware.

- ✔ If you can throw it out a window and it comes back, it's a cat.

- ✔ Computer *software* is nothing more than instructions that tell the hardware what to do, how to act, or when to mangle your data.

- ✔ Contrary to what most people think, between hardware and software, the software is more important. Just as a director tells actors what to do in a play, software directs hardware, telling it what to do, where to go, and how best to convey the emotional context of the scene. Software's importance is especially valuable to note when first buying a computer because most people dwell on the new computer's hardware rather than on the software controlling the hardware.

- ✔ Without the proper software, your computer's hardware has nothing to do. That's when the powerful computer magically transforms itself into an expensive paperweight.

The computer's operating system

The most important piece of software in your computer system is its *operating system*. It has several duties:

- ✔ **Control the computer's hardware:** Hardware does nothing without software to tell it what to do, and the operating system *is* that software.

- ✔ **Manage all the computer programs:** The operating system isn't the only software in your computer, but it is the software in charge of all the other software. It's the head honcho, the big cheese, *el numero uno*.

- ✔ **Organize the storage system:** The operating system is in charge of the computer's memory, both long-term and short-term. For the long-term storage system, the operating system organizes and maintains, in files, the stuff you create on the computer.

- ✔ **Interface with you:** The operating system must also provide a way for you, the human, to use the computer.

Doing all these tasks is a major feat. Be thankful that computer designers have seen to it that only one program does everything! The operating system is no slacker.

On PCs, the most common operating system is Microsoft Windows, or often just Windows. Other operating systems are available (though Windows dominates the marketplace), each of which does the things just listed and can handily control the PC's hardware. This book assumes that Windows is your PC's operating system.

How the operating system does its various jobs is covered elsewhere in this book.

- ✔ The operating system is the most important piece of software in your computer. It's in charge, the hardware's Fearless Leader, *le roi*.

- ✔ The computer hardware surrenders control of itself to the operating system mere moments after you turn on the computer. See Chapter 4 for information on turning the computer on and off.

- ✔ The operating system typically comes with the computer when you buy it. You never need to add a second operating system, although operating systems are updated and improved from time to time.

- ✔ When you buy software, you buy it for an operating system, not for your brand of computer. So, rather than buy software for your Dell, Compaq, or Crazy Larry's PC, you look in the Windows section of the software store.

Other software

The operating system isn't the only software you use on your computer. The typical computer user has lots of software on the computer. Some of that software runs specific pieces of hardware, but a lot of it is productivity software, designed to get work done. Oh, and some of it is entertainment software, which is for the fun stuff.

Computer software is known by several different names. In addition to the general term *software,* you find

Program: An individual piece of software. To use a musical example, all software is like all music. A program is the "music" for a specific song.

Application: A category of software used for productivity or to create things. Applications are the software that does the work.

Game: A program for fun, of course.

Utility or tool: A program designed to help you manage the computer or diagnose or fix problems. For example, you may use a tool to optimize the performance of your computer's storage system.

Driver: A special type of program that allows specific hardware to work. For example, a specific *video driver* program is required for the operating system to use your PC's graphics hardware. This type of software comes with the hardware it supports.

Part IV of this book goes into more detail on computer software.

The stuff you make (files)

You use a computer to create things, such as a document in a word processor, a painting from a graphics program, a movie, or any of a number of interesting things. The stuff you create is stored on the computer in a digital container known as a *file*. You should understand the concept of files to get the most benefit from your PC.

A *file* is basically a storage unit for computer stuff. Files are created by computer programs. The file is born in the computer's temporary storage area, or *memory.* That's where the program, directing the PC's processor, manipulates information. When you're pleased with the results, the file is *saved* to long-term storage.

Programs can also *open* files you've previously worked on and saved to the PC's storage media. After a file is opened, it's read from long-term storage and placed back into memory. After the file's contents are in memory, you can continue to work on the file, modify it, print it, or mangle it completely.

Knowing about files and how they fit into the computer picture is vital to getting the most from your PC. Be sure to check out Chapter 20 for more detailed information on the useful topic of computer files.

Boring PC History

Computers have been around for a long time. Ancient computers were programmable devices used mostly for entertainment value, such as Leonardo da Vinci's knight, named "Leonardo's Robot."

The first modern, electronic computers appeared in the 1940s and were mostly used for government or military purposes. In the 1960s, computers found favor in screwing up people's phone bills.

The PC was spawned from the microcomputer craze of the mid-1970s, as shown by the timeline in Figure 1-2. Though those microcomputer systems were generically known as *personal computers*, it was the IBM Personal Computer, or IBM PC, introduced in 1981, that proved the most popular.

Figure 1-2:
Timeline of the personal computer.

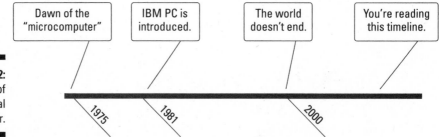

The success of the IBM PC led to many copies, or *clones,* for many years. Almost 90 percent of the computer industry now develops personal computers modeled after the descendants of the original IBM PC. Because of that lineage, the computer systems are dubbed, generically, *PCs.*

- ✔ The term *PC* is now used to specifically refer to any computer that can run the Windows operating system.

- ✔ Though your car, sewing machine, or the kidney dialysis machine at the hospital may contain computer electronics, those devices are not PCs.

- ✔ Curiously, IBM got out of the PC manufacturing business in the early 2000s.

- ✔ The success of the PC is based on its use of off-the-shelf parts that are easily replaced. The PC can also be configured and upgraded with ease, which is another reason it's so popular.

- ✔ The only thing not officially considered a PC is Apple's Macintosh computer. Although the Mac is a *personal* computer and *can* run the Windows operating system, Mac users go all verklempt when you call their computers PCs.

An Important Thing to Remember

Computers aren't evil. They harbor no sinister intelligence. In fact, when you get to know them, you see that they're rather dumb.

Chapter 2

Your Basic PC Tour

The very first PCs were not known for their stunning, aerodynamic designs. They were hefty metal boxes — intimidating, beige. By contrast, today's PCs have a sleek, almost aerodynamic, design to them. They can come in a wide array of bold colors. Some newer models sport ominous internal lighting, an evil glowing red or a cool blue, hinting at some internal, hideous intelligence.

Well, forget anything about computer hardware being intelligent. In a computer system, the hardware plays a subservient role to software, which is the real brain. Still, it's important to know about basic computer hardware. This chapter provides a quick overview, showing things you'll find on a PC that can be interesting and useful.

Even though your PC may sport an aerodynamic design, that doesn't imply flightworthiness — despite any desire you may have to hurl the computer out a window.

The Mundane PC

Figure 2-1 shows a typical personal computer system. Try to avoid the urge to yawn.

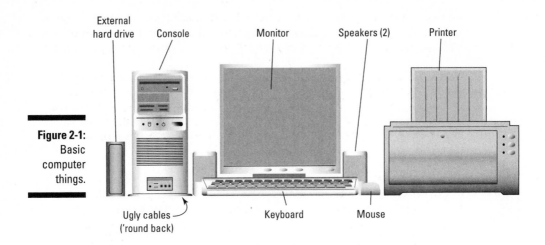

Figure 2-1:
Basic
computer
things.

The big, important pieces have been labeled in Figure 2-1 for your enjoyment. You should know which piece is which and what the proper terms are:

Console: The main computer box is the console, although it may also be called the system unit (geeky) or the CPU (incorrect). The box contains your computer's soul, its electronic guts. Adorning the outside of the console are various buttons, lights, and holes into which you plug the rest of the computer system.

Monitor: The monitor is the device where the computer displays information — its output. A common mistake made by new computer users is to assume that the monitor is the computer. Nope. The console is the computer. The monitor merely displays stuff.

Keyboard: It's the thing you type on; it's the primary way you communicate with the computer, with input.

Mouse: No rodent or pest, the computer mouse is a helpful device that lets you work with graphical objects displayed on the monitor.

Speakers: PCs bleep and squawk through a set of stereo speakers, which can be external jobbies you set up (refer to Figure 2-1), speakers built into the console or monitor, or perhaps even headphones. Pay more money and you can even get a subwoofer to sit under your desk. Now, *that* will rattle the neighborhood's windows.

External hard drive: You may or may not have one (yet), but an external hard drive is used to *back up*, or create a safety copy, of the important stuff you store on your computer.

Printer: It's where you get the computer's printed output, also called *hard copy*.

You may find, in addition to these basic items, other items clustered around your computer, such as a scanner, a digital camera, a gamepad or joystick, a high-speed modem, or many, many other toys — er, vital computer components.

One thing definitely not shown earlier, in Figure 2-1 — and something you will never see in a computer manual and especially not in advertisements — is the ganglion of cable that lives behind each and every computer. What a mess! These cables are required in order to plug things into the wall and into each other. No shampoo or conditioner on Earth can clean up those tangles.

✔ Ensure that you know where the console, keyboard, mouse, speakers, monitor, and printer are in your own system. If the printer isn't present, it's probably a network printer sitting in some other room.

✔ Chapters in Part II of this book go into more detail on the individual computer components just introduced and illustrated in Figure 2-1.

✔ CPU stands for *central processing unit*. It's another term for the computer's processor (see Chapter 6). Even so, some folks foolishly refer to the console as the CPU. Boy, are they wrong!

The Console Tour

Of all the computer hardware that makes up a computer system, the console is the most important (refer to Figure 2-1). But what exactly is a console?

Thanks to major conspiracies and a generally evil sense of humor in the computer industry, not all consoles look the same. Not only that, vital locations are found on the console, useful places that each manufacturer deliberately puts in a different spot. You need to know where those things are if you want to add them and use them. The following sections help.

There is no typical console

All PC consoles feature the same basic hardware, doodads, and goobers spotting the case like warts on a witch. But, just as there's no typical car, there's no typical computer console. You can't say, "If you've seen one, you've seen 'em all!" That's because one PC can look as different from another as a sports car looks different from a pickup truck.

Figure 2-2 illustrates six common PC configurations, and the following list describes them.

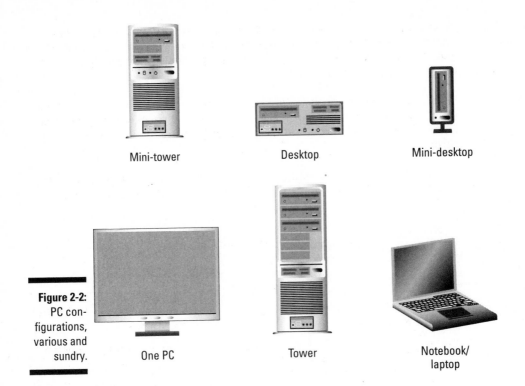

Mini-tower   Desktop   Mini-desktop

One PC   Tower   Notebook/
laptop

Figure 2-2:
PC con-
figurations,
various and
sundry.

Mini-tower: The mini-tower is the most popular console type. It can sit on top of a desk, right next to the monitor (refer to Figure 2-1). It can also be tucked away out of sight, below the desk.

Desktop: Once the most popular type of console, the desktop PC sits flat on the desk. The monitor usually squats on top of the console in the standard desktop configuration.

Mini-desktop: The mini-desktop console is just too cute and tiny, about the size of a college dictionary. That makes it ideal for places where space is tight, and where budgets are tight. The downside is that these consoles lack internal expansion options.

One PC: A popular and trendy computer design combines the console and monitor into a single unit. From the front, the console looks like a monitor, though it's thicker. On the sides, you find the optical drive plus the myriad of connectors and other computer doodads.

Tower: The tower console is essentially a taller version of the mini-tower. The bonus with the tower is internal expansion options, making this type of console ideal for power-mad users. A tower typically sits on the floor, often propping up one end of the table.

Notebook/laptop: A specialty type of computer that folds into a handy, light-weight package, ideal for slowing down the security checkpoints in airports. Laptop PCs work just like their desktop brethren; any exceptions are noted throughout this book.

Choosing the proper PC configuration depends on your needs. Power users love the expandability of the tower. Those on a budget may go for a mini-desktop. Folks on the go love laptops.

✔ No matter how big your computer, the amount of clutter you have always expands to fill the available desk space.

✔ Though you can find separate mini-tower and desktop configurations, many of the mini-tower PCs are often sold as "desktop" models.

✔ Another type of laptop is the *tablet*, which lets you enter information by writing on the screen using a special tool called a *stylus*.

✔ For the highly mobile Internet crowd, a special teensy-laptop category is the netbook. Lilliputians love 'em.

✔ More laptop (and tablet) information is in my book *Laptops For Dummies* (Wiley), available at fine bookstores all over planet Earth.

✔ The amount of space a PC console occupies is often referred to as its *footprint.* Smaller consoles are *small footprint* PCs.

Major points of interest on the console, front

After many years, PC manufacturers discovered that it works best to put those items designed for you, the human, on the *front* part of the console. I'm not joking: Early PCs had nearly everything on the console's back side. So consider yourself blessed and use Figure 2-3 as your reference as you go hunting for the following items:

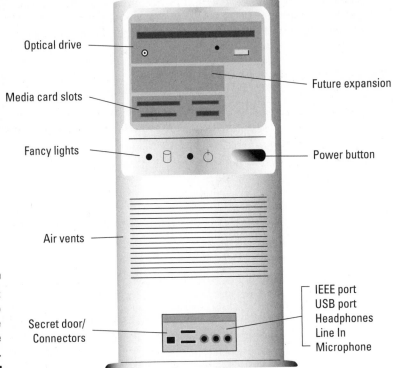

Optical drive

Future expansion

Media card slots

Fancy lights

Power button

Air vents

Figure 2-3:
Items to
note on the
front of the
console.

Secret door/
Connectors

IEEE port
USB port
Headphones
Line In
Microphone

Optical drive: The computer's primary removable storage media is the optical disc. The optical drive reads optical discs, computer CDs, or DVDs, just like music CDs or movie DVDs. Read more about this topic in Chapter 9.

Future expansion: Most consoles feature blank spots. They may look interesting or useful, but they're not! They're simply blanks that cover holes used for adding new features to your PC.

Media card slots: These slots are used for reading common media cards, such as those used by digital cameras or portable electronic gizmos. See Chapter 9 for more information about media cards.

Air vents: Air vents aren't impressive, but they're necessary. They keep the console cool by helping air circulate inside. Don't block the air vents with books or sticky notes!

The secret panel: Whether it's covered by a door or not, your PC most likely features a clutch of various connectors somewhere on its front. Nestled in that area, you find places to connect joysticks, microphones, headphones, digital video, or other handy gizmos you may need to plug and unplug from time to time.

Buttons and lights: Most computer buttons are on the keyboard. A few of the more important buttons are on the console, and on fancier PCs are accompanied by many impressive, tiny lights. These buttons and lights include

✔ **Power button:** No longer a plain on–off button, the *power button* can do more than just turn the computer off or on. See Chapter 4 for the details.

✔ **Reset button:** Rare but still found on some consoles is a button that forces the computer into a restart during times of woe. Consider it a plus if your PC features this button.

✔ **Hard drive light:** This wee light flashes when the PC's primary storage media, the hard drive, is being accessed. A light that's sometimes on the optical drive does the same thing.

You might be lucky and find other fun and unusual items living on the front of your PC's console. They're probably particular to a certain computer brand or model. Consider them a bonus.

✔ The front of the console may also boast a brand label or manufacturer's tattoo.

✔ Some newer computers have stickers that show the secret Windows installation number or proclaim such nonsense as "I was built to run Windows Optimus Prime" or "A Pentium hoohah lurks inside this box."

✔ For more specific information on the connectors lurking behind a secret panel, see the section "The I/O panel," later in this chapter.

✔ Don't block the air vents on the front of the console. If you do, the computer may literally suffocate. (It gets too hot.)

✔ A hard drive light can be red or green or yellow, and it flickers when the hard drive is in use. Don't let it freak you out! It's not an alarm; the hard drive is just doing its job.

Stuff found on the console's backside

The console's backside is its busy side. That's where you find various connectors for the many devices in your computer system: a place to plug in the monitor, keyboard, mouse, speakers, and just about anything else that came in the box with the PC, or which you might add later.

Use Figure 2-4 as a guide for finding important items on the back of your PC's console. Note that some things may look different and some may be missing; not every console is the same.

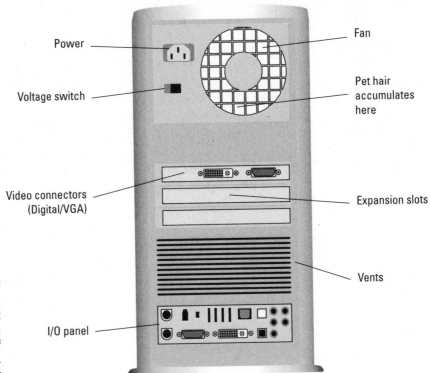

Power

Fan

Voltage switch

Pet hair accumulates here

Video connectors (Digital/VGA)

Expansion slots

Vents

Figure 2-4:
Important doodads on the back of the console.

I/O panel

Power: The console needs power, and the power connector is where you plug in the power cord. The other end plugs into the wall.

Fan: Air gets sucked in here. Or it might be blown out. I forget which.

Voltage switch: Use this switch to change power frequencies to match the specifications for your country, region, or planet.

Expansion slots: These slots are available for adding new components on *expansion cards* to the console and expanding your PC's hardware. Any connectors on the expansion cards appear in this area, such as the video connectors on a graphics adapter (refer to Figure 2-4).

Vents: The breathing thing again.

I/O panel: Aside from the power cord, and anything attached to an expansion card, the rest of your PC's expansion options and plug-in-type things are located in a central area that I call the I/O panel. Details of what you can find there are covered in the next section.

The I/O panel

To either help keep all connectors in one spot or just create the most intensely cable-crammed location on the console, your PC's console features an I/O panel on its rear. That location is where you add various expansion options to the PC as well as plug in the standard devices shown way over in Figure 2-1.

Use Figure 2-5 as your guide for what's what. The items you find on your PC's I/O panel may be labeled with text, or they may include the symbols listed later, in Table 2-1. Also keep in mind that Figure 2-5 is only a guide; your PC console may have a different layout and sport more or fewer items on the I/O panel.

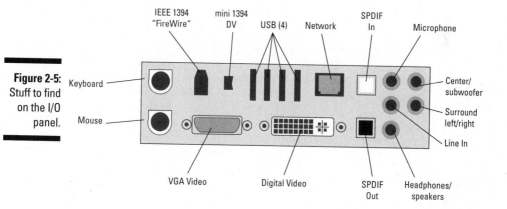

Figure 2-5: Stuff to find on the I/O panel.

Center/subwoofer: For a surround sound audio system, you plug the center speaker or subwoofer, or both, into this jack.

Headphones/speakers: Into this hole you plug in your PC's external speakers or headphones, or it's where you hook up the PC to a sound system. (Also check the "secret panel" on the front of the console for a headphone connector.)

IEEE 1394 (FireWire): This type of versatile connector is similar to USB. See Chapter 7.

Keyboard: The keyboard plugs into this little hole.

Line In: You use this jack to plug a traditional audio-producing device (stereo, phonograph, or VCR, for example) into the PC for capturing sound.

Microphone: The computer's microphone plugs into this jack. A similar jack might also appear on the front side of the console.

Mini 1394: This special version of the IEEE 1394 connector is designed specifically for digital video.

Mouse: This hole is generally the same size and shape as the keyboard connector, although a mouse icon nearby lets you know that the mouse plugs in here.

Network: Plug in a local-area network (LAN) connector or attach a broadband modem to the PC.

SPDIF In, SPDIF Out: These connectors are used for digital audio. Special fiber optic cable is required: Audio coming into the computer plugs into the In hole; the sound the computer generates goes out the Out hole.

Surround left/right: Also for surround sound, this jack is the one in which you plug the rear left and right speakers.

USB: Plug snazzy devices into these Certs-size Universal Serial Bus (USB) slots. See Chapter 7 for more information about USB.

Video: Your PC's monitor can plug into one of the video adapters on the I/O panel, either the traditional VGA adapter or, if you have a digital monitor, the Digital video adapter. Newer PCs may even sport an HDMI adapter for super-duper digital video. See Chapter 10 for more information on computer video.

The good news? You connect all this stuff only once. Then your PC's butt faces the wall for the rest of its life and you never have to look at it again (well, unless you add something in the future or you just enjoy looking at PC butts).

 ✔ The keyboard and mouse connectors *are* different! Be certain that you plug the proper device into the proper hole, or else the keyboard and mouse don't work!

 ✔ See Chapter 7 for more information on these holes and what plugs into them.

 ✔ The I/O panel might also feature a jack for connecting a dial-up modem, though such jacks are more common on laptop computers than on desktop models.

 ✔ Older PCs may sport ports not shown in Figure 2-5. These ports include the serial or COM port, the printer port, and the joystick port. The functions of these ports have been replaced with USB ports, which are plentiful on modern PCs.

Helpful hints, hieroglyphics, and hues

Even though most PC connectors are different, manufacturers have relented and agreed upon a set of common colors and symbols used to label the various holes, connectors, and ports on the console's rump. They're listed in Table 2-1 to help you find things, in case the need arises.

Table 2-1	Shapes, Connections, Symbols, and Colors		
Name	*Connector*	*Symbol*	*Color*
Center/subwoofer			Brown
COM/Serial			Cyan
Digital video			White
eSATA	SATA	eSATA	None
HDMI	HDMI	HDMI	None
IEEE 1394			None
IEEE 1394 mini			None
Infrared			None
Joystick			Mustard
Keyboard			Purple
Line In (audio)			Gray
Microphone			Pink
Modem			None
Monitor			Blue
Mouse			Green
Network			None

(continued)

Table 2-1 *(continued)*

Name	Connector	Symbol	Color
Power			Yellow
Printer			Violet
SPDIF In		**IN**	Pink or white
SPDIF Out		**OUT**	Black
Speakers/head-phones			Lime
S-Video			Yellow
Surround left/right			Black
USB			None

Chapter 3

Computer Assembly

. . . .

In This Chapter

▶ Putting together your PC

▶ Understanding computer cables

▶ Plugging things into the console

▶ Using a power strip

▶ Managing with a UPS

. . . .

*T*he PC holds a hallowed place in the pantheon of Incredibly Difficult Devices to Assemble. In fact, I would say that the computer is perhaps chief god of the pantheon, more dreaded than the backyard grill, stereo equipment, pressboard Scandinavian furniture, bicycles, hammocks, and kids' toys combined.

I could lie to you and say that setting up a PC is so simple that a child could do it. Well, perhaps a child with an IQ of 210 could. So, though the PC isn't the easiest thing to put together, the truth is that millions of people have survived the PC assembly ordeal, with quite a few of them armed with only their wits and perhaps a glass of wine to calm their nerves. You have a leg up on all of them, of course: You have the helpful information in this chapter, which should help you get your PC assembled and running in no time.

✔ Even though this chapter carefully and cheerfully assists you with PC setup, feel free to enjoy the experience with your favorite beverage. Mind that you keep the beverage far enough away from the PC so as not to spill your drink into the electronics.

✔ This chapter covers basic computer setup. Turning the computer on is covered in Chapter 4.

✔ See Chapter 7 for additional information on how to connect external USB devices to the computer system.

Unpack the Boxes

Computers can come in one or two boxes, or multiple sets. If you're lucky, one of the boxes says Open Me First. Open that one first. Otherwise, attempt to locate the box containing the console. Open that one first.

Be sure to look through all the packing materials inside the box. Sometimes, manufacturers stick important items inside boxes inside boxes, or nestled in the Styrofoam. Look over everything.

As you open boxes, check to ensure that you have all the pieces necessary for your computer system. (Refer to Chapter 2 for a review of the pieces.) If you're missing anything, call someone!

- ✔ Your computer runs faster when you take it out of the box.
- ✔ Keep the packing slip, warranty, sales receipt, and other important pieces of paper together.
- ✔ Don't fill out the warranty card until after the computer is set up and running fine. If you have to return the computer, the store prefers that the warranty card *not* be filled in.

- ✔ Keep all boxes and packing materials. You need them if you have to return the computer. Also, the boxes are the best way to ship the computer if you ever have to move. Some movers don't insure a computer unless it's packed in its original box.
- ✔ Your computer may have come with a road map or flowchart diagram that tells you how to set everything up. If so, follow those instructions first and use my advice here as a helpful suggestion.

Set Up the Console First

The *console* is the main computer box, the locus of all PC activities, so you should set it up first. Put it on the desktop or in the location where you've always dreamed it would be. If you plan to put the console beneath your desk, put it there now.

Don't back the console up against the wall just yet. You need to start plugging things into the console's back. Not until everything is connected to the console do you want to push it up against the wall. (Even then, leave some room so that you don't crimp the cables.)

- ✔ The console needs to breathe. Don't set up the computer in a confined space or inside a cabinet where there's no air circulation.

- ✔ Avoid setting the console by a window where the sun will heat it up. Computers don't like to operate in extreme heat — or cold, for that matter.

- ✔ A PC is happiest when it operates at temperatures between 40 and 80 degrees Fahrenheit, or between 4 and 27 degrees Celsius.

- ✔ Also avoid humidity, which can gum up a computer. Readers in tropical climes have reported mold growing inside their PCs — the humidity was that bad! If you compute where it's humid, do so in an air-conditioned room!

- ✔ Don't put the console in a cabinet unless the cabinet is well ventilated.

- ✔ A computer by a window also makes a tempting target for a smash-and-grab thief.

A General Guide to Plugging Things into the Console

All major parts of your computer system plug directly into the console, which means that after you set up the console, the next step in assembling your computer is to unpack other pieces-parts and connect them into the console.

Don't plug anything into the wall just yet! Even so, as you begin to set up your computer system and attach various gizmos, ensure that devices with on–off switches have the switches in the Off position.

This section covers the basics of connecting many popular items to the console. Use this information when you first set up the computer, as well as later when you expand or add to your computer system.

It's generally okay to plug in most computer gizmos while the computer is on. There are some exceptions to this rule, so carefully read this section!

Audio

Computer audio involves both output and input — the famous I/O you probably read about in Chapter 1 or maybe sang songs about when you went to computer camp as a teen.

Know your computer cables

Most common devices (the nonwireless kind) in your computer system connect to the console by using cables. The cable is known by which hole, or *port,* it plugs into. For example, USB cables plug into USB ports.

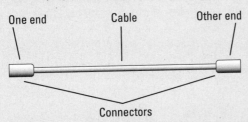

One end   Cable   Other end

Connectors

The ends of a computer cable are configured so that you cannot plug the cable in backward: The connector for the console is one shape, and the connector for the gizmo is another shape. When the connectors are the same shape, it doesn't matter which end plugs in where.

All cables plug in snugly. Network cables have little tabs on them that snap when the cable is properly inserted. You must press the tab to remove the cable. The video connector has tiny thumbscrews on the side, which help attach and tighten the cable to the connector.

Some cables are permanently attached to their devices: The mouse and keyboard have this type of cable, for example. Other cables are separate. You just have to remember to plug in both ends.

Extra cables, if you need them, can be purchased at any computer or office supply store or over the Internet. As a suggestion, measure the distance for which you need a cable and then double it to get a cable of the proper length. For example, if it's 2 feet between your console and where you want a microphone, get a 4-foot cable.

All computer audio uses the standard *mini-DIN* connector, which looks like a tiny pointy thing. Audio input is supplied by a microphone, which connects to the computer's microphone jack. Audio output is supplied by either headphones, left–right speakers, or full-on-wake-up-the-neighbors surround sound, also using the mini-DIN connector and the appropriate jacks on the console.

- ✔ Refer to Chapter 13 for more information on PC audio, including some speaker layout instructions.

- ✔ Both headphones and speakers use the Line Out, headphone, or speakers jack. Furthermore, speakers may need to be plugged into the wall for more power; see the section "It Must Have Power," later in this chapter.

- ✔ Be sure to check the front of the console for another spot to plug in the headphones or microphone. It's much handier than using the connector on the back.

- ✔ The Line In connector is used to connect any non-amplified sound source, such as your stereo, TV, Victrola, or other antique audio devices.

✔ The difference between the Line In and microphone jacks is that Line In devices aren't amplified.

✔ USB speakers or headphones plug into one of the PC's USB ports. See "USB," later in this chapter.

✔ If your audio equipment lacks a mini-DIN connector, you can buy an adapter at any audio store or Radio Shack.

✔ Some PCs have special audio hardware, which you can determine by looking at the console's rear for audio connectors on an expansion slot cover. If your PC is configured that way, be sure to plug the speakers into the audio card's output jacks, not the standard audio output jacks on the I/O panel.

If your PC sports SPDIF connectors, you can use digital audio devices for your computer sound. The digital audio devices must also have SPDIF connectors, and you must use special (and not cheap) fiber optic cable to connect these high-end toys.

✔ Plug optical audio input cables into the computer's SPDIF In connection. To use the computer's optical audio output, plug the cable into the SPDIF Out connector.

✔ Be careful not to bang, touch, or taunt the clear glass ends of the optical cable. Better cables come with little protective caps that you can keep on the ends when the cable isn't connected.

✔ SPDIF stands for Sony/Philips Digital Interconnect Format. It's also written S/PDIF or S/P-DIF.

IEEE, 1394, FireWire

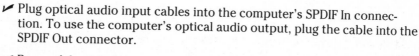

On a PC, the IEEE port is used most notably for a digital video camera. Or, an external scanner or disk drive might use the IEEE port. (See Chapter 7.)

You can plug any IEEE device into the computer at any time. The computer or the device can be on or off when you plug things in or remove them. Be sure to check with the device's documentation for any exceptions to this rule.

✔ IEEE connectors come in two shapes: regular and mini. The smaller, mini connector is used specifically with digital video and is often labeled DV. Be sure to look for one of these connectors in the secret panel on the front of the console (if the console has such a panel).

✔ See Table 2-1, in Chapter 2, for a visual description of the IEEE connector shapes.

✔ IEEE devices require an IEEE cable, which may or may not come with the device.

✔ See Chapter 7 for more information on all things IEEE.

Gamepads, controllers, joysticks

Here's a quick way to tell how old you are. If you call the thing a joystick, you're probably pushing geezerhood. If you're younger, you call the gizmo a *gamepad* or *game controller*. Nomenclature aside, the thing plugs into the PC console by using a USB port.

See Chapter 11 for more information on joysticks — er, gamepads.

Keyboard and mouse

Set up the keyboard right in front of where you sit when you use the computer, between you and where the monitor goes. The mouse lives to the right or left of the keyboard, depending on whether you're right- or left-handed.

The PC keyboard either plugs into the keyboard port on the back of the console or into a USB port. Likewise, the mouse plugs into the mouse port or a USB port. How can you tell? Look at the end of the cable.

 ✔ The mouse and keyboard ports look identical, but they are not. Yes, they're different colors, but more importantly, they're different *electronics*. Don't plug the keyboard or mouse into the wrong port or else neither device works.

 ✔ Don't plug the keyboard or mouse into the keyboard or mouse port while the computer is on. It may damage the keyboard, mouse, or computer. This warning doesn't apply when plugging a keyboard or mouse into a USB port.

Modem

A dialup modem connects to the phone company's wall jack by using a standard telephone cord. It works just like plugging in a telephone, and you leave the cord connected all the time, just like a telephone.

You can use the modem's second phone jack, if available, to connect a real telephone to the computer so that you can use the phone when the computer isn't on the line. The second phone jack is labeled Phone and may have a telephone symbol by it. (The first jack is labeled Line.)

 ✔ Broadband modems — either cable, DSL, or satellite — plug into the computer's networking jack. See "Network," a little later in this chapter.

 ✔ Be careful not to confuse the modem's jack with the network jack. They look similar, but the network jack is slightly wider.

Monitor

Set the monitor atop your desk, generally back away from where you sit, to accommodate room for the keyboard.

The monitor's cable may be attached or separate. If separate, attach the cable to the monitor. Plug the monitor's cable into the console's graphics adapter jack. If the monitor is digital, plug it into the white digital adapter. Otherwise, connect the monitor to the VGA adapter.

The monitor also requires power. See the section "It Must Have Power," later in this chapter.

- ✔ If the console has two VGA connectors, use the one on an expansion card rather than the one found on the console's I/O panel. That expansion card jack indicates a high-end graphics adapter, which offers better features.

- ✔ You can use digital-to-VGA adapters when you have a VGA monitor and a digital graphics adapter.

- ✔ You can also connect a monitor using an HDMI digital video connector. HDMI, which stands for High Definition Multimedia Interface, can be used to attach a large flat-panel TV to use as your PC monitor.

- ✔ The S-Video adapter can be used to attach a monitor to the console or a television or any video gizmo that has S-Video input. Keep in mind that S-Video is for video output only; it doesn't transmit any audio.

- ✔ See Chapter 10 for more information about PC monitors and graphics.

Network

Plug the network cable into the network jack on the back of the console. This is how you connect your PC to a network, a router, a broadband modem, or any of a number of oddly named networking things.

- ✔ The network jack is similar in size to the modem's jack, so try not to confuse them.

- ✔ Network jacks are commonly, though incorrectly, called RJ-45.

- ✔ Setting up a network involves more than just connecting the network cable to the console. Part III of this book covers computer networking.

Printer

Set up the printer where it's within arm's reach of the console. This isn't a necessity; it's just handy to have the printer nearby so that you can reach over and pluck out whatever it is you're printing.

To make the printer and console talk to each other, you need to formally introduce them. No invitation is necessary; all you need is a USB cable. When you're blessed with a wireless printer, keep it close enough to the console to ensure that it's within range of the signal.

The printer requires power, so you need to plug it into a wall socket. See the section "It Must Have Power," later in this chapter.

 ✔ The printer's USB cable has unique ends. One goes into the printer; the other goes into the console. You cannot plug the thing in backward.

 ✔ Older printers and PCs could use what's called, surprisingly, a *printer cable* to connect the console to a PC. Like a USB cable, the printer cable cannot be plugged in backward. If you're cursed with such a setup, be sure to use a bidirectional cable. And, if you have the option of using a USB cable rather than the old printer cable, use the USB cable.

 ✔ Printers can also be accessed via the computer network. See Part III of this book for more information on networking.

USB

USB devices plug into the USB port — any USB port. Fortunately, the USB cable has unique ends; you cannot plug in anything backward.

Examples of USB gizmos to attach to the console include the printer, scanner, digital camera, Webcam or video camera, speakers, headset, disk drives, thumb drives, keyboard, mouse, and on and on.

 ✔ Some USB devices need extra power, such as some portable external hard drives. Those *USB-powered* devices must be plugged directly into the console or into something called a USB-powered hub. See Chapter 7 for more information on USB-powered hubs, as well as a general discussion of USB phenomena.

 ✔ Some devices come with USB cables; some do not. Most notoriously, computer printers do not come with USB cables.

Wireless gizmos

Just because the gizmo says that it's wireless, don't think that it means wire-free. For example, a wireless keyboard or mouse may not connect to the console by using a wire, but a wireless transmitter *is* wired to the console, to either the USB or the keyboard and mouse ports. Beyond that point, however, you don't find any more wires.

Wireless networking is more or less truly wireless. The networking adapter on the console has a tiny antenna — no wires. But the rest of the network will, at some point, require a wire or two. See Chapter 15 for wireless networking nonsense.

It Must Have Power

The last thing you need to do, after plugging your computer components into the console and setting them all up, is to plug all those gizmos into the wall. Those things need power!

The mighty power strip

You may have noticed that you have far many more devices that need to be plugged in than you have available wall sockets. No problem! That's why power strips were invented! The idea is to plug everything into a power strip and then plug that single power strip into the wall, as illustrated in Figure 3-1.

Follow these steps:

1. **Ensure that all your gizmos with on–off switches are in the Off position.**

2. **Ensure that the power strip is in the Off position.**

3. **Plug everything into the power strip.**

4. **Turn your gizmos to the On position.**

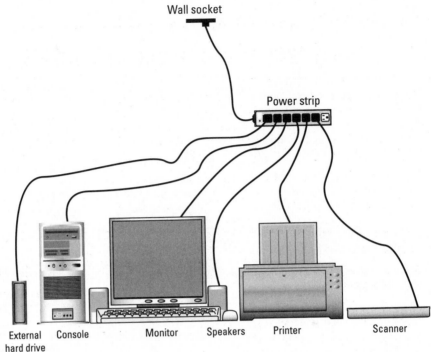

Wall socket

Power strip

Figure 3-1:
Plug your
stuff in like
this.   External   Console   Monitor   Speakers   Printer   Scanner
        hard drive

Now you're ready to turn on the computer system, by turning on the power
strip. But not yet! The official on–off information is in Chapter 4. See that
chapter for more information, although I highly recommend finishing this
chapter before you plow ahead.

✔ Yes, sometimes it's difficult to tell whether an electronic gizmo's power
button is "in the Off position." Just plug it into the power strip anyway.

✔ Most power strips have six sockets, which is plenty for a typical computer system. If not, buy a second power strip, plug it into its own wall
socket, and use it for the rest of your computer devices.

✔ Try to find a power strip with line noise filtering. Even better, pay more
to buy a power strip that has line conditioning! That's super nice for
your electronic goodies.

✔ I recommend the Kensington SmartSockets-brand power strips. Unlike
cheaper power strips, the SmartSockets brand lines up its sockets in an
arrangement that makes it easier to plug in bulky transformers.

✔ Don't plug one power strip into another power strip; it's electrically unsafe!

✔ Don't plug a laser printer into a power strip. The laser printer draws too
much juice for that method to be effective — or safe. Instead, you must
plug the laser printer directly into the wall socket. (It says so in your
laser printer's manual — if you ever get around to reading it.)

Surges, spikes, and lightning strikes

The power that comes from the wall socket into your computer isn't as pure as the wind-driven snow. Occasionally, it may be corrupted by some of the various electrical nasties that, every now and then, come uninvited into your home or office. Here's the lowdown:

Line noise: Electrical interference on the power line, most commonly seen as static on the TV screen when someone uses the blender.

Surge: A gradual increase in power.

Serge: Some guy from Europe.

Spike: A sudden increase in the power, such as what happens when lightning strikes nearby.

Dip: The opposite of a surge; a decrease in power. Some electrical motors don't work, and room lights are dimmer than normal. It's also known as a *brownout.*

Power outage: An absence of power coming through the line. People in the 1960s called it a *blackout.*

If possible, try to find a power strip with surge protection for your computer. You have a price to pay, but it's worth it. For an even better power strip, find one with both surge protection and noise filtering or line conditioning.

The most expensive form of protection is spike protection. That causes the power strip to lay down its life by taking the full brunt of the spike and saving your computer equipment.

Spikes, because they're particularly nasty, come through not only the power lines but also the phone lines. So, if lightning strikes are a common occurrence in your area, use a power strip with phone line protection, as well as network protection if you're using a broadband modem.

For more information about nasty things that can walk into your house through your wall sockets, contact your electrical company. It may offer its own solutions to help you keep your valuable electronics safe, such as power protection right at the breaker box.

The UPS power solution

UPS stands for *uninterruptible power supply*, and it's the best thing to have for hooking up your computer system to the wall socket. Basically, a *UPS* is a power strip combined with a battery to keep your computer running when the power goes out.

The notion behind a UPS isn't to keep computing while the power is out. Instead, the UPS is designed to keep your basic computer components — the console and monitor — up and running just long enough for you to save your work and properly shut down the computer. That way, you never lose anything because of a power outage.

Figure 3-2 illustrates the proper way to set up your computer system with a UPS and power strip. Not shown is a USB cable, which is used on some UPS systems to alert the computer about a power outage. Refer to Chapter 14 for information on how it works.

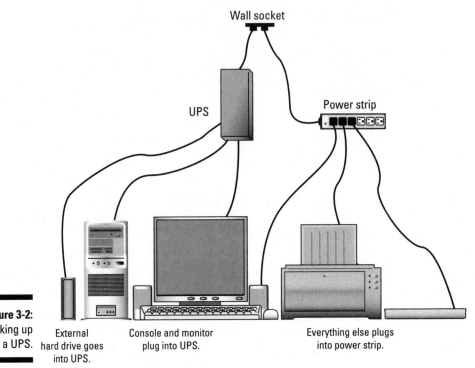

Figure 3-2:
Hooking up
a UPS.

External
hard drive goes
into UPS.

Console and monitor
plug into UPS.

Everything else plugs
into power strip.

✔ Also see Chapter 14 for information on having your computer shut down automatically when the power goes out.

✔ Ignore what it says on the box: A UPS gives you *maybe* five minutes of computer power. Most often, you get only two minutes of power.

✔ Some UPS systems also have non-battery-backed-up plugs so that you can plug everything into the UPS directly. Just be sure to plug the monitor and console into the battery-backed-up sockets.

✔ I also recommend plugging any external hard drives into the UPS's battery-backed-up sockets.

✔ Leave the UPS on all the time. Turn it off only when the power is out and the computer has been properly shut down.

✔ In addition to providing emergency power, a UPS provides higher levels of electrical protection for your equipment. Many models offer surge, spike, and dip protection, which keep your PC running smoothly despite any nasties the power company may throw your way.

Using the UPS (a short play)

Interior upscale kitchen. A thunderclap is heard. The lights flicker and then go out. ROGER, 40ish and nerdy, is left sitting in the dark, his computer is still on. The UPS beeps once every few seconds. FELICIA rushes in. She is pretentious but not insufferably so.

FELICIA: The power is out! The brioche I put in the toaster oven is ruined! Did you lose that urgent doodle you were creating in Paint?

ROGER: No, darling, I'm still working on it. See? Our UPS has kept the computer console and monitor turned on despite the power outage.

FELICIA: Oh! That explains the beeping.

ROGER: Yes, the UPS beeps when the power has gone out. It does that just in case I don't notice the pitch darkness.

FELICIA: Well, hurry up and print your doodle!

ROGER: Nay! I shan't print. Printing can wait, which is why I did not connect the printer to the UPS. It's as powerless as the toaster oven.

FELICIA: What can you do? Hurry! The UPS battery won't last forever!

ROGER: Relax, gentle spouse. I shall save to disk, thus. *(He presses Ctrl+S on the keyboard.)* Now I may shut down the computer, assured with the knowledge that my urgent doodle is safely stored on the PC's mass storage system. There. *(He turns off the computer and monitor. He shuts off the UPS and the* beeping *ceases.)* Now we can weather the storm with peace of mind.

Two hours later, after the power is back on, FELICIA and ROGER are sipping wine.

FELICIA: Honey, you sure are smart, the way you used that UPS.

ROGER: Well, I'm just thankful I read Dan Gookin's book *PCs For Dummies, Windows 7 Edition,* from Wiley Publishing, Inc. I think I shall buy more of his books.

FELICIA: Who knew that we could find such happiness, thanks to a computer book?

They canoodle.

Chapter 4

On and Off

. . . .

. . . .

*N*o doubt about it: Evil computers cannot be turned off. To prove it, I turn to the canon of *Star Trek*, Episode 53: When Scotty tried to turn off the malevolent M5 computer, it actually *killed* the crewman trying to pull the plug. Nope, you just can't turn off an evil computer.

Your PC is probably not evil. *Probably*. If it were, you could try to use Captain Kirk's infallible logic to reason the computer into committing suicide. I regret to tell you, however, that this book doesn't have any information on arguing a computer to death. That's because your PC has a power button, which is used to turn the computer both on and off. Though that might sound confusing, this chapter helps clear up the issue.

Turn On Your PC

You turn on the computer this way:

1. **Turn on everything but the console.**

2. **Turn on the console last.**

Or, if everything is plugged into a power strip, just turn on the power strip.

If the console and monitor are plugged into a UPS (which should be kept turned on all the time) and everything else is plugged into a power strip, do this:

1. **Turn on the power strip, which turns on all the computer's external devices, or *peripherals*.**

2. **Press the monitor's power button to turn it on.**

3. **Press the console's power button to turn it on.**

Success is indicated by your computer system coming to life; you can hear the fan whine, and various lights on the console, keyboard, and other devices may flash at you or glow softly. The scanner and printer may whir and grind their servos. Your computing day is at hand.

✔ By turning the console on last, you allow time for the other devices in the computer system to initialize and get ready for work. That way, the console recognizes them and lets you use those devices in your computer system.

✔ Not all computer devices have their own on–off switches. For example, some USB devices — scanners and disk drives — use the USB port's power. To turn off these devices, you must unplug the USB cable, although that's not necessary unless the device is behaving improperly.

✔ You don't have to turn everything on when the computer starts. For example, if you don't plan on printing, there's no need to turn on the printer. Ditto for the scanner.

✔ Some devices can be left on all the time. For example, the printer may have a special low-power mode that allows you to keep it on all the time, yet it uses little (if any) energy. It's often better to keep these devices on than to turn them on or off several times a day.

✔ It's generally a good idea to keep the DSL or cable modem on all the time. See Chapter 14 for more information on modems.

✔ The largest button on the front of the monitor turns it on. Some older models may have the on–off switch in back. Indeed, many computer devices have their switches in the back, usually next to where the power cord attaches.

✔ When something doesn't turn on, check to see whether it's plugged in. Confirm that all the cables are properly connected, at both ends.

✔ For times when Windows fails to start smoothly, or whenever the computer goes hinky, consider checking out my book *Troubleshooting Your PC For Dummies* (Wiley) or its hefty companion *Troubleshooting & Maintaining Your PC All-In-One For Dummies* (Wiley).

Ugly terms for starting a computer

Pay no attention to these other terms that refer to the process of starting a computer: boot, cold start, cycle power, hard start, power on, power up, reboot, reset, restart, soft boot, warm boot.

Windows, Ahoy!

Starting a computer is a hardware thing. But the hardware is dumb, remember? It needs software to keep things hopping, and the most important piece of software is your computer's operating system. For most PCs, that operating system is *Windows*. So, after starting your computer's hardware, the next thing you have to deal with is Windows.

The first thing you must do in Windows is identify yourself. The process is called *logging in* or *loggin on*, depending on which side of the Mississippi you live. Think of it as entering your name into a logbook as you board a ship. In fact, internally, Windows does just that: It keeps track of when you use the computer.

You log in by using your computer account name. That might be your own name, a nickname, some kind of computer superhero name, or something totally odd, like User117.

The computer must not only know who you are but also be reassured that you are who you say you are. You do that by entering a password. Only you should know the password for your computer account.

Figure 4-1 shows the standard logon screen in Windows, which is where the computer's prisoners identify themselves to the warden, and where you start your computer day. The following steps outline the process:

1. **If presented with a list of multiple accounts (pictures), choose yours from the list.**

   This step is optional. When you're the only one using your computer, your account is the only one that comes up.

2. **Enter your password into the box, if one appears.**

   Carefully type your password in the box. The password doesn't appear on the screen. Instead, tiny dots show up. Therefore, be careful when typing your account password.

3. **Click the blue arrow button or press the Enter key to have Windows check your password.**

Figure 4-1:
You log in
to Windows
here.

If everything goes well, you're logged in! You next see the Windows *desktop*, which is where you can start using your computer. See Chapter 5 for information about the desktop, stuff too distracting to reveal at this point in the book.

✔ Both the account name and password were set up when Windows was first configured on your computer. You probably forgot when you did that, but you did do it.

✔ When you goof up typing your password, try again. You can use the Password Hint link to remind you of your password — but you must type a password to get into the system!

✔ Mind the Caps Lock key on the keyboard! Your password is *case sensitive*, which means that the computer sees upper- and lowercase letters differently.

✔ The *user account* identifies who you are and keeps your information separate from anyone else who may be using the same computer. By adding a password, you ensure that your information on the computer stays safe and protected.

Turn the Computer Off

Common sense would dictate that the button you use to turn the computer off would be the same button you use to turn the thing on. But computers are all about logic, not common sense.

Your computer doesn't have an on–off switch. It has a *power button*. That sounds okay for turning the computer on, yet the same button can be used to turn the thing off. This concept fails to pass the "makes sense" test for a lot of people. But wait, there's more!

Not only does the power button turn the computer both on and off, but you also have numerous other ways to turn the computer off. Yep, it's not a question of just turning the darn thing off.

Here are the various ways you can end your computing session:

Don't end your computer day: This choice is the one the computer prefers, and the one you will invariably make after the computer has full control over your mind. It's *digital demonic possession,* and you'll need a pagan priest and an unblemished goat to rid yourself of the scourge. Seriously: One option for turning the computer off is not to turn it off ever. See the section "Should You Leave the Computer On All the Time?" toward the end of this chapter.

Log Off: Tell Windows that you're done without having to turn the computer off and then on again. You quit doing all your work, and the computer just sits with bated breath, waiting for you — someone, anyone — to log in again.

Lock the computer: Use this quick way to suspend computer operations and present the login screen, but without logging off or quitting any programs. I use this option most often.

Switch User: Allow another user on the same computer to access their account without logging off from your own account or quitting any programs.

Sleep Mode: The computer slips into a special power-saving Sleep mode, like going into a low-power coma.

Hibernate: The computer turns itself off, but when you turn it back on again, it comes back to life much faster. Think "suspended animation."

Restart: You turn the computer off and on again in one step, mainly when installing or upgrading software or sometimes to fix minor quirks — like slapping Windows upside its head.

Shut Down: This is the one true option that turns the darn thing off.

Yank the power cord out of the wall: This method is satisfying, but not recommended.

Many of these options are on the official Shutdown menu, located on the Start button's menu, as shown in Figure 4-2. To open the Shutdown menu, follow these steps:

Control Panel

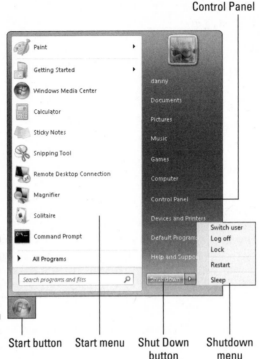

Figure 4-2:
Where the
Shutdown
menu lurks.

Start button   Start menu   Shut Down   Shutdown
                              button   menu

1. **Pop up the Start button's menu.**

   You can pop up the menu by clicking the Start button with the mouse or by pressing the Windows key on the keyboard.

2. **Click the Shutdown menu's triangle button in the lower-right corner of the Start button menu.**

Using the various options on the Shutdown menu is covered in the sections that follow.

   ✔ If you just want to shut down the computer, you can click the Shut Down button (refer to Figure 4-2).

   ✔ In Windows Vista, the Shutdown menu appears in basically the same location as shown in Figure 4-2, though the Start menu appears differently.

   ✔ The Windows XP shutdown options are selected from the Start button in their own manner. The sections that follow describe the pertinent details.

Log yourself off

When several people have accounts on the same computer, you can log off to keep the computer on, toasty, and ready for someone else to use it. To do so, follow these steps:

1. **Click the Start button.**

2. **Click the Shutdown menu button on the Start menu.**

   Refer to Figure 4-2.

3. **Choose the Log Off command.**

As the computer logs you out, you're prompted to save any unsaved files, and then your programs and windows are closed. You're done for the day. Windows once again displays its initial logon screen.

✔ Logging yourself off does not turn off the PC.

✔ In Windows XP, choose the Log Off button at the bottom of the Start menu, and then click the Log Off button in the Log Off Windows window that appears.

✔ When you're the only person who has an account on the computer, logging off is an utter waste of time. A better option break is to lock the computer, as covered in the next section.

Lock the computer

When you *lock* the computer, you're directing Windows to display the initial logon screen, similar to the one shown in Figure 4-1. You prevent anyone from seeing what you're doing, as well as keep out anyone who doesn't have an account on your PC.

To lock the computer, press the Win+L key combination, where Win is the Windows key on the computer keyboard and L is the L key. The computer is locked.

✔ Lock the computer whenever you need to step away for a bit.

✔ Press Win+L, where L stands for *lock*.

Switch users

The Switch User command allows you to temporarily log out so that another user on the same computer can log in. This option is faster than logging out because it doesn't require you to save your stuff or close your programs. When you return (log in again), all your stuff is waiting for you just as you left it.

- ✔ The Switch User command is on the Shutdown menu (refer to Figure 4-2).

- ✔ In Windows XP, choose the Log Out command from the Start button menu, and then click the Switch User button in the Log Off Windows dialog box.

- ✔ As with logging off, there's no point in using the Switch User command when you're the only person who has an account on the computer.

Sleep mode

Sleep mode is an energy-saving way to not quite turn off the PC. In Sleep mode, Windows saves what you're doing and then puts the computer into a special low-power mode. The computer isn't exactly off, and it restores itself quickly, which makes Sleep mode more effective as a way to shut down the computer.

To put your PC to sleep, choose the Sleep command from the Shutdown menu, beautifully illustrated in Figure 4-2.

To wake the computer from its slumber, you can wiggle the mouse or press a key on the keyboard. Be patient! Sometimes the PC takes a few seconds to wake up.

- ✔ Sleep mode was once known as Stand By mode. Sometimes the term Suspend was used instead.

- ✔ In Windows 7 and Windows Vista, Sleep mode is officially known as *Hybrid Sleep*. In Windows XP, Sleep mode puts the computer into a low-power state, but information isn't saved before the PC goes to sleep.

- ✔ To "sleep" the computer in Windows XP, click the Shut Down button at the bottom of the Start button menu. In the Turn Off Computer dialog box, click the Stand By button.

- ✔ Sleep mode is part of the computer's power management features. See Chapter 14 for more information.

Hibernation

The most dramatic way to save power and not-quite-exactly turn off the PC is to use *hibernation*. It saves all the computer's memory — everything the system is doing — and then turns off the computer. (It's turned off, not just sleeping). When you turn on the computer again, things return to the way they were. So hibernation not only saves electricity but also provides a faster way to turn the computer off and then on again.

- ✔ To hibernate your computer, you must program the console's power button to become the Hibernation button. That information is found in Chapter 14.

- ✔ In Windows XP, you can enter Hibernation mode by choosing Shut Down from the Start button menu. When the Turn Off Computer dialog box appears, press the Shift key, which reveals the Hibernate button. Click that button.

Restart Windows

You need to reset or restart Windows in two instances: First, Windows may direct you to restart after you install something new or make a change. Second, restarting is a good idea whenever something strange happens. For some reason, a restart clears the computer's head like a good nose blow, and things return to normal.

To restart Windows, choose the Restart command from the Shutdown menu (refer to Figure 4-2). Windows shuts itself down — almost as though it were turning off the computer. But, just at the moment the system would have turned off, it starts back up again — a restart.

- ✔ If any files are unsaved, you're asked to save them before shutting down.

- ✔ In Windows XP, restart by popping up the Start button menu and clicking the Shut Down button. Click the Restart button in the Turn Off Computer dialog box.

- ✔ Windows may initiate a restart on its own; or, when upgrading, you may have to click a button in a window to restart the computer.

Regarding that bonus power button (the secret one)

Some PC cases have a true on–off switch in addition to a power button. You can find the on–off switch on the back of the console, usually by the place where the power cord connects to the PC's power supply. The switch is often labeled | and O, for on and off, respectively. Use this button rather than the power button only in times of dire emergency. Also note that the on–off switch must be in the on position for you to turn on your computer (using the power button).

Turn the darn thing off

Yes, it's absolutely possible: Despite having only one of several options, you can turn off your computer. From the Shutdown menu, click the Shut Down button (refer to Figure 4-2). If you have any unsaved documents or files, Windows asks you to save them. Then it slowly unwinds and your computer turns itself off.

After the console turns itself off, go ahead and turn off the other components in your computer system: monitor and scanner and any other external devices. Or, if you have a power strip, simply flip its switch to turn everything off.

- ✔ The computer may also turn off when you press the console's power button. Well, it doesn't turn off right away; the power button simply issues the Shut Down command and Windows closes your programs, and then the computer turns itself off.

- ✔ Keep in mind that the console's power button can be programmed to perform a variety of shutdown options. If you're interested in changing the console power button's function, see Chapter 14.

- ✔ In Windows XP, you can turn off the computer by choosing the Shut Down command from the Start button menu and then clicking the Turn Off button in the Turn Off Computer dialog box.

- ✔ If the computer shuts down and then immediately restarts, you have a problem. Ask your dealer or computer manufacturer for assistance, or check out my other PC book, *Troubleshooting Your PC For Dummies* (Wiley).

- ✔ You can always use it to turn off the PC in a panic: Simply press and hold the console's power button for about three or four seconds, and the computer turns off. Although this trick is a handy one to know, you should use it only in times of desperation. Otherwise, shut down the PC properly, as described in this section.

Should You Leave the Computer On All the Time?

I've been writing about computers for more than 20 years, and this debate has yet to be settled: Should you leave your computer on all the time? Does it waste electricity? Is it better for the PC to be on all the time — like the refrigerator or a lava lamp? Will we ever know *the truth?* Of course not! But people have opinions.

"I want to leave my computer off all the time"

It's an excellent solution, but one that renders nearly all of this book unnecessary.

"I want to leave my computer on all the time"

I say Yes. If you use your computer often, such as for a home business, or you find yourself turning it on and off several times during the day, just leave it on all the time.

The only time I ever turn off my computers is when I'll be away for longer than a weekend. Even then, I just hibernate the computers rather than turn them off.

Does my method waste electricity? Perhaps, but most computers have Sleep mode and save energy when they're not being used. Modern PCs don't use that much electricity, especially when you have an LCD monitor (see Chapter 10), and having a PC on all the time doesn't raise your electric bill significantly, not like a Jacuzzi or a Tesla coil does.

Also, computers enjoy being on all the time. Having that fan whirring keeps the console's innards at a constant temperature, which avoids some of the problems that turning the system off (cooling) and on again (heating) cause.

- ✔ If you use your PC only once a day (during the evening for e-mail, chat, and the Internet, for example), turning it off for the rest of the day is fine.

- ✔ Most businesses leave their computers on all the time, though a medium-size business can save thousands of dollars a year by shutting down their computers overnight. Just a thought.

✔ Whatever you do with your PC, always turn off the *monitor* when you're away. Some monitors can sleep just like PCs, but if they don't, turning them off saves electricity.

✔ If you leave your computer on all the time, don't put it under a dust cover. You'll suffocate the thing.

Chapter 5

The Windows Tour

*I*remember that Microsoft originally wanted to call its new PC operating system *Doors* and not Windows. That was because, as a graphical operating system, Doors opened the doors of access to the vast power of the computer. Also, doors are easier to walk through than windows. Sadly, the estate of the late Jim Morrison sued, so Microsoft had to settle on Windows instead.

Yeah, I made up that entire paragraph.

Software controls the hardware, and the primary piece of software that controls the hardware is the operating system, Windows. Though this book is primarily about hardware, you have to use Windows to get things done with PC hardware, such as adjusting the mouse, getting on the network, and using the storage system. Rather than scatter that important information about Windows all over this book, I thought I'd put it here, in this chapter. Welcome to your Windows tour.

Windows and Its Gooey, Glorious Graphical Interface

You aren't required to read Chapter 1 before you read this chapter, but if you did so, you might recall that one of a computer operating system's primary duties is to interface with you, the human. Windows does that by presenting you with a graphical visage, spackled with interesting items given unusual names:

✔ Desktop

✔ Taskbar

✔ Start button

✔ Start button menu

✔ Notification area

The key to manipulating your computer is to know what those names refer to and how to use each of them to get things done. This section explains the details.

The desktop

Because hell already has a vestibule, the folks who designed Windows were forced to make its lobby, its home base, its starting point something called the *desktop*. That's the place where you really start using your computer, getting stuff done, or just goofing off.

Essentially, the desktop is the main screen in Windows, shown in Figure 5-1. It's where the actual windows appear, the windows containing your programs, games, and other fun computer whatnot.

The desktop also features *icons*, or tiny pictures that represent information or programs stored on your computer. System icons represent fun and interesting places to visit in Windows, as well as shortcut icons, which you can use to start programs, visit Web sites, and more.

Figure 5-1 also shows some Windows Sidebar gadgets. The gadgets display information such as the time or stock quotes or images or games or other diversionary items. The gadgets may appear along the edge of the desktop; they can "float" anywhere; or they might not even show up.

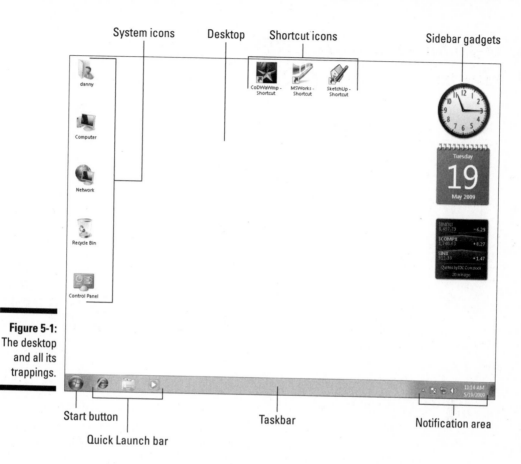

System icons Desktop Shortcut icons Sidebar gadgets

Figure 5-1:
The desktop
and all its
trappings.

Start button Taskbar Notification area

Quick Launch bar

Finally, the desktop background can be a fancy image or picture, a slide
show, or the famous *Snowbank* painting, shown in Figure 5-1.

- Not shown in Figure 5-1 is the *mouse pointer*, the tiny arrow that manipulates the graphical goodies you see on the screen. The mouse pointer is
  controlled by the mouse, covered in Chapter 11.

- The *desktop* is merely the background on which Windows shows you
  its stuff — like that pale blue bedsheet they use as a backdrop for any
  elementary school's production of *Eat Your Vegetables*.

- *Icons* are tiny pictures representing files or programs on your computer.
  See Chapter 20 for more information on icons.

- You can do lots of fun things with the desktop background image, as well
  as specify screen resolution and other graphical things. See Chapter 10 for
  the details.

✔ When you connect two monitors to a single PC, the desktop appears on both monitors but the taskbar appears on only the main monitor. Again, see Chapter 10 for more information on the dual-monitor thing.

✔ The desktop is called a desktop for traditional reasons. Several generations of computers ago, it did look like a desktop, complete with paper pad, clock, glue, scissors, and other desktop-y things.

The taskbar

A lot of stuff happens on the Windows desktop, but a majority of the time the action starts at the taskbar. The taskbar is normally found lining the bottom of the computer screen, as shown in Figure 5-2. On the taskbar dwell various interesting and useful items:

Start button   Window buttons   Notification area

Figure 5-2:
The taskbar.

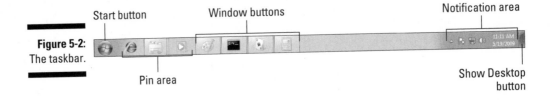

Pin area   Show Desktop
button

Start button: This is where you control Windows, which is covered in the next two sections.

Pin area: The icons, or tiny pictures, on this part of the taskbar are used to quickly start programs or perform common tasks in Windows.

Window buttons: A button appears on the taskbar for each window or program running in Windows. Those things are called *tasks*, which is why the taskbar is called the taskbar and not the candy bar.

Notification area: This part of the taskbar contains tiny icons (pictures) that help you run your computer or alert you to certain things going on. It's covered in detail later in this chapter.

Show Desktop button: Clicking this button with the mouse hides all windows and programs on the display so that you can easily see the desktop.

The taskbar is locked into position, held at the bottom of the desktop by digital bolts made of the strongest bits. Still, the taskbar can be unlocked and moved, so it might not always be at the bottom of the screen. Further, the taskbar can be configured to be hidden, though it pops up automatically if you point the mouse at the edge of the screen where the taskbar was last seen or when you press the Windows button on your PC's keyboard.

The Start button and Start menu

 The Start button lives on the left end of the taskbar, assuming that the task-bar is docked at its usual spot on the bottom of the screen. As its name suggests, the Start button is used to start things in Windows. What kinds of things? Everything!

More important than the Start button is the menu that appears when you click the Start button with the mouse. That menu, the Start button menu or just Start menu, is shown in Figure 5-3. That's where the fun — or anguish — starts!

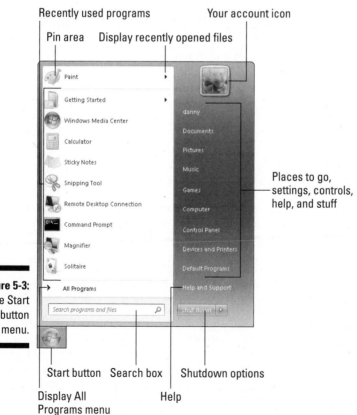

Figure 5-3: The Start button menu.

Important things to find on the Start button menu are listed in Figure 5-3. The Start button menu can be customized, so it may not appear exactly like what you see in the figure, but it's close.

One of the most important items on the Start button menu is the All Programs menu. When you click the All Programs triangle (refer to Figure 5-3), the left side of the Start button menu is replaced with a list of programs and folders. You can either choose a program from the list to run the program or choose a folder to see additional programs. Chapter 23 offers more information on the Start button menu and your programs.

- ✔ In Windows XP, the Start button has the word *Start* on it.

- ✔ A quick way to pop up the Start button menu is to press the Win key on your computer's keyboard. For older computers or laptops that lack a Win key, press Ctrl+Esc to pop up the Start button menu.

- ✔ You make the Start button menu go away by pressing the Esc key on the keyboard.

- ✔ The Start button menu is customized by using the Taskbar and Start Menu Properties dialog box. To see that dialog box, right-click the Start button and choose Properties from the pop-up menu. Click the Customize button to adjust how the Start button menu looks and behaves.

The notification area

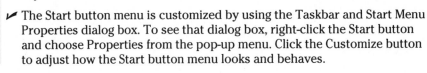

Those teensy icons on the far right side of the taskbar aren't just sitting around waiting for a bus. Nope, they are part of a thing called the *notification area*. The icons, along with the current date and time, allow you to control various things in Windows, check in on running programs, adjust the volume, and other miscellaneous chores.

As with just about everything in Windows, the notification area can be customized. You can see a lot of icons there, a few, or none. Also, icons may come or go. Don't let that random nature of the notification area vex you.

- ✔ You can see more information about the special programs by clicking, double-clicking, or right-clicking the wee icons.

- ✔ Some icons display pop-up bubbles with messages in them as various things happen in Windows. Click the X in the pop-up bubble to dismiss the message.

- ✔ Once upon a time, the notification area was known as the *system tray*. You may still find it referred to that way in various documentation.

The Control Panel

The operating system is also in charge of all your PC's hardware. It controls everything. Therefore, it makes sense that the one place where all the computer hardware is controlled is called the *Control Panel*.

Figure 5-4 shows the Control Panel. It's organized by categories, with various links and such that you can click to examine or adjust various aspects of the computer system. By clicking a link, you see even more categories, though eventually you get down to a window that lets you manipulate something specific. It's somehow both organized and confusing, which seems to be a common combination in Windows.

Figure 5-4:
The Control
Panel Home.

To display the Control Panel window, follow these steps:

1. **Click the Start button.**

2. **Click the Control Panel menu item on the right side of the Start button menu.**

Later chapters in this book offer specific directions for things to do in the Control Panel. As long as you know how to open the Control Panel window, you'll be okay.

You can close the Control panel window by clicking the X (Close) button in the window's upper-right corner.

✔ And now, the bad news: You have several ways to view the Control Panel. In Figure 5-4, you see Category view, and also Icon view, which comes in both small and large presentations. To switch between views, choose the proper view from the View By menu, found near the upper right corner of the Control Panel's window.

✔ This book assumes that you're using the Control Panel in Category view.

✔ In older versions of Windows, you choose Category view by clicking the proper link from the left side of the Control Panel window.

Where Your Stuff Goes

Windows provides special folders where you can store the things you create on the computer — files and folders. Files are covered in Chapter 20, but for now, a few specific locations are worthy of note:

 Computer: This main icon details all long-term storage in your computer, which includes disk drives, CD/DVD, media storage, as well as any network drives you're using. You display the Computer window by opening the Computer icon on the desktop or accessing it from the Start button menu.

 User Profile: The main folder for your stuff is named after your account, and it's officially called the User Profile folder. I prefer to call it your account folder. Within this main folder, you find various subfolders to help you organize your stuff. The subfolders are named according to their content, which surprisingly makes sense.

 Libraries: All files on your computer of a certain type are organized into a broad category called a *library*. There are libraries for your documents, music, videos, and pictures, plus libraries can be created to store your computer games, specific projects, or your collection of racy salt shaker photos, for example.

 HomeGroup: The HomeGroup provides a way to share stuff with other computers on a network so that you can all listen to music, watch videos, or steal each other's files with ease. More information about networking is in Part III of this book.

 Recycle Bin: This icon represents the place where files go after they're deleted — kind of like File Hell but nondenominational. Normally, this icon is found on the desktop.

✔ Windows Vista does not use the My prefix for the Music, Pictures, and Video folders.

✔ See Part IV of this book for more information about the stuff you create on your computer, including a discussion of what the heck a "folder" is.

Windows Tries to Help You

Historically speaking, Windows never came with a full manual. Originally, it had just a feeble *Getting started* type of booklet that wasn't much help. That's because the real "help" exists inside the program in what's called the Windows Help System. There are two ways to use it:

First, press the F1 key while you're in the midst of doing anything in Windows. You see a window appear with (supposedly) helpful information about what you're doing.

Second, choose the Help and Support command from the Start button menu, shown in Figure 5-3.

Either way you get there, the Windows Help and Support window opens, listing help topics, some tutorials, plus a search box where you can type a question or term to get more information. At least that's the theory.

When you're done with the help, or simply exasperated, close its window by clicking the X (Close) button in the window's upper-right corner.

- ✔ Help can also be found in just about every Windows program. Most often, you find a Help menu near the top of the window on the menu bar. Some programs feature a tiny question mark in a circle instead of the Help menu. Just click the question mark to get help.

- ✔ Windows may have to contact the Internet to display its helpful information. You notice that it's doing so only when you have a dial-up Internet connection. See Part III of this book for more information on the Internet.

Part II
The Nerd's-Eye View

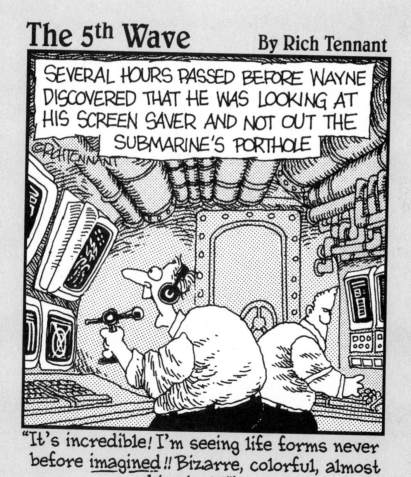

The 5th Wave   By Rich Tennant

SEVERAL HOURS PASSED BEFORE WAYNE DISCOVERED THAT HE WAS LOOKING AT HIS SCREEN SAVER AND NOT OUT THE SUBMARINE'S PORTHOLE

"It's incredible! I'm seeing life forms never before _imagined_!! Bizarre, colorful, almost whimsical!!!"

In this part . . .

For a moment, dare to pretend that you're a computer
nerd. Now imagine that you're looking at a computer.
Of course, you see only the hardware, but that hardware
beckons to you, drawing your attention like a seductive
siren lures a storm-tossed ship into a rocky shoal. Indeed,
computer hardware can be alluring; it can entice you,
seduce you, overwhelm you with its sweet-smelling,
throbbing plastic beauty. Oh, my!

Okay! You can stop pretending that you're a computer
nerd now.

This part of the book discusses the true guts of your computer system: its hardware. Though software rules the PC
roost, it's the hardware that sets the tone for what the
software does. By discovering what computer hardware is
and how it fits into the big picture, you get more from
your PC. And, yes, it's entirely possible to do that without
ever becoming a computer nerd.

Chapter 6

Deep Inside the Console

. . . .

In This Chapter

▶ Studying the console's insides

▶ Examining the motherboard

▶ Understanding the processor

▶ Working with expansion cards

▶ Setting the clock

▶ Knowing about the chipset

▶ Supplying the console with power

. . . .

Some people have a certain fascination with wanting to know what makes things tick. They take stuff apart and look at the pieces and somehow glean understanding. Then, amazingly, they put everything back together and it all still works. I've tried that approach myself: taking apart various household items, understanding how they work, and putting them back together. The technique works well for appliances, less so for pets.

The computer console isn't something you want to completely take apart and put back together. It's just too important to risk such a thing, especially if you mistrust computers in the first place. Still, the console is the heart of your PC. Though opening it up may not be appropriate, it does help to know what goes on inside the box.

Console Guts

A lot of interesting doodads and goobers dwell safely inside the PC's bosom. You can't see them (well, unless the case is translucent), but they exist. Despite their concealment, those components play a key role in your computer system. As the master of the PC, you should know what those doodads and goobers are, what they do, and — most importantly — what their real names are and how to properly pronounce them.

Looking under the hood

If you dared to remove the cover from your PC, you would see a clutch of mysterious technology, from large metal boxes to tiny pointed and dangerous raw electronics. There's no need to remove the PC's cover to witness such miracles, however, because I provide a safe and lovely illustration of what you'd see inside the console, shown in Figure 6-1.

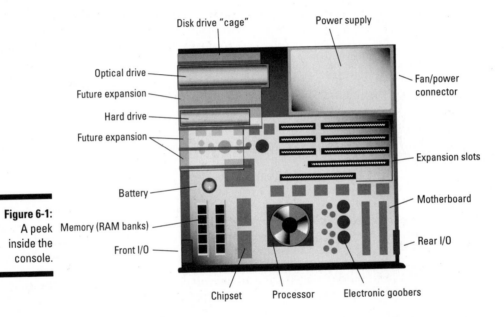

Disk drive "cage"
Power supply
Optical drive
Future expansion
Hard drive
Future expansion
Fan/power connector
Expansion slots
Battery
Motherboard
Figure 6-1:
A peek inside the console.
Memory (RAM banks)
Front I/O
Rear I/O
Chipset
Processor
Electronic goobers

The figure illustrates the PC's internals as though you're looking inside a typical mini-tower console. The front of the computer is on the left.

Though lots of things are inside the console's tummy, here are the important items to note:

- ✔ The power supply
- ✔ The disk drive cage
- ✔ The motherboard

The *power supply* feeds the console that all-important stuff called electricity. You can read more about the power supply in the section "The Source of PC Power," at the end of this chapter.

The *disk drive cage* is a contraption used to hold internal disk drives, an optical drive, a hard drive, plus maybe a media card reader. The cage also has room for even more disk drives (the so-called "future expansion"), usually right behind some knockout panels on the console's front.

Finally, the *motherboard* is the computer's main circuitry board. It's important, as are its many important residents, so I talk about it later in this chapter, starting with the section "The Mother of All Boards."

✔ Everything inside the PC's case is a *modular* component: Individual pieces can be replaced without having to toss out the entire console. Modularity is one of the keys to the PC's success as a computer system.

✔ What you don't see in Figure 6-1 are the miles of cables that festoon the console's interior space. Also missing is a thin layer of dust and perhaps some pet hair.

Going inside the console (not recommended)

There is no sane reason to open your PC's case. Nope. In fact, I've owned computers for years without ever popping their hoods. Even when it's a necessary task, such as when performing an upgrade or a repair, I highly recommend that you have someone else do it.

If you were going to open the PC's console, which I'm still not recommending, you'd probably follow these general steps:

1. **Turn off the computer.**

   Refer to Chapter 4.

2. **Unplug the console; remove the power cord.**

   Turning off the console isn't enough: You need to unplug the power cord. Unplugging other cables isn't necessary unless you need to do so to move the console around, or when replacing an expansion card that has cables attached.

3. **Move the console out from the wall or locate it in a place where you have room to work.**

4. **Open the console's case.**

That last step isn't as easy as it sounds. There's no universal way to open a computer console: Some cases require a screwdriver and the removal of several screws. Other cases may just pop up, slide off, or swing open. Someone who is good with tools can figure out the operation in a jiffy. And, by "good with tools," I don't mean good with a blow torch or the Jaws of Life.

When you finish doing whatever motivated you to open the console, close it up! Heed these cautious steps:

1. **Check to ensure that all wires and cables have been properly reconnected.**

2. **Confirm that no tools or parts are left loose inside the case.**

3. **Reattach the lid or console cover.**

4. **Reattach the power cord to the console.**

5. **Turn the computer on.**

6. **Pray that it still works.**

    This step is optional in case you don't believe in a higher, divine being. But why risk it now?

When the case is open and the computer's guts are visible, you're ready to work inside the console. Use Figure 6-1 as a general reference — but mind the cables!

- ✔ Never plug in the console when the case is open. If you need to test something, close up the case!

- ✔ Typically, you open the case to do one of three things: Add memory; add an expansion card; or replace the PC's battery.

- ✔ While you work in the console, try to keep one hand touching the case or, preferably, something metal, like the disk drive cage. That way, your electric potential is the same as the console's and you reduce the chances of generating static electricity — which can damage your computer.

The Mother of All Boards

The computer's largest circuitry board is the *motherboard*. It's where the computer's most important electronics dwell. The motherboard is home to the following essential PC components, many of which are illustrated earlier in this chapter (refer to Figure 6-1):

- ✔ Processor
- ✔ Chipset
- ✔ Memory

- ✔ Battery
- ✔ Expansion slots
- ✔ I/O connectors
- ✔ Electronic goobers

The processor, chipset, battery, and expansion card items all have their own sections in this chapter. Refer to them for more information. Computer memory is a big deal, so it's covered exclusively in Chapter 8.

The *I/O connectors* are simply places on the motherboard where various internal options plug in and communicate with the rest of the computer system. For example, on the motherboard, you find an I/O connector where the internal disk drives plug in and an I/O power connector for electricity from the power supply.

The electronic goobers are those miscellaneous pieces of technology that engineers put on the motherboard to make their work look impressive.

The Processor Rules

It's a common mistake for folks to refer to the computer's processor as its *brain*. That's not true. Software is the brain in a computer; it controls all the hardware, which means that it also controls the processor.

- ✔ The processor is your PC's main chip. Just about everything else on the motherboard exists to serve the processor.
- ✔ Another term for a processor is CPU. *CPU* stands for central processing unit.
- ✔ Modern PC processors run very hot and therefore require special cooling. If you ever look inside the PC console, you'll notice that the processor wears a tiny fan as a hat. That helps keep the thing cool.

What does the processor do?

Despite its importance, what the processor does is rather simple: Beyond basic math (addition, subtraction, division, multiplication), the processor can fetch and put information to and from memory, and it can do basic input/output (I/O) stuff. That doesn't seem impressive, yet the key to the processor's success is that, unlike your typical brooding teenager, the processor does things *very fast*.

Try to imagine the processor as a combination adding machine and traffic cop, though the traffic is traveling 64 lanes wide and at the speed of light.

Name that processor!

Once upon a time, computer processors were named after famous numbers, like 386 and 8088. The trend now is toward processor names, but not human names, like John or Mary, or even dog names like Rover or Chomps. No, now processors are named after potential science fiction heroes, pharmaceuticals, or sounds made by a baby rhinoceros in distress.

Seriously, the primary processor found in a typical PC is the Pentium, developed by industry leader Intel. Other processor names include Athlon, Itanium, Opteron, Phenom, and Xeon. (Six more names and you have a galactic pantheon.)

The number-name thing is difficult for the computer industry to completely break with, so you also see processor names followed by numbers and other strange words. Honestly, the processor name and number matter only when you first buy the computer, and even then the only numbers that truly matter are the dollars you plunk down for the thing.

Beyond the name, the truly important yardstick used to judge a processor (aside from price) is its speed, which is covered in the next section.

✔ The Pentium processor exists in various flavors. It's those flavor names that adorn a PC's console, often found on a little "Intel Inside" sticker.

✔ Popular Pentium variations include the Core 2 Duo, Core 2 Quad, and Core i7. I'm sure there are more, but as I already wrote, most of this stuff plays a role only when you first buy the computer.

✔ Little difference exists between a true Intel and a non-Intel processor. As far as your PC's software is concerned, the processor is the same no matter who made it.

Processor muscle and speed

Processors are gauged by two factors: their muscle power and how fast they go.

Processor muscle is measured in bits — specifically, how many bits at a time the chip can toss around. The more bits at a time a processor can deal with, the better. For a typical PC processor, that's 32, 64, or 128 bits, and 64 bits is the most common.

Think of bits in a processor like lanes on a freeway: The more you have, the more traffic (information) the processor can play with and the faster it can go. More bits equals faster processor.

Processor speed is measured in *gigahertz (GHz)*, or billions of cycles per second. The higher the value, the faster the processor, with average speeds between 2.0 GHz (slower) and 4.0 GHz (faster). Yep, faster processors cost more. Lots more.

Sadly, speed isn't a realistic gauge of how fast a processor does its processing. Speed is a relative measurement when it comes to computers. So although a Pentium running at 2.4 GHz is technically slower than a Pentium running at 3.0 GHz, you probably wouldn't notice the difference between the two.

Which processor lives in your PC?

Believe it or not, it's difficult to tell by looking at it which processor is found inside your PC's console. That's because the processor wears a little fan as a hat, and you shouldn't pull off that little hat just to read the gibberish printed on top of the processor that you probably wouldn't understand anyway.

The best way to determine which processor is busy working away inside your PC is to use Windows. The System window shows a brief processor and RAM summary, similar to the one shown in Figure 6-2. To summon that window, press Win+Break on your keyboard (that's the Windows key plus the key labeled Break or Pause Break).

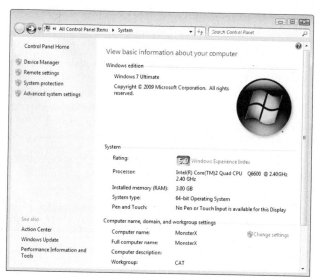

Figure 6-2:
The System window.

In Figure 6-2, you can see that the PC sports an Intel Core 2 Quad CPU, which is a Pentium processor. It runs at 2.40GHz. The computer sports 3GB of RAM. All that information jibes with what I paid for, so my dealer is off the hook.

✔ Not every System window displays information as complete as is shown in Figure 6-2. When Windows doesn't know, it may say something vague, as in "x86 Family."

✔ See Chapter 8 for more information on RAM.

Expansion Slots

The success of the original IBM PC was due to the ability to expand the computer internally by adding circuitry boards. Those boards, or *expansion cards*, plugged directly into *expansion slots* on the motherboard. The idea is that you can expand your computer system by adding options not included with the basic PC.

Expansion slots, as well as the cards that plug into those slots, are known by their type. The most popular type of expansion slot is now PCI Express, also written as PCIe. Without boring you, the PCI Express type of expansion slot communicates with the motherboard, and therefore with the processor, both quickly and efficiently. That makes it an ideal way to add circuitry to your computer system.

Older expansion slot types might also be found in your PC on the motherboard. They exist primarily for compatibility with older PC hardware.

✔ The number and type of slots available in your computer depend on the size of the console's case as well as on the motherboard's design. Small-footprint PCs have the fewest expansion slots. Mini-desktop systems, all-in-one PCs (where the console and monitor are the same), and nearly all laptops lack expansion slots. Tower computer models have the most — sometimes up to eight expansion slots!

✔ Expansion cards are sometimes called *daughterboards*. Get it? Motherboard, daughterboard? I'm looking forward to *auntboard* or perhaps *secondcousinboard*.

✔ Most expansion cards come squirming with cables. This mess of cables makes the seemingly sleek motherboard look more like an electronic pasta dish. Some cables are threaded inside the PC; others are left hanging limply out the back. The cables are what make the internal upgrading and installation process so difficult.

✔ The backsides of most expansion cards stick out the rear of the consoles; the card's back replaces the metallic slot cover to reveal special connectors or attachments for the expansion card.

✔ When your PC has PCI Express expansion slots, you must be sure to buy only PCI Express expansion cards. For example, if you choose to add an internal TV adapter, you have to buy a PCI Express TV adapter.

✔ A common type of PCI Express card to add to a PC is a high-end graphics card. See Chapter 10 for more information on graphics.

✔ Other expansion card types include the following acronyms: AGP, ISA, and PCI. If you want to get antique, there once were the MCA, VESA Local Bus, NuBus, EISA, and LEGO expansion slots.

✔ I'm just kidding about LEGO.

✔ If you're faced with a choice between PCIe and an older expansion option, use the PCIe card and slot.

✔ PCI stands for Peripheral Component Interconnect, in case that issue ever comes up in a crossword puzzle.

Your Computer Is Also a Timepiece

All PCs come equipped with internal clocks. Don't look for a dial, and don't bother leaning into the console to hear the thing going "tick-tock." Trust me: The clock exists. Specifically, clock circuitry exists somewhere on the motherboard.

The amazing thing is that the PC keeps track of the time even when you unplug it. That's because the motherboard sports a teensy battery (refer to Figure 6-1). That battery helps the computer hardware keep track of the date and time all the time.

✔ See Chapter 5 for more information about the notification area.

✔ Computers need clocks just like humans do: to keep track of time. Computers use clocks for scheduling, to time-stamp information and events, and generally to prevent everything from happening all at once.

✔ Here's a secret: Computers make lousy clocks. A typical PC loses about a minute or two of time every day. Why? Who knows! You can set the clock, as discussed in the next section, or have Windows automatically set the date and time, covered in the section "Using the Internet to set the clock," a little later in this chapter.

✔ On the positive side, the computer's clock is well aware of daylight savings time: Windows automatically jumps the clock forward or backward, and does so without having to know the little ditty "Spring forward, fall back." Or is it the other way around? Whatever — the computer knows and obeys.

✔ The date-and-time format is based on your country or region, which was set when you first configured Windows. You can change the date-and-time format by using the Control Panel: Open the Control Panel and click the Clock, Language and Region link. On the next screen, click the link Change The Date, Time or Number Format. Use the Region and Language dialog box to set things up properly.

Viewing the date and time

Windows reads the PC's hardware clock and displays a software clock for you. It's found in the notification area, usually in the lower right corner of the screen. To see a pop-up clock and calendar, click that time display once.

Setting the clock

To set the date and time on your PC, heed these steps:

1. **Right-click the time display in the notification area on the taskbar.**

2. **From the pop-up menu, choose the command Adjust Date/Time.**

   The Date and Time Properties dialog box appears.

3. **Click the Change Date and Time button.**

   The Date and Time Settings dialog box appears, as shown in Figure 6-3.

4. **Manipulate the controls in the Date and Time Properties dialog box to change or set the date or time.**

5. **Click OK when you're done.**

6. **Close the Date and Time dialog box.**

You can also have the computer automatically set time by using something called a *time server* on the Internet. That's covered later in this — oh! Why, it's covered next.

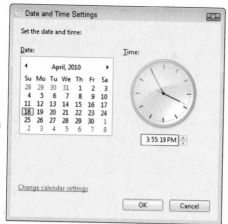

Figure 6-3:
The Date
and Time
Settings
dialog box.

Using the Internet to set the clock

One way to tame the wild computer clock is to have the computer itself auto-matically synchronize the time with one of the many worldwide time servers. A *time server* is a computer designed to cough up accurate time information for any computer that checks in on the Internet.

Your PC should be configured to automatically set itself to Internet time. To confirm that option, or to set up Internet time, follow these steps:

1. **Right-click the mouse on the date-and-time display in the taskbar's notification area.**

2. **Choose the command Adjust Date/Time from the pop-up menu.**

   The Date and Time dialog box shows up.

3. **Click the Internet Time tab in the Date and Time Properties dialog box.**

   If you see the text telling you that the computer is set to automatically synchronize on a scheduled basis, you're set. Skip to Step 8. Otherwise:

4. **Click the Change Settings button.**

   The Internet Time Settings dialog box appears.

5. **Click to place a check mark by the option Synchronize with an Internet Time Server.**

6. **(Optional) Choose a time server from the drop-down list.**

7. Click the Update Now button to ensure that everything works.

When a problem occurs, repeat Steps 6 and 7 by choosing another time server.

8. Click OK to close the Internet Time Settings dialog box.

9. Click OK to close the Date and Time dialog box.

On Internet time, Windows automatically adjusts the PC's clock whenever you're connected to the Internet. There's nothing else you need to do — ever!

About the PC's Battery

All PCs have internal batteries, which are found on the motherboard. The battery's primary purpose is to help the PC's internal clock keep time even when the computer is turned off or unplugged.

A typical PC battery lasts for about six years, possibly more. You'll know when it dies because the computer's date and time go screwy, or perhaps the PC even has a message telling you that the motherboard's battery needs replacing. You can get a replacement at any Radio Shack.

✔ Yes, you have to open the console's case to get at the battery. Don't expect it to be easy to find, either!

✔ The motherboard's battery is in addition to any other batteries in the computer, such as the main battery used to power a laptop.

The Chipset

Rather than refer to the galaxy of computer chips on the PC's motherboard as The Galaxy of Chips on the Motherboard, computer scientists have devised a single descriptive term. All those chips comprise the chipset.

The *chipset* is what makes up your computer's personality. It contains instructions for operating the basic computer hardware: keyboard, mouse, networking interface, sound, and video, for example.

Different chipsets are available depending on which types of features the computer offers. For example, some motherboards come with advanced graphics in the chipset or maybe wireless networking. Sadly, there's no easy way to tell based on the chipset's weirdo names or numbers; you must refer to the chipset's documentation to see what you're getting. (Even then, the info is interesting only to the engineers who design computers.)

✔ Different PCs use different chipsets, depending on which company manufactured the motherboard.

✔ An older term for the chipset, particularly the main ROM chip in a PC, is *BIOS,* which stands for Basic Input/Output System. There's a BIOS for the keyboard and mouse, one for the video system, one for the network, and so on. Altogether, they comprise the *chipset.* See Chapter 8 for more info on ROM.

The Source of PC Power

Lurking inside your PC's console is something incredibly dumb, which is based on 19th century technology: the PC's *power supply.* Despite my disrespect, the PC's power supply does several wonderful things for Mr. Computer. It

✔ Brings in electricity from the wall socket and converts the electricity from wild AC current into mild DC current

✔ Provides electricity to the motherboard and everything living on it

✔ Provides juice to the internal disk drives

✔ Contains fans that help cool the inside of the console

✔ Contains or is directly connected to the PC's power button

The power supply is also designed to take the brunt of the damage if your computer ever suffers from electrical peril, such as a lightning strike or power surge. In those instances, the power supply is designed to die, and to sacrifice itself for the good of your PC. *Don't panic!* You can easily have the power supply replaced and discover that the rest of your PC is still working fine.

✔ Thanks to the fan, the power supply is the noisiest part of any PC.

✔ Power supplies are rated in *watts.* The more internal hardware stuff your PC has — the more disk drives, memory, and expansion cards, for example — the greater the number of watts the power supply should provide. The typical PC has a power supply rated at 150 or 200 watts. More powerful systems may require a power supply upward of 750 watts.

✔ One way to keep your power supply — and your computer — from potentially going poof! (even in a lightning strike) is to invest in a surge protector, or UPS. Refer to Chapter 3 for details.

Chapter 7

Connect This to That

*Y*our PC is a computer system, which means that it can consist of more than just the basic parts. How much more? Well, the answer depends on available technology and how much you're willing to spend. The point is that your computer system can be expanded both internally and externally. The number of gadgets available is nearly limitless, as is the number of tasks they perform.

Expanding your PC externally happens by taking advantage of the available and various connectors found on the console. Basically, you plug a gizmo directly into the console and — presto! — it's added to your computer. Well, maybe it's not that easy, but almost. This chapter explains how it works.

✔ The devices you attach to the console are *peripherals*. The printer is a peripheral, a scanner is a peripheral, even the keyboard and monitor are peripherals.

✔ Internal expansion takes place in a PC by using expansion cards, covered in Chapter 6.

It's a Port

Connectors have always been used on a PC, to add various gizmos to the computer system. The connectors go by a number of names. The names that can be printed in this family-friendly book include *connector*, *hole*, *jack*, and *port*. Only one of these names is accurate.

A hole is just a hole, of course. The computer case may have holes in it, but they're not all for connecting new components.

A *connector* is simply a general term for something that plugs into something else. It's descriptive, but not useful (just like the Windows Help System!). Likewise, a *jack* is simply a term applied to a connector, usually an audio connector.

No, for computers, the proper term for "the thing that gets a cable plugged into it" is a *port*.

A port is more than a hole. It defines the shape of the hole and its connector, the type of devices that can be plugged in, and all sorts of technology required to control the device or devices being connected. It's a big deal.

Your PC's console features a variety of ports into which a variety of devices can be attached. The goal is to expand your computer system. When you know what all the ports do and how they work, you can easily expand your system's potential.

- Officially, a *port* is a place on the computer where information can be sent or received, or both.

- Ports are often called *I/O ports* because they're used for both input and output. Information flows out of the computer through the port, and into the computer from whichever gizmo is attached to the port.

- For technological as well as historical reasons, the typical PC has a variety of ports. The current and most popular slate of ports includes the versatile USB and IEEE 1394 ports, discussed in this chapter. Those ports can handle a variety of gizmos.

- Your PC might also feature what are called *legacy ports*, originally designed for specific devices, such as the printer, mouse, and keyboard. See the section "Legacy Ports," toward the end of this chapter.

- Also refer to Chapter 3 for information on finding the various PC ports.

USB, a Most Versatile Port

The most popular and useful port on your PC is the USB port, where the *U* stands for *u*niversal and means that this port can be used to plug in an entire universe of peripherals. I could also make up that the *S* in USB stands for cinchy, but cinchy is spelled with a *C,* so that one won't fly.

Since I brought it up, USB stands for Universal Serial Bus. Pronounce it letters-only: "yoo-ess-bee."

USB ports, as well as USB devices, sport the USB symbol, shown in the margin. (To see what the USB hole looks like, see Chapter 2.)

The variety of USB devices is legion: printers, speakers, headsets, joysticks, scanners, digital cameras, video cameras, Webcams, disk drives, media storage, keyboards, networking gizmos, pointing devices, tiny fans, lamps, tanning beds, time machines — the list goes on and on. More and more USB devices are appearing every day.

The best news about USB? It's *easy.* Just plug in the gizmo. Often, that's all you need to do!

Playing with USB cables

Whereas a few USB devices attach directly to the computer, such as a USB thumb drive, most USB devices need cables. The name of the cable is, surprisingly, *USB cable*.

USB cables are judged by their length and the type of connector on each end.

As far as length goes, you can get a USB cable up to 3 or 4 meters long. Any longer and the signal may be compromised. Any shorter and I'd have to use English measurements, like one or two feet.

A standard USB cable has two different ends, dubbed A and B, illustrated in Figure 7-1. The A end is flat, and it plugs into the console or a USB hub. The B end has a trapezoidal shape and plugs into the USB device.

Figure 7-1:
The A and
B ends of a
USB cable.

 The A end   The B end

You may also see mini-USB connectors, though those ports are often found only on portable devices, such as cellphones and video cameras. The cables used to connect those devices to your PC feature a mini-USB connector for the device but then the standard A connector for the PC.

Special USB extension cables are available with two A ends, so try not to confuse them with the standard A-B cables.

Connecting a USB device

One reason that the USB port took over the world is that it's smart. Dumb things never take over the world. That's why you don't see more cheese-flavored ice cream. But I digress.

Adding a USB device to your computer is easy: Just plug it in. You don't need to turn off the computer first, and often times you don't even need to install special software. When you plug in a USB device, Windows instantly recognizes it and configures the device for you.

Of course, it pays to read the directions! Some USB gizmos require that you first install software before connecting the device. The only way to tell is to read the quick-setup guide or the manual that came with the USB device.

Using USB-powered gizmos

Another advantage of USB is that many types of USB devices don't require separate power cords. Instead, they use the power supplied by the USB port, making them *USB-powered* devices.

When you have a USB-powered device, you need to plug it into one of two places: directly into the console or into a USB-powered hub. When you don't plug the device into the console or a USB-powered hub, it doesn't work properly. See the section "Expanding the USB universe with hubs," a little later in this chapter, for information on powered-versus-unpowered hubs.

✔ Some folks are uncomfortable that USB-powered devices lack an on–off switch. That's okay; it's fine to leave the device on, as long as you keep the computer on. But, if you really, *really* want to turn the gizmo off, simply unplug the USB cable.

✔ USB devices that require lots of power, such as printers and certain external disk drives, also have their own power cords.

Removing a USB device

This task is cinchy: To remove a USB device, just unplug it. That's it! Well, unless that device is storage media, such as an external disk drive or a thumb drive. In that case, you must officially *unmount* the gizmo before you unplug it. Refer to Chapter 9 for information on removing USB storage media.

Expanding the USB universe with hubs

There never seem to be enough USB ports when you need them. Fortunately, when you need more USB ports, you can quickly add them by plugging a USB hub into your computer system.

A USB *hub* allows you to greatly expand your PC's USB universe. A typical expansion hub, shown in Figure 7-2, connects to the console's USB port. By plugging in the thing, you increase the number of USB gizmos you can attach to your computer system.

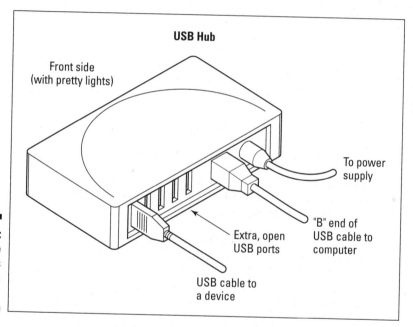

USB Hub

Front side
(with pretty lights)

To power
supply

"B" end of
USB cable to
computer

Extra, open
USB ports

USB cable to
a device

Figure 7-2:
Add more
USB ports
with a USB
hub.

✔ If one hub isn't enough, buy another! You can connect hubs to hubs, if you like. As long as the cables fan out from the PC and nothing loops back on itself, it all works.

✔ You can also add a hub to the console internally by installing a USB expansion card.

✔ Sometimes, you don't have to buy a separate USB hub. Some USB devices act as their own hubs, providing connectors for plugging in additional USB devices.

✔ Using hubs, you can expand your PC's USB universe to the maximum 127 USB devices. You'll probably run out of desk space before that.

✔ Some USB devices prefer to be plugged directly into the console. These types of devices say so on their boxes and in their manuals.

✔ A hub that also plugs into the wall socket is known as a *powered* USB hub. (The console is also a powered USB hub.) This type of hub is necessary for some USB devices to operate.

 ✔ An example of an unpowered hub is a keyboard that has USB ports on it. Those ports are designed to connect non-USB-powered devices, such as mice.

 ✔ The first hub (your PC) is the *root* hub.

The IEEE or 1394 or FireWire Port

About the time the USB port was taking over the computer world, a second, "universal" computer port standard appeared. Sadly, this port lacks a clever acronym. Instead, it's named the IEEE port or IEEE 1394 port (after the technical standard) or the 1394 port. It was once known as I.Link in the Macintosh world, and it's known as the FireWire port. No matter what you call it, it's the same port.

The IEEE port works similarly to the USB port: IEEE devices can be plugged and unplugged at any time, just like USB gizmos. You can find IEEE hubs, just as you can find USB hubs.

On the downside, there just aren't as many IEEE devices as there are USBs. In fact, IEEE is pretty much limited to high-speed gizmos such as external storage devices, scanners, and video cameras.

Some PCs come with an IEEE port standard; most don't. If you need an IEEE port on your computer system, you can easily add one by installing an IEEE expansion card in the console.

 ✔ The IEEE port comes in two sizes: regular and Mini DV. Refer to Chapter 2 for information about the different connector sizes.

 ✔ When your PC has both IEEE and USB ports and the gizmo you're installing uses both IEEE and USB connectors, choose USB. I find that USB is more reliable than IEEE, at least on the external storage media where both options are available.

 ✔ IEEE uses its own, unique cables, which aren't the same as USB cables. Also, unlike USB cables, IEEE cables use the same type of connector on both ends.

 ✔ Unlike USB cables, IEEE cables are quite expensive. Maybe that's when you pronounce it "Ieeeee"?

 ✔ Some IEEE ports are marked by the FireWire symbol, shown in the margin.

 ✔ IEEE is officially known as the High Performance Serial Bus.

The eSATA port

A relatively new port on the port scene is eSATA. SATA is the standard for connecting disk drives inside the console to the PC's motherboard. eSATA is basically an external version of that port standard, allowing you to connect eSATA hard drives and optical drives to your computer.

Not every PC comes with eSATA ports, and most external disk drives that use eSATA can also be connected using the USB port. For now, eSATA is an option, one that may either become more popular in the future or join a long line of once-upon-a-time port standards for the PC.

To properly pronounce eSATA, say "ee-SAY-tuh."

Legacy Ports

When the PC was first designed, external thingamajigs were attached to the console by using ports named after the gizmos you attached to them. If you wanted to attach a keyboard, mouse, or printer, for example, you would use a specific keyboard, mouse, or printer port.

As more and more peripherals became available to computers, it became obvious that you couldn't have a unique port for every gizmo. So, eventually, ports such as the USB and IEEE were developed, which handle a variety of devices.

Despite the USB and IEEE standards, your PC may still support a handful of these older ports, or *legacy ports*. Here's the round-up:

Mouse port: The computer's mouse plugs into the mouse port.

Keyboard port: The computer's keyboard plugged into the keyboard port.

Printer port: The printer plugged into the printer port — though, because of the printer port's nature, people commonly added other devices to the printer port, including external scanners and hard drives. That madness ended when the USB port became standard.

COM port: The old COM port was the most versatile of the legacy ports. You could plug an external modem or computer mouse into the COM port and into a serial printer.

Other legacy ports exist, standards from the rubble and detritus that follow in the computer industry's wake. One of my favorites was the old SCSI port standard. The funnest thing about SCSI was its pronunciation: "skuzzy."

Otherwise, the standard was clunky and difficult to configure. Living through such things reminds me how nice the computing world is now, with its pleasant and flexible USB port.

- ✔ Despite the fact that both the keyboard and mouse ports look alike, they're unique. Strange things happen when you connect things improperly.

- ✔ Some wireless keyboards and mice still use the traditional keyboard and mouse ports. You plug the wireless base station into the keyboard or mouse port (or both), and then you can use the wireless keyboard and mouse.

- ✔ The printer port was also known as the LPT port. (LPT is an IBM acronym-thing for Line Printer.) It may also be called a PRN port, which is how the word *printer* looks when the keyboard is broken.

- ✔ The serial port is also known as the COM or COM1 port. Some old-timers may call it the RS-232C port.

- ✔ The serial port connector is about the same size as the standard video connector on a PC's rump. The difference is that a serial port has 9 holes in it and the video connector has 15. Be careful not to confuse the two!

The magical KVM switch

KVM is an acronym for *keyboard, video,* and *mouse.* The *KVM switch* is a box you can use to attach a single keyboard, monitor, and mouse to two (or more) computers. That way, you can use two computers without having to buy each one its own keyboard, monitor, or mouse. Often, people use the KVM switch so that they can use their current computers as well as access older computers or second computer systems.

Alas, there's no inverse-KVM switch, or a device that lets a single computer have two keyboards, monitors, and mice attached so that two people can use a single computer at the same time. That's possible with the Linux and Unix operating systems, but not with Windows.

Chapter 8

PC Memory

*M*emories, like a PC full of RAM. . . .

Your computer craves memory for its temporary storage. With plenty of memory installed in the console, your PC has ample elbow room to handle a variety of tasks easily and swiftly. When the computer lacks enough memory, things get cramped worse than a tour bus overflowing with sweaty-drunk PhDs returning from an all-you-can-eat kimchi bar. But, I digress. When it comes to PC memory, more is better. This chapter tells you why.

What Is Computer Memory?

If your computer were a sport, memory would be the field on which competition would take place. Memory is where the action is.

Your computer needs memory because the processor has no storage. Well, it has *some* storage, but not a lot. Basically, the processor works like a calculator but without the paper tape. Computer memory acts like that paper tape to help the processor store information and work on data.

The reason that memory is only temporary storage is that memory chips require electricity in order to maintain their information. So, when you're done creating something in memory, you must *save* that information to long-term storage in the PC's mass storage system. But for working on things, creating stuff, and engaging in general computer activity, memory is where it's at.

- ✔ All computers need memory.

- ✔ Memory is where the processor does its work.

- ✔ The more memory in your PC, the better. With more computer memory on hand, you can work on larger documents, work graphics programs without interminable delays, play games faster, edit video, and boast about having all that memory to your friends.

- ✔ The term *RAM* is used interchangeably with the word *memory*. They're the same thing.

- ✔ RAM stands for *random access memory*, in case you have been working any crossword puzzles lately.

- ✔ Turning off the power makes the *contents* of memory go bye-bye. The memory chips themselves aren't destroyed, but the chips require electricity in order to maintain their contents.

- ✔ Computer memory is *fast*. The processor can scan millions of bytes of memory — the equivalent of Shakespeare's entire folio — in fractions of a second, which is far less time than it took you to even trudge through *Hamlet* in the 11th grade.

- ✔ The PC's storage system — disk drives and media cards — provides long-term storage for information. See Chapter 9.

- ✔ Memory is reusable. After creating something and saving it to disk, the computer wipes memory clean and lets you start afresh.

- ✔ Yes, Mr. Smartypants, some types of computer memory do not require electricity in order to maintain information. The problem is that this type of memory isn't fast enough. Only fast RAM, which requires electricity, is best used as temporary storage in your PC.

Delicious Chocolate Memory Chips

Physically, memory dwells on the PC's motherboard, sitting very close to the processor for fast access and ready dispatch. The memory itself resides on a tiny memory expansion card, or *DIMM*, which stands for Dual Inline Memory Module. On the DIMM, you find the actual memory chips.

Boring details on RAM, ROM, and Flash memory

RAM, which stands for *random access memory*, refers to memory that the processor can read from and write to. When you create something in memory, it's done in RAM. RAM is memory and vice versa.

ROM stands for *read-only memory*. The processor can read from ROM, but it cannot write to it or modify it. ROM is permanent. ROM chips contain special instructions or other information that the computer uses — important stuff that never changes. For example, the chipset on

the motherboard is in ROM (refer to Chapter 6). The processor can access information stored on a ROM chip, but unlike with RAM, the processor cannot change that information.

Flash memory is a special type of memory that works like both RAM and ROM. Information can be written to flash memory, like RAM, but like ROM the information isn't erased when the power is turned off. Sadly, flash memory isn't as fast as RAM, so don't expect it to replace standard computer memory anytime soon.

A typical DIMM is illustrated in Figure 8-1, although in real life the chips are often covered by a sheet of metal. A DIMM also has chips on both sides, which is why it's a DIMM and not a SIMM, or Single Inline Memory Module.

Figure 8-1:
A semi-
sweet
DIMM.

Each DIMM card contains a given chunk of RAM, measured in megabytes or gigabytes using one of the magical memory quantities of 1, 2, 4, 8, 16, 32, 64, 128, 256, or 512. See the later section "Measuring Memory One Byte at a Time" for information on megabytes and gigabytes. See the later sidebar "The holy numbers of computing" for information on memory quantities.

A DIMM card is plugged into a DIMM slot on the motherboard, where it forms a *bank* of memory. So, a PC with 2GB of RAM may have four banks of 512MB DIMMs installed or two banks of 1GB DIMMs. That's all trivial, however; unless you plan to upgrade the memory yourself, the physical allocation of memory on the DIMMs doesn't matter. The bottom line is the total amount of RAM in your PC.

✔ The most common type of memory chip installed in a PC is the DRAM, which stands for *d*ynamic *r*andom *a*ccess *m*emory. It's pronounced "dee-ram."

✔ Other types of memory chips exist, each with a name similar to DRAM, such as EDORAM or BATTERINGRAM or DODGERAM. And then there's DDR2 and GDDR2 and WRAM and on and on. Most of these are merely marketing terms, designed to make one type of memory sound spiffier than another.

✔ Yes, I'm just kidding about the "chocolate" part of RAM. Memory has no flavor, although it has been reported on the Internet that memory chips are difficult to chew, are generally bitter, and often taste like blood.

Measuring Memory One Byte at a Time

Computer memory is measured by the byte. So what is a byte?

Think of a byte as a storage unit, but very small. A *byte* can store a single character. For example, the word *cerumen* is seven characters long and requires seven bytes of computer memory storage. The word *earwax* is six characters long and requires six bytes of memory to store. How many letters in your name? That's how many bytes of storage your name would occupy in computer memory.

Bytes are useful but puny. Back in the 1970s, having a few thousand bytes of computer storage was *really something!* Today's PCs need *millions* of bytes just to run the operating system. That's okay for many reasons, the first of which is that computer memory is relatively cheap. More importantly, it's easy to reference large quantities of memory, thanks to handy and confusing computer jargon, as shown in Table 8-1.

Table 8-1		Memory Quantities	
Term	*Abbreviation*	*About*	*Actual*
Byte		1 byte	1 byte
Kilobyte	K or KB	1 thousand bytes	1,024 bytes
Megabyte	M or MB	1 million bytes	1,048,576 bytes
Gigabyte	G or GB	1 billion bytes	1,073,741,824 bytes
Terabyte	T or TB	1 trillion bytes	1,099,511,627,776 bytes

TECHNICAL STUFF

The holy numbers of computing

Computer memory comes in given sizes. You see the same numbers over and over:

1, 2, 4, 8, 16, 32, 64, 128, 256, 512, 1024, 2048, 4096, and so on.

Each of these values represents a *power of two* — a scary mathematical concept that you can safely live your entire life knowing nothing about. To quickly review: $2^0 = 1$, $2^1 = 2$, $2^2 = 4$, $2^3 = 8$, and up to $2^{10} = 1024$, and so on, until you get a nosebleed.

These specific values happen because computers count by twos — ones and zeros — the old binary counting base of song and legend. So, computer memory, which is a binary-like thing, is measured in those same powers of two. RAM chips come in quantities of 256MB or 512MB, for example, or maybe 2GB.

Notice that, starting with 1024, the values take on a predictable pattern: 1024 bytes is really 1K; 1024K is really 1M, and 1024M is 1G. So, really, only the first 10 values, 1 through 512, are the magical ones.

Although it's handy to say "kilobyte" rather than mouth out "1,024 bytes," it's hard to visualize how much data that is. For comparison, think of a kilobyte (KB) as about a page of text from a novel.

One *megabyte* (MB) of information is required in order to store one minute of music in your computer, a medium-resolution photograph, or as much text information as in a complete encyclopedia.

The *gigabyte* (GB) is a huge amount of storage — 1 billion bytes. You can store about 30 minutes of high-quality video in a gigabyte.

The *terabyte* (TB) is 1 trillion bytes, or enough RAM to dim the lights when you start the PC.

A *trilobite* is an extinct arthropod that flourished in the oceans during the Paleozoic era. It has nothing to do with computer memory.

Other trivia:

✔ The term *giga* is Greek, and it means *giant*.

✔ The term *tera* is also Greek. It means *monster!*

✔ Hard disk storage is also measured in bytes; see Chapter 9.

✔ A PC running Windows 7 requires at least 1GB of memory in order to work well. Having 2GB of memory is better.

✔ The PC's processor can access and manipulate trillions and trillions of bytes of memory. Even so, because of limitations in hardware design as well as the operating system, your computer can use, practically, only a given amount of RAM. The exact number depends on the motherboard design as well as on the version of Windows.

Memory Q&A

It doesn't matter where I am — greeting people at church, working off my community service, or leaving detox — folks still stop and ask me questions about computer memory. Over the years, I've collected the questions and have distilled the answers in this section. That should help clear up any loose ends or random access thoughts you may have about computer memory.

"How much memory is in my PC right now?"

You may not know how much RAM resides within your PC's bosom, but the computer knows! Summon the System window to find out: Press Win+Break on the computer keyboard to summon the System window (refer to Figure 6-2, over in Chapter 6).

The amount of memory (RAM) appears right beneath the type of processor that lives in your PC. In Figure 6-2, it says that the computer has 3.00GB of RAM — a goodly amount for Windows 7. Close the System window when you're done checking your PC's memory.

"Do I have enough memory?"

If you have to keep on asking this question, the answer is No.

"Does my PC have enough memory?"

Knowing how much memory is in your PC is one thing, but knowing whether that amount is enough is entirely different.

The amount of memory your PC needs depends on two things. The first, and most important, is the memory requirement of your software. Some programs, such as video-editing programs, require lots of memory. It says right on the box how much memory is needed. For example, the Adobe Premier Pro video-editing program demands 2GB of RAM to run properly.

- ✔ Generally speaking, all PCs should have at least 1GB of RAM, which is what you need, at minimum, to run Windows 7 (but not run it well).

- ✔ Here's one sure sign that your PC needs more memory: It slows to a crawl, especially during memory-intensive operations, such as working with graphics.

- ✔ Not enough memory? You can upgrade! See the upcoming section "Can I add memory to my PC?"

"Can I test whether my PC has enough memory?"

Your computer is designed to function even when it lacks a sufficient amount of memory. To test whether your PC has enough memory installed, you make the computer *very* busy, by loading and running several programs simultaneously. I'm talking about *big* programs, like Photoshop or Word or Excel. While all those programs are running, switch between them by pressing the Alt+Esc key combination.

If you can easily switch between several running programs by using Alt+Esc, your PC most likely has plenty of memory. But, if you press Alt+Esc and the system slows down, you hear the hard drives rumbling, and it takes a bit of time for the next program's window to appear, your PC could use more memory.

Close any programs you have opened.

"Can I add memory to my PC?"

You bet! The best thing you can do for your PC is to add memory. It's like putting garlic in a salad. *Bam!* More memory provides an instant boost to the system.

Adding memory to your computer is LEGO-block simple. Well, *expensive* LEGO-blog simple. Knowing how much memory and which type to buy is the tough part. Because of that, I highly recommend that you have a dealer or computer expert do the work for you.

If you opt to perform your own PC memory upgrade, I can recommend Crucial at www.crucial.com. The Web site uses special software to determine which type of memory you need and how much. You can then buy the memory directly from the site.

"Will the computer ever run out of memory?"

Nope. Unlike the hard drive, which can fill up just like a closet full of shoes and hats, your PC's memory can never truly get full. At one time, back in the dark ages of computing, the "Memory full" error was common. That doesn't happen now, thanks to something called virtual memory.

"What is virtual memory?"

Windows uses a clever technique to prevent your computer's memory from ever becoming full: It creates virtual memory.

Virtual memory is a fake-out. It lets the computer pretend that it has much more memory than it has physical RAM. It does that by swapping out vast swaths of memory to the hard drive. Because Windows manages both memory and hard drive storage, it can keep track of things quite well, by swapping chunks of data back and forth. *Et, voila!* — you never see an "Out of memory" error.

Alas, there's trouble in paradise. One problem with virtual memory is that the swapping action slows things down. Although it can happen quickly and often without your noticing, when memory gets tight, virtual memory takes over and things start moving more slowly.

  ✔ The solution to avoiding the use of virtual memory is to pack your PC with as much RAM as it can hold.

  ✔ Windows never says that it's "out of memory." No, you just notice that the hard drive is churning frequently as the memory is swapped into and out of the disk drive. Oh, and things tend to slow down dramatically.

  ✔ You have no reason to mess with the virtual memory settings in your computer. Windows does an excellent job of managing them for you.

"What is video memory?"

Memory used by your PC's video system is known as *video memory*. Specifically, memory chips live on the display adapter card. Those memory chips are used specifically for the computer's video output and help you see higher resolutions, more colors, 3D graphics, bigger and uglier aliens, and girlie pictures that your husband downloads from the Internet late at night but says that he doesn't.

As with regular computer memory, you can upgrade video memory if your PC's display adapter has room. See Chapter 10 for more information on display adapters.

Shared video memory is used on some low-end computers to save money. What happens is that the computer lacks true video memory and instead borrows some main memory for use in displaying graphics. This strategy is fine for simple home computers but not nearly good enough to play cutting-edge games or to use photo-editing software.

"What are kibi, mebi, and gibi?"

Because the world loves standards, there's an international attempt to standardize what K, M, G, and other abbreviations mean when it comes to numbers. Specifically, according to the standard, KB should refer to 1,000 bytes, not to the actual 1,024 bytes that it more accurately references. To differentiate between 1,000 and 1,024, the standards people are proposing that *kibi,* or *Ki,* be used to refer to 1,024 bytes. Ditto for *mebi* and *Mi* and *gibi* and *Gi;* for example:

> 1MB = 1,000,000 bytes
>
> 1Mi = 1,048,576 bytes

Both these values are correct, according to the standard. One megabyte (MB) is one million bytes. But on a computer, they want to use one *mebibyte* (*Mi*) to refer to the actual value, which is 1,048,576 bytes.

Weird? You bet! And you can probably guess why this change is slow to happen and why many in the computer industry are reluctant to adopt the new terms. Don't fret! If and when it happens and knowing about it becomes important, you can read about it in a future edition of this book.

Chapter 9

The Mass Storage System

In This Chapter

▶ Understanding mass storage

▶ Recognizing the hard drive

▶ Using the optical drive

▶ Working with media cards and thumb drives

▶ Adding external storage

▶ Using storage media in Windows

Call it junk or call it treasure, we humans tend to accumulate a lot of it. Some people hoard it. They have so much of it that they fill their closets, attics, and garages to overflowing. Some rent even more storage space. It's not really a question of whether that stuff is worth anything; the issue at hand is storage itself. Given that you like your stuff, where will you put it?

Just as in real life, you accumulate a lot of stuff in your computer: stuff you create and stuff you collect, plus stuff such as programs, the operating system, and all sorts of delicious digital data. The place to put, keep, and store that stuff is in the PC's mass storage system, which is this chapter's subject.

What Is Mass Storage?

Mass storage is the second half of the PC's storage system. The first half is temporary storage, or computer memory (refer to Chapter 8). *Mass storage* is permanent storage, required for keeping information for the long term.

The stuff placed in mass storage is information the computer needs every time you turn on the PC. The mass storage system is where the operating system is stored, where all your PC programs are kept, and where you keep the stuff you create and collect. Yes, it's the PC's closet.

Briefly, the computer manages its storage system by creating things in memory, or temporary storage. The information is then copied, or *saved*, in mass storage by the operating system. When you need the information again, the operating system takes it from mass storage and loads, or *opens,* it back into memory. The operation happens quickly, and it saves you the chore of having to type in the computer's programs every time you start the machine.

Storage media roundup

In the olden days, mass storage was referred to as the computer's "disk drives." But on today's computers, mass storage consists of more than just spinning disks. Here's a quick summary of the different types of storage media found in a typical PC:

Hard disk drives: Your PC has one or more hard disk drives. The hard drive is the computer's primary mass storage device.

Optical drives: Your PC probably has at least one optical drive, used to read and write to optical discs.

Media cards: Your PC probably has a media card reader, which accesses these solid state mass storage devices and allows your computer to easily exchange information with digital cameras and other portable gizmos, as well as with other computers.

Later sections in this chapter go into detail on these various forms of storage, where to find them in Windows, and how to use them.

All storage media is measured by its capacity in bytes. Refer to Chapter 8 for more information on bytes, megabytes, gigabytes, and other related terms.

Mass storage technical drivel

Yeah, you don't need to know this stuff, but occasionally the terms may rear their ugly heads. Here's the short list:

Media: The media is where information is recorded. It's the disk part of a hard disk or the CD or DVD for an optical drive, or it consists of *flash memory* in a media card.

Drive: The drive mechanism reads the media. It spins the hard disk or optical disc so that information can be read from or written to the media. For a media card, the drive is the gizmo that accesses the information stored on the media card's flash memory chip.

Interface: The final word in the media storage trifecta is *interface,* or the hardware and software used to transfer information between the storage media and the rest of the computer.

Though it's rare, sometimes it helps to know these terms. You may never use them yourself, but when shopping for new computer toys or dealing with technical support, knowing the proper terms comes in handy.

- ✔ *Flash memory* is a special type of computer memory that isn't erased when the power turns off.

- ✔ The current standard for hard drive and optical drive interface is *SATA,* or Serial Advanced Technology Attachment.

- ✔ Other interface standards for storage media include USB, IEEE, and eSATA. Media card readers and external hard drives and optical drives typically use the USB interface.

- ✔ See Chapter 7 for more information on USB and IEEE.

The Hard Disk Drive

The primary place for storing stuff on your PC is its hard drive. It's the PC's main source of permanent storage. That's because the hard drive is capable of storing the greatest amount of information and accessing it quickly.

Hard drives are measured by their capacity, and the standard computer unit of a *byte* is the yardstick. So much information can be stored on a hard drive that the bytes have to be counted by the billions, or gigabytes. A typical PC hard drive can store between 120GB and 500GB of information — or more.

Hard drives dwell primarily in the PC console. All PCs have at least one, and you can add a second hard drive in your PC, if you like, as long as you have room for it.

- ✔ Unlike other types of mass storage, the hard drive cannot be removed from the computer's console. The hard drive is fixed in its position (which is why some old-timers called it a *fixed disk*).

- ✔ The hard drive is simply a storage device. It isn't *everything* inside the console.

- ✔ The main consumers of hard drive storage space are media files: music and video.

- ✔ The PC's main hard drive is known as "drive C" or "the C drive." See the section "Permanent Storage ABCs," later in this chapter, for more information.

- ✔ External hard drives can be added to a PC. See the section "External Storage," later in this chapter.

- ✔ The hard drive is where Windows lives, where you install software, and where you keep the stuff you create or save on your computer. That's what the hard drive is designed for.

Which storage media is the *boot* disk?

One job of your computer's hardware is to find and locate an operating system. That happens every time you start your PC. To find the operating system, the computer looks for a mass storage device that contains an operating system, a mass storage device that's identified as a *boot disk*.

The traditional boot disk in a PC is the first hard drive, known as Drive C. If an operating system isn't found there, the computer might look for an optical drive with an operating system, or an external drive or even another computer on the network. Yes, the PC can become quite desperate to find an operating system.

Depending on how your PC is set up, it may try to start itself using an optical disc rather than the hard drive. You see the text, something like "Press Enter to boot from the CD/DVD", when the PC first starts. If you want to start the computer from the optical disc, press Enter. Otherwise just wait, and the computer starts normally.

To change the way the computer searches for a boot disk, or to set the PC to always and only start from the hard drive, you need to access something called the PC Setup program. A handy nerd or other computing professional will be happy to set up such a thing for you.

The Optical Drive

The PC's primary form of removable mass storage is its optical drive. It's also called a DVD drive, but because it can read both DVDs and CDs, I prefer the term *optical drive*. Both the DVD and the CD are optical disc technologies.

The primary purpose of the optical drive is to let your PC access removable media (optical discs). You use the optical drive as the primary method of installing software on your computer. The discs also let you view movies or listen to music, as well as access information created by other people.

- ✔ You can also use your PC's optical drive to create, or *burn,* your own optical discs. It's a big topic, so Chapter 24 is devoted to the subject.

- ✔ The typical PC has at least one optical drive installed.

- ✔ Some consoles can have a second optical drive installed. In fact, the tower consoles favored by computer gamers have spots for several optical drives. That's because many computer games require an optical disc to be in the drive while the game is being played.

- ✔ The optical drive can also be used to read high-capacity Blu-ray discs; they're optical as well. To make that happen, you need an optical drive that can specifically read Blu-ray discs.

Observe the optical drive

Your PC's optical drive can be found lurking somewhere on the front of the PC console. If you can't see the optical drive, it's hidden behind a panel or door, which seems to be a common PC design element. If so, you can open the door or panel to see the optical drive, illustrated in Figure 9-1.

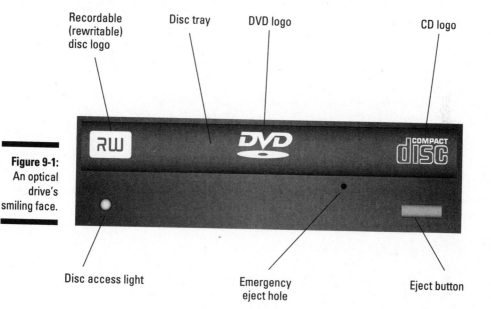

Recordable (rewritable) disc logo   Disc tray   DVD logo   CD logo

Disc access light   Emergency eject hole   Eject button

Figure 9-1: An optical drive's smiling face.

The key elements of the drive are the disc tray, which slides out to accept a disc, and the Eject button, which pops out the tray. Some drives may not have a tray, but instead a slot into which you jam the disc.

Also on the front of the drive is a light that blinks when the drive is in use. The teensy hole is used to eject a stubborn disc or to open the tray when the drive isn't functioning or is turned off: You simply jab a bent paper clip into the hole, press, and the tray pops open or the disc pushes itself out.

In addition to the button, light, and tray, the optical drive might be adorned with various tattoos (refer to Figure 9-1). Each tattoo helps explain which types of disc the optical drive can read. Here's a list of the logos you might see:

DVD: The drive can read both CD and DVD discs. The logo is shown earlier, in Figure 9-1.

Disc: The drive can read CDs. Even when the CD logo (refer to Figure 9-1) doesn't appear on a DVD drive, that DVD drive can still read CDs.

Blu-ray Disc: The drive can read high-capacity Blu-ray discs as well as DVDs and CDs.

RW: The drive is capable of creating rewritable discs.

DL: The DVD drive can read dual-layer discs. The label *R DL* means that it can also create dual-layer discs.

R: A single R indicates a drive that can create optical discs. The R may be suffixed with a + or – or the ± thing, which means that you can create discs in the + or – (or both) formats.

RAM: The DVD drive can read or create the DVD-RAM disc format.

The big deal with all these labels comes into play when you create optical discs on the computer. Refer to Chapter 24 for more information on creating discs and some hints about the various optical disc recording formats.

- ✔ A CD optical drive might feature a headphone jack and a volume control, used for listening to musical CDs.
- ✔ Laptop optical drives are found on the front or sides of the unit, but note that many ultramobile laptops, or *netbooks*, lack optical drives altogether. In that case, you can attach and use an external optical drive.

The speed rating (the X number)

Optical drives have speed ratings measured in *X*. The number before the *X* indicates how much faster the drive is than the original PC CD-ROM drive (which plays as fast as a musical CD player). So, a 52X value means that the drive is 52 times faster than the original PC CD-ROM drive.

You commonly see an optical drive rated with three *X*s:

- ✔ The first X represents the drive's write speed, or how fast a disc can be written to.
- ✔ The second X specifies how fast the drive can rewrite to a rewritable (RW) disc.
- ✔ The final X indicates how fast the drive can be read from.

DVD drives, especially combo drives that can write a variety of disc formats, come with multiple X ratings, one for each of the various types of discs they create.

All about optical discs

An *optical disc* is circular plastic, about 5 inches in diameter, and coated with a Mylar film on which data is stored. All in all, it's a rather ho-hum thing. In fact, it's so ho-hum that you can't readily tell the difference between a CD and a DVD by looking at the disc.

Other than its boring physical description, an optical disc can be rated by its capacity. As you would suspect, a DVD holds more information than a plain ol' CD. Here are the stats:

✔ DVD is an acronym for *d*igital *v*ersatile *d*isc. Or, it may be *d*igital *v*ideo *d*isc.

✔ CD stands for *c*ompact *d*isc.

✔ A typical CD holds as much as 640MB of data or 80 minutes of music.

✔ A DVD is capable of storing 4GB of information on one side of a disc, or 8GB on one side of a dual-layer (DL) disc.

✔ A Blu-ray disc can store as much as 25GB on a single side of the disc, or 50GB on a dual-layer (DL) disc.

✔ The British spelling of *disc* is used for historical reasons, most likely because it was part of some elaborate palindrome that has long since been forgotten.

Put the disc into the drive

Generally speaking, the disc is always inserted label side up. Aside from that, how you stick the disc into the drive depends on how the drive eats discs:

Tray: The most popular type of optical drive uses a slide-out tray to hold the disc. Start by pressing the drive's Eject button, which pops out the tray (often called a *drink holder* in computer jokes). Drop the disc into the tray, label side up. Gently nudge the tray back into the computer. The tray slides back in the rest of the way on its own.

Slide-in: Another type of disc drive works like the CD player in most automobiles; the drive is merely a slot into which you slide the disc: Pushing the disc (label side up) into the slot causes a gremlin inside the drive to eventually grab the disc and suck it in all the way. Stand back and be amazed!

What happens after you insert the disc depends on the disc's content. You may see a prompt to install software, play a movie, or play or import music —

or sometimes you don't see anything. In that case, to find out what to do next, you have to heed whatever directions came with the optical disc.

- ✔ A disc properly inserted into an optical drive is used just like any other storage media in your computer.

- ✔ When you insert the disc upside down (label side down), the drive can't read it and most likely simply ejects the disc automatically. No harm done.

- ✔ Most laptops lack a disc tray that automatically slides in or out. In that case, you must pull out the disc tray, put in (or remove) the disc, and then push the tray all the way back inside the laptop.

- ✔ An exception to the label-side-up rule is an optical disc with data recorded on both sides. For example, some DVD movies have the TV version on one side and the wide-screen, or *letterbox,* version on another. If so, make sure to put the proper side face up in the drive.

- ✔ Some discs are clipped. That is, they aren't round discs but, rather, are business card size or some other odd shape. These discs work fine in the tray type of optical drive, but don't insert them into the slide-in type of drive.

Eject the disc

Follow these steps to eject a disc from a DVD drive:

1. **Click the Start button on the taskbar, or press the Win key on your PC's keyboard.**

   The Start button menu pops up.

2. **Choose Computer from the Start button menu.**

   The Computer window appears, which lists all mass storage devices available to your PC.

3. **Click to select the optical drive icon.**

   Just click once; you want to select the icon, not open it.

4. **Click the Eject button on the toolbar.**

   The disc spits out of the optical drive.

You may be tempted to eject the disc by punching the Eject button on the front of the drive. Don't! If Windows is using the drive, you see an ugly error message on the screen when you try to eject a disc this way.

Weird disk drives from long ago

The PC's history is littered with piles of alternative forms of disk drives. You have a veritable salad bar of options and choices, depending on which part of computer history you're looking at.

The original PC mass storage device was the floppy disk drive and its removable floppy diskettes. You may still see computers with floppy drives, but they're either older PCs or PCs with floppy drives included for compatibility. Because of their low storage capacity and unreliability, I don't recommend that you use floppy disks.

For the longest time, removable hard drives were popular in the PC realm. Before the CD-R appeared, the magneto-optical (MO) disk was popular. Various removable cartridge drives came and went, such as the Bernoulli disk, Zip disk, and Jaz disk. The SuperDrive and its high-capacity SuperDisk were popular for a while. Many of these alternative disk drives tried to replace the once-standard PC floppy drive, but none succeeded.

Media Cards and Flash Drives

The next generation of computer mass storage is the solid state drive, or SSD. It comes in two flavors:

Media cards: I use the term *media card* to describe the various memory cards, sticks, and wafers commonly used with portable electronic devices. The cards themselves come in a variety of shapes and are referred to by a slew of different names. Because the cards are used primarily by portable devices to store media (pictures, music, video), the generic term *media card* seems apt.

Flash drives: Widely known as a *thumb drive* because of its shape, a flash drive plugs directly into a computer's USB port. It's designed specifically as removable PC storage.

SSDs are made using special *flash* memory chips. Those chips allow information to be accessed quickly and retained for long periods. Unlike regular computer memory, the contents of an SSD aren't erased when the power goes off. So you can remove a media card or thumb drive from your PC and store it in a drawer without losing any information.

✔ Media cards and thumb drives can be used for regular PC storage, to help transfer files between computers and portable electronic gizmos, for backup, or for a bunch of other interesting tasks.

✔ Media cards and flash drives can also be used to speed up your computer. The technology is ReadyBoost, and you can find more information in my book *Troubleshooting & Maintaining Your PC All-In-One For Dummies* (Wiley).

✔ Media cards need a special reader for the PC to access their information. See the later section "The media card reader," for details. A thumb drive doesn't need a special reader because it plugs directly into a USB port.

✔ Eventually, the SSD will replace the hard drive as the PC's primary form of mass storage. The issues are capacity and price. Though you can get an SSD to replace a hard drive today, the cost is terribly expensive. Like most things electronic, however, the prices will drop and eventually computer hard drives will become a thing of the past.

The media card reader

To use a media card, your PC must come equipped with a *media card reader*. Individual card readers are out there, each of which is customized to accommodate a specific type of media card. More common are media card readers that have cubbyholes for all types of media cards. This type is often called the "19-in-1" media card reader, as shown in Figure 9-2.

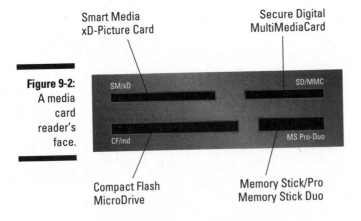

Smart Media
xD-Picture Card

Secure Digital
MultiMediaCard

Figure 9-2: A media card reader's face.

SM/xD

SD/MMC

CF/md

MS Pro-Duo

Compact Flash
MicroDrive

Memory Stick/Pro
Memory Stick Duo

The 19-in-1 media card readers come in both internal and external flavors. If your PC doesn't have an internal media card reader, you can buy an external media card reader (cheap), and easily attach it to your PC by using a USB port.

The typical media card reader contains four slots, which, surprisingly, let you access as many as 19 different types of media cards — hence the 19-in-1 name. The reader is labeled, as shown in Figure 9-2, though you can pretty much figure out which card goes in which hole. See the section "Insert a media card or thumb drive," later in this chapter.

Each hole in the media card reader is represented by a drive icon and drive letter in Windows. You can view the icons and their letters in Windows in the Computer window; see the section "Permanent Storage ABCs," later in this chapter, for more info.

Media card roundup

Like other storage media, media card capacity is measured in bytes. Smaller-capacity cards store a few megabytes, although 32MB seems to be the smallest media card available these days. At the high end, media cards can hold as much as 32GB of data — or more! They aren't cheap.

The other way to judge a media card is by its type. There are seven types, names, and sizes, shown in Table 9-1.

Table 9-1	Media Card Types	
Card Name	*Abbreviation*	*Sample*
CompactFlash	CF	
Memory Stick/Pro	PRO	
Memory Stick Duo	Duo	

(continued)

Table 9-1 *(continued)*

Card Name	Abbreviation	Sample
MultiMediaCard	MMC	MultiMedia Card
Secure Digital	SD	SD
SmartMedia	SM	SmartMedia
xD-Picture Card	xD	xD

In addition to the seven formats shown in Table 9-1 are other, subtle variations. For example, the two types of CompactFlash media cards are Type
I and the thicker Type II. Likewise, you can find several sizes and types of
memory sticks and Secure Digital cards as well as other differences in the
other card types — nothing worth memorizing.

You can choose any card type to use with your PC, though more commonly
you use the type of card designed for your digital camera or video recorder.

Insert a media card or thumb drive

To use a media card, just plug it into the proper card slot, located either directly on the PC's console or via a media card adapter attached to a USB port. Likewise, to add a thumb drive to your PC's storage system, plug the thumb drive into any USB port.

Windows instantly recognizes the storage device you attached to your computer. A pause occurs while Windows mulls things over. Eventually, the card is *mounted* into the computer system, making the card available for use. You can then access whatever information is stored on the device or use it to store new information.

As with other mass storage devices, you access the media card or thumb drive from the Computer window. See Part IV of this book for more information.

- ✔ Do not force a media card into a slot! If the media card doesn't fit into one slot, try another.

- ✔ Media cards are inserted label side up. For vertically mounted media card readers, try label-left (although this may not always work).

- ✔ Information stored on a media card or thumb drive is accessed using the same methods you use to access files and folders in Windows. See Part IV of this book for the details.

- ✔ Media cards and thumb drives added to your computer system are given a drive letter, just like any other permanent storage device in Windows. See the section "Permanent Storage ABCs," later in this chapter.

- ✔ After inserting the media card or thumb drive, you may see the AutoPlay dialog box. You can use the dialog box to choose how to view the card's contents, or you can close the dialog box if it's pestering you.

Eject a media card or thumb drive

You cannot just yank out a media card. I know: It's tempting. And, often, nothing prevents you from being naughty and yanking out the card. But if you do so, you run the risk of damaging the card or destroying the information stored on the card, not to mention having to endure a nasty warning message from the PC.

No, just be proper! Follow these steps to remove a media card or thumb drive the safe, happy way:

1. **Ensure that you're done using the media card or thumb drive.**

   Windows doesn't want you to eject any storage device that's in use. So, be sure that none of your programs or windows are accessing information on the storage device.

2. **Pop up the Start button menu: Click the Start button on the taskbar, or press the Win key on your PC's keyboard.**

3. **Choose the Computer item.**

   Choosing the Computer item from the Start button menu displays the Computer window, which lists all mass storage gizmos attached and available to your PC.

4. **Choose the icon representing the media card or thumb drive to remove.**

   This step is tricky; it's not always obvious which icon in the Computer window represents the media card or thumb drive. Sometimes, you can tell because the name below the icon is something other than Removable Disk.

5. **Click the Eject button on the toolbar.**

6. **Pull out the media card or detach the thumb drive.**

Be sure to store the media card in a safe, static-free location when you're not using it.

When the media card is canceled

Just like other types of storage media, media cards wear out. Media cards use flash memory to store information, and flash memory is limited in how many times it can be written to and read from. The limitation is quite high, and the media cards are manufactured to use storage as efficiently as possible, to put off that inevitable death date. Even so, eventually the media cards err and stop working. When that happens, dispose of the media card properly and buy a replacement.

External Storage

Your PC's permanent storage isn't limited to what's available inside the console. Using the smarts of the USB port, you can expand your computer system externally, by adding peripheral hard drives, optical drives, flash drives, or media card readers to your heart's content.

Oh, you can also use the IEEE port or an eSATA connector to add external storage, although it's more common to use the USB port.

Adding external storage

To add another storage media device to your computer simply plug it in. The drive attaches to the console by using a USB connector. It may also require power, so plug the drive into the wall — or better, into a UPS. (See Chapter 3.)

When you plug the drive into the USB connector, and assuming that the drive has power and is turned on, Windows instantly recognizes the drive and adds it to your computer's list of permanent storage devices, found in the Computer window. You can immediately start using the drive.

Removing external storage

Although you can easily unplug any USB device from your computer at any time, I don't recommend doing so for external storage. Because the computer may be using the storage, you should always properly remove the external drive *logically* before you remove it physically. Here's how:

1. **Click the Start button to pop up the Start button menu.**

2. **Choose the Computer command to open the Computer window.**

3. **Right-click the external storage device's icon.**

   A pop-up menu appears.

4. **From the pop-up menu, choose the command Safely Remove.**

   Windows displays a message (in the notification area), informing you that the device can be safely removed.

5. **Disconnect the external storage device.**

If you see an error message, the disk drive is either busy or being used. You have to wait and try again. If the error is persistent, you should turn off the computer. Detach the device. Then restart the computer.

Permanent Storage ABCs

Windows lets you view all permanent storage devices in the computer in one central location, a place called the Computer window, shown in Figure 9-3.

To see the Computer window, choose the Computer command from the Start button menu. You see the storage devices available to your computer shown in the window, similar to the one shown in Figure 9-3. (Your PC may not have as many storage devices as shown in the figure.)

Figure 9-3:
Assorted
storage
devices
in the
Computer
window.

In Figure 9-3, the storage devices are listed in categories. The categories are Hard Disk Drives and Devices with Removable Storage. To see the storage devices listed by drive letter, which is more useful, right-click in the window and choose the command Group By⇨(None). Then, to sort the storage devices alphabetically, right-click in the window and choose Sort By⇨Name.

- ✔ A quick way to see the Computer window is to press Win+E on the keyboard, where Win is the Windows logo key.

- ✔ Disk drives on a computer network might also appear in the Computer window. See Part III of this book for more information on networking.

Describing and naming storage devices

The storage devices available to your computer, and shown in the Computer window (refer to Figure 9-3), are assigned three different forms of identification: an icon, a name, and a drive letter.

Unique icons are used to represent the various types of mass storage devices. In Figure 9-3, you can see different icons for hard drives, the optical drive, as well as the various media card drives. Note that the boot disk, where the operating system is stored, is shown with a Windows flag on its icon.

The disk name can help identify the disk, though the name isn't used much in Windows. In Figure 9-3, the main hard drive is named Windows 7, Drive F is named RECOVERY, and Drive J: is named KINGSTON. Sometimes, the name is descriptive, as in the names of the media card storage drives, found near the bottom of the window.

The most important aspect of the storage device's descriptions is the drive letter, covered in the following section.

Assigning storage devices a drive letter

Mass storage devices in Windows are referred to by letters of the alphabet, from A to Z. Knowing the drive letter is how you access the drive and the information stored there.

Though each PC's storage media setup is different, Windows follows a set of rules regarding how the drive letters are assigned. Here's the skinny:

Drive A: On a PC, Drive A is the first floppy disk drive, which is how the first IBM PC was configured. Because floppy drives are no longer used, drive letter A is no longer used — unless you attach an external floppy drive to your PC.

Drive B: The letter *B* is reserved for the PC's second floppy drive, whether it has one or not. Few did, even back in the early days.

Drive C: The letter *C* represents the PC's first hard drive; generally, the drive where Windows dwells.

After letter *C,* the storage devices in a PC get their letter assignments based on their drive type and whether they're external or internal. Here are the rules:

- ✔ Any additional internal hard drives are assigned the next letters of the alphabet after *C.* So, if you have a second internal hard drive, it becomes Drive D. (Most PCs use Drive D as their recovery drive.) A third internal hard drive would be Drive E.

- ✔ The internal optical drive is given the next drive letter after the last internal hard drive has been given a letter. Any additional internal optical drives are given the next letter (or letters) of the alphabet.

- ✔ After the optical drive, any internal media card readers are given the next few drive letters.

- ✔ After all internal storage has been assigned drive letters, Windows begins assigning letters to external storage devices in the order in which they're found when the PC was first turned on, or when the drives were attached. Each new storage device is given the next letter in the alphabet.

Not every PC will have the same drive letter assignments. For example, on your PC, Drive D may be the optical drive, but that doesn't mean that Drive D on *all* PCs is the optical drive.

Make a note of your PC's disk drive assignments on the printable Cheat Sheet available for download at www.dummies.com/cheatsheet/pcs.

Chapter 10

The PC's Display

Contrary to what you've seen on TV and film, text makes no noise when it appears on a computer screen. Text also appears rather quickly, not one letter at a time. If you really want a noisy computer, you need to return to the deafening days of the teletype, which served as the main input and output gizmo for the ancient, steam-powered mainframe computers of the 1960s. Things today are much better, and quieter.

The computer's main output gizmo is the monitor. The thing that drives the monitor is the PC's video system, which is rather spritely, full of color, and far quieter than an old teletype. It also wastes a lot less paper. This chapter covers the computer monitor, as well as the electronics and software that control the monitor, which serves as the PC's primary output device.

The PC's Display System

You may stare at it during the entire the time you use your computer (unless you can't touch-type), but the monitor is only the visible half of your computer's video system. Inside the PC console, you find the other half, a bit of electronics called the *display adapter*.

The monitor is the dumb part. All it does is display information.

The display adapter is the heart of the PC's display system. It tells the monitor what to display and where, plus how many colors to use and the overall resolution of the image. It's the display adapter that determines your PC's graphics potential.

Figure 10-1 illustrates the relationship between the monitor and the display adapter. Keep in mind that the display adapter lives inside the console, not free-floating in space, as shown in the figure.

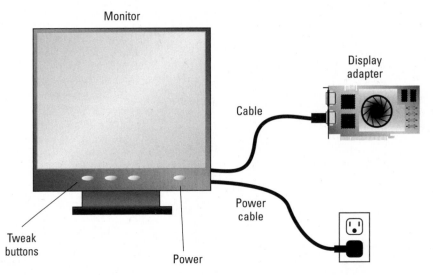

Monitor

Display adapter

Cable

Power cable

Figure 10-1:
The monitor and display adapter.

Tweak buttons

Power

The display adapter can be a separate expansion card, as shown in Figure 10-1, or its circuitry is commonly found on the motherboard. A cable then connects the monitor to the console. The monitor, of course, plugs into the wall for power.

Finally, the PC's display system involves software to control the video hardware. The software is part of Windows, which tells the display adapter what kind of graphical goodness to toss up on the monitor. You also use Windows to control various aspects of the display, as covered elsewhere in this chapter.

- ✔ The display adapter is also known as a *video card*.
- ✔ Sometimes the monitor and console are the same thing, such as the "One PC" type of design. Even so, the monitor and display adapter are separate items in that single unit.

✔ The term *integrated video* is often used to describe a display adapter that's part of the motherboard, not a separate expansion card.

✔ You can have more than one monitor attached to your PC. See the section "The second monitor," later in this chapter.

✔ The PC's video system is its standard output device.

The monitor

The standard type of PC monitor is the LCD monitor, where LCD stands for *l*iquid *c*rystal *d*isplay. It isn't a hallucinogenic.

LCD monitors are flat. They're also thin, and they don't use much power, which keeps the bearded, sandal-wearing Seattle crowd happy.

The older type of PC monitor, which you may see squatting by a PC, is the *CRT* monitor. It's the traditional, glass-screen, television-set-like monitor. At one time, CRTs were plentiful and cheap, but prices on LCD monitors have dropped so much, and they're so much more efficient, that the CRT monitor is pretty much a thing of the past.

Beyond the three-letter acronyms to describe them, not much is going on with computer monitors. Check out the later section "Merry Monitor Mayhem" for more monitor information.

✔ CRT stands for *cathode ray tube*, not *catheter ray tube*.

✔ Some CRT monitors are advertised as "flat screen." This term isn't misleading: The glass on the front of the monitor is indeed flat, and it provides a better viewing surface than the traditional convex glass. But it's *not* an LCD monitor.

✔ All LCD monitors are flat.

✔ CRT monitors are still favored by folks who work in graphic design. Apparently, the CRT monitor is better than the LCD monitors at rendering real-world colors. Also, the CRT monitors are faster at refreshing the screen, so some hard-core gamers prefer them.

✔ You don't need to have the same brand of computer and monitor. You can mix and match. You can even keep your old PC's monitor with a new console you may buy — as long as the monitor is in good shape, why not?

Jargon Department

Where does text appear? Is it on the monitor? On the screen? What is the display? Sadly, several confusing terms are often used interchangeably to refer to the stuff the computer displays. Here's a handy lexicon for you:

✔ The *monitor* is the box.

✔ The *screen* is the part of the monitor on which information is displayed.

✔ The *display* is the information that appears on the screen.

These are the terms as I use them. Other folks, manuals, and Web pages probably mix and match them to mean whatever. In this book, however, I use these terms consistently.

The display adapter

The smarter and most important half of the PC's display system is the graphics hardware itself, known as the *display adapter*. It's the circuitry that runs the monitor and controls the image that the monitor displays.

Display adapters come in various price ranges and have features for artists, game players, computer designers, TV junkies, and regular Joes like you and me and guys named Joe. You should look for three key characteristics in a display adapter:

✔ The amount of memory

✔ The type of GPU

✔ The type of interface

PC graphics require special memory that's separate from the computer's main memory. This memory is known as *video RAM,* or, often, *VRAM.* The more memory, the more colors and high resolutions and fancier tricks the display adapter is capable of.

Display adapters can have from 0M (no memory) to 1024MB (1 gigabyte) and beyond. Even so, more video memory isn't necessarily better. Only when your applications demand more memory, or can take advantage of the extra video memory, is the price worth it. Otherwise, a typical PC has between 32MB and 512MB of video RAM. That's enough.

Another measure of a display adapter's muscle is made by judging its own processor, or graphics *p*rocessing *u*nit (GPU). That processor is specially geared toward graphical operations, and, by having it, the display adapter takes a load of work away from the PC's main processor and things fly on the screen. Two common models of GPU are available: the ATI Radeon and the NVIDIA GeForce. Both are approximately equal in power and popularity.

Finally, there's the interface, or how the display adapter plugs into the motherboard. The best models use the PCI Express slot, which is the most efficient. Some low-end display adapters are included on the chipset found on the PC's motherboard. They provide adequate graphics for general computer use and Web browsing, but little else.

✔ The more memory the display adapter has, the higher the resolutions it can support and the more colors it can display at those higher resolutions.

✔ Some video adapters "share" memory with main memory, such as adapters listed with 0MB of memory. Obviously, for anyone interested in playing games or creating computer graphics, it's a bad deal.

✔ Another term for GPU is VPU, or *visual processing unit*.

✔ You can always upgrade your PC's video adapter. In some cases, you can even add more memory directly to the adapter.

✔ Refer to Chapter 6 for more information on expansion slots, such as the PCI Express slot.

✔ See Chapter 8 for more information on computer memory.

✔ Many display adapters are advertised as supporting 3D graphics or having a "physics engine." That's okay, but they work only if your software supports those features. If so, the side of the software box should say so.

✔ Display adapters may also be judged on their ability to capture or process standard television signals. See Chapter 26 for more information on computers and television.

Merry Monitor Mayhem

Yes, the PC's monitor displays wonderful graphical stuff, but when you boil it down to the basics, it's merely a peripheral. Yeah, it's an important one, a vital part of the basic computer system. But aside from looking at the monitor, you don't spend much time pressing its buttons or studying it intently. When you do, the information in this section will prove handy.

The physical description

Monitors are judged primarily by their picture size, measured on a diagonal, just like a TV set. Common sizes for PC monitors are 15, 17, 19, or 21 inches. Some monster-size monitors, dubbed wide-screen or cinema monitors, measure as much as 23 inches or larger. Oooooooo! (That's me swooning.)

Another characteristic of a PC's monitor is its *aspect ratio*, or the relationship between the monitor's width to its height. There are two common PC monitor aspect ratios:

4:3: Traditional computer monitors had a ratio of four units of width for three units of height, known as the *Academy Standard* and commonly used in film and television. This aspect ratio is also called the "square" ratio.

16:9: More common today is the *wide-screen* monitor format, also known as cinema or HDTV (high-definition television). The screen is 16 units wide for every 9 units in height.

Figure 10-2 illustrates both ways of measuring a monitor, diagonally as well as by its aspect ratio.

4:3 aspect ratio

16:9 aspect ratio

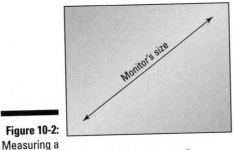

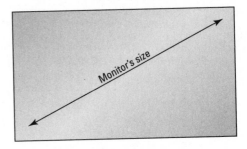

Figure 10-2:
Measuring a
PC monitor.

Standard "square"
computer monitor

Wide-screen
computer monitor

Other physical attributes of a monitor include its video cable, or power cable. The power cable is a plug, but the video cable ends in either a standard VGA connector, digital video or DVI connector, or an HDMI connector. See Chapter 2 for more information on these connectors, and specifically, what their holes might look like.

You also discover a swath of buttons on the monitor; hopefully, right on the front, where they're handy. If not, look for the buttons on the sides of the monitor or behind a door or panel. The most important button is the power button, which is how you turn the monitor on and off.

Other features that have, optionally, found their way onto modern PC monitors include integrated stereo speakers as well as integrated cameras. Generally, these devices are adequate; better options for speakers and PC video exist.

> ✔ Monitors display a message when the monitor is turned on and the PC is not (or the monitor isn't receiving a signal from the PC). The message may read No Signal or Power Save Mode or something like that, or it may urge you to check the connection. That's okay. The monitor pops to life properly when you turn on the console and it receives a video signal.

✔ A relationship exists between a monitor's diagonal measurement and its aspect ratio. Square monitors, or those with the traditional 4:3 aspect ratio, have more screen area than wide-screen monitors of a similar diagonal size. That's because the diagonal on a wide-screen monitor is more acute and, recalling your high school trigonometry, that makes for a smaller display area than on an equivalent standard screen monitor. It also makes the wide-screen monitors cheaper to manufacture than their square cousins.

Adjust the monitor's display

There's an art form to adjusting the display on your PC's monitor. Not that such an action is difficult to understand — it's just difficult to perform. Borrowing from the school of thought that has you use only two buttons to set time on a digital clock, usually four buttons are used to set a multitude of functions on a computer monitor.

The key to adjusting the display is locating a main button, sometimes labeled Menu or with the number 1. Pressing that button pops up an on-screen display, such as the one shown in Figure 10-3.

The onscreen display appears over other information on the screen; don't let that freak you out. After the display is up, use the control buttons on the monitor — plus, minus, up, down, or whatever — to select items from the menu and adjust the settings.

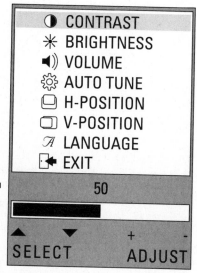

Figure 10-3: A typical onscreen display.

◑ CONTRAST
✳ BRIGHTNESS
◀)) VOLUME
⚙ AUTO TUNE
⬭ H-POSITION
⬭ V-POSITION
𝓐 LANGUAGE
↩ EXIT

50

▲ ▼   +   -
SELECT   ADJUST

The best way to adjust the settings is to look for an Auto option on the menu and choose it.

When you're done messing with the display and adjusting the monitor, either choose an Exit menu item or just wait long enough and the onscreen display vanishes.

The second monitor

Windows comes in several versions: Home, Professional, Business, Ultimate, Stupendous, and so on. The more expensive versions offer a feature that lets you use two monitors on a single PC. As long as your computer's video hardware can support two monitors, you're in business.

On the hardware side, the video adapter must support two monitors. It does that by either having two separate video connectors or by your obtaining a splitter cable to attach two VGA (analog) monitors to a single digital video connector. Either way, you still have to buy and connect the second monitor.

On the software side, you need to use Windows to confirm that using two monitors is possible on your computer, and to set things up. Obey these steps:

1. **Right-click the mouse on the desktop.**

   Right-click a blank part of the desktop, not any icon or window.

2. **Choose the Screen Resolution command from the pop-up menu.**

   In Windows Vista, you need to choose the Personalize command and then choose the Display Settings option.

   The Screen Resolution dialog box appears, as shown in Figure 10-4.

3. **Click the Detect button.**

   Assuming that the second monitor is attached and you have the proper version of Windows, clicking the Detect button activates the second display.

   If you don't see the second monitor after clicking the Detect button, then your computer system (hardware or software) isn't capable of using two monitors.

4. **From the menu button next to Multiple Displays, choose the option Extend These Displays.**

   In Windows Vista, put a check mark by the option Extend the Desktop Onto This Monitor.

5. **Configure the second display. (Optional)**

   Instructions are elsewhere in this chapter.

Drag monitor icons around to position them   Detect sound monitor

First monitor   Second monitor   Show which monitor is which

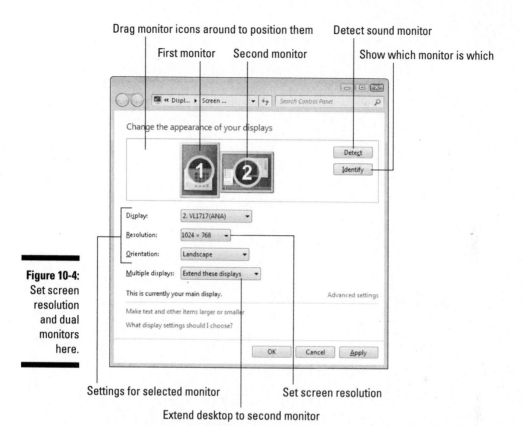

Figure 10-4:
Set screen
resolution
and dual
monitors
here.

Settings for selected monitor   Set screen resolution

Extend desktop to second monitor

6. Use the mouse to adjust the two monitor icons so that they line up onscreen as they do in the real world.

7. Click OK.

The two monitors share the desktop, but the taskbar stays on only the main monitor. Otherwise, you can use both monitors in Windows, dragging a window from one monitor to the second — which is something to see, and definitely impresses folks who've never seen two monitors on a single PC.

✔ Icons stick to only the first monitor's desktop. If you place any icons on the second monitor's desktop, they hop back to the first monitor when you restart Windows.

✔ See Chapter 2 for information on VGA and digital video connectors.

Windows Controls What You See

Don't look now, but the thing controlling what you see on the computer's monitor isn't the monitor. It isn't even the display adapter. Nope, the thing in charge is software, and the software that controls what you see on the monitor is Windows itself. This section describes how to use Windows to control what you see on the screen.

✔ Additional control over your display may be available by using custom software that came with your PC's display adapter. For example, ATI adapters come with a special control center that you can access from the notification area.

✔ The specific software that controls the display is something called the *video driver.*

Setting display size (resolution)

The monitor's physical dimensions cannot change, but you can control the amount of stuff you see on the screen by adjusting the screen *resolution.* That's the number of dots, or *pixels,* the monitor displays, measuring horizontally by vertically.

To set the screen's resolution, follow these steps:

1. **Right-click the desktop and choose the Screen Resolution command from the pop-up menu.**

   In Windows Vista, right-click the desktop and choose Personalization, and then, from the Personalization window, choose Display Settings.

   The Screen Resolution dialog box appears (refer to Figure 10-4).

2. **Click the Resolution menu button.**

   Use Figure 10-4 as your guide.

3. **Use the slider gizmo to set the resolution.**

   As you adjust the slider, the preview monitor in the Screen Resolution dialog box adjusts the size to reflect how things will appear on the screen.

   The recommended resolution is the option that works best for your PC's combination of monitor and display adapter.

4. **Click the Resolution button again to lock in your choice.**

5. **Click the Apply button to preview the new resolution.**

6. **Click the Keep Changes to accept the new resolution.**

   Or, if you opt not to choose the new resolution, click the Revert button and the screen's original resolution is restored.

The maximum resolution and color settings depend on the amount of video memory available to the display adapter. Resolution isn't based on the monitor's size.

- ✔ *Pixel* is a contraction of *pic*ture *el*ement. On a computer display, a *pixel* is a single dot of color.

- ✔ Higher resolutions work best on larger monitors.

- ✔ Some computer games automatically change the monitor's resolution to allow the games to be played. This change is okay, and the resolution should return to normal after you play the game.

Going for a new look

Windows lets you mess with the way its windows appear on the screen. You can change the basic color scheme, transparency, effects, and other time-wasting endeavors — including options to change the sounds you hear when you screw up.

The whole-new-look effort begins with the Personalization window, as depicted in Figure 10-5. To access that window, right-click the desktop and choose the Personalize command from the pop-up menu.

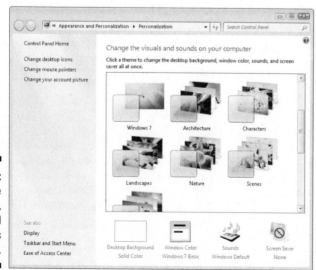

Figure 10-5:
Change the look, sound, and smell of Windows here.

Make things easier to see

If you have trouble seeing small things, adjust your display so that they appear as big as possible: Choose a low resolution, such as 800 x 600. Take advantage of the various View⇨Zoom commands available in applications, which greatly enlarge the text or subject matter.

You can also direct Windows to help you: From the Control Panel, choose Appearance and Personalization, and then, beneath the Display heading, choose the link Make Text and Other Items Larger or Smaller.

Choose a new theme, or an overall look and design for Windows, from the big scrolling gallery in the center of the Personalization window. The change to the new look is instant after you click a theme icon.

You can click the Sounds button to change sounds in Windows.

You can click the Screen Saver button to set up a screen saver, which is covered in the next section.

✔ The Desktop Background button, at the bottom of the Personalization window (refer to Figure 10-5) lets you pick a specific image for the background, or a solid color for the desktop, such as the Titanium White background, ordered upon me by the brutal Wiley Production department.

✔ To set an image from the Web as the desktop background, right-click the image in Internet Explorer and choose the Set As Background command from the pop-up menu.

✔ Windows lets you change the desktop background by using a slide show feature. Click the Desktop Background button, and then choose something other than a solid background. Use the controls in the Desktop Background window to specify whether the images change or stay the same.

✔ Click the link Change Desktop Icons on the left side of the Personalization window to choose a new look for the desktop icons or to hide them altogether.

✔ Clicking the Change Mouse Pointers link opens a fun, time-wasting dialog box where you can choose a new mouse pointer. See Chapter 11 for more information on configuring the mouse in Windows.

Saving the screen

A *screen saver* is an image or animation that appears on the monitor after a given period of inactivity. After your computer sits there, lonely and feeling ignored, for 30 minutes, for example, an image of a fish tank appears on the monitor to amuse any ghosts in the room.

To set up your computer to display a screen saver, obey these steps:

1. From the Personalization window, choose Screen Saver.

Refer to the preceding section (and to Figure 10-5) for information on opening the Personalization window. The Screen Saver Settings dialog box appears, as shown in Figure 10-6.

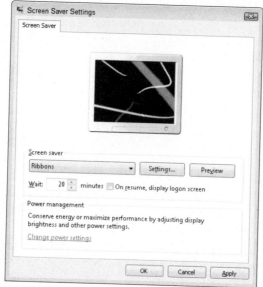

Figure 10-6:
Select a
screen
saver here.

2. Choose a screen saver from the Screen Saver area.

The screen saver is previewed in the tiny monitor window.

3. Click the Settings button to adjust any options for the individual screen saver you chose.

The options vary, depending on the screen saver.

4. Enter the number of minutes to wait before the screen saver kicks in.

If you're impatient, click the Preview button to see the full-screen screen saver. (Click the mouse to end the screen saver.)

5. Click the OK button.

After you haven't touched the mouse or keyboard for the given length of time, the screen saver appears on your monitor. To return to Windows, press a key on the keyboard or jiggle the computer mouse.

✔ To disable the screen saver, choose (None) from the screen saver menu button.

✔ Beware of downloading screen saver files from the Internet. Although some of them are legitimate screen savers, most of them are invasive ads or programs that are impossible to uninstall or remove. If you download this type of screen saver, you're pretty much stuck with it. Be careful!

✔ You may never see the screen saver, especially if you're using the PC's power management system to put the monitor to sleep. See Chapter 14 for more information.

✔ For extra security, in the Screen Saver Settings dialog box, put a check mark by the option On Resume, Display Logon Screen.

✔ The problem the original screen savers tried to prevent was known as *phosphor burn-in* on the old CRT monitors. Such a thing can still happen on monitors, but only if the same image is displayed for months.

Chapter 11

Input This!

Your computer doesn't do anything useful without proper input. For your PC, that input comes primarily from the keyboard. Assisting the keyboard in working the graphical fun and folly that is Windows is another input device: the computer mouse. Yet another type of input device is the joystick or gamepad, which I've also tossed into this enjoyable chapter on PC input.

Meet Mr. Keyboard

The PC's keyboard comes from its history — specifically, the shotgun marriage between the electric typewriter and the calculator. Yes, a lot of using the computer is about typing. You have to live with that. Sure, you could try talking to the computer. It's therapeutic, but not productive.

✔ The keyboard is the computer's standard input device. Refer to Chapter 1 for more information on computer input.

✔ Although you can talk to the computer, it doesn't work as smoothly as you see on those science fiction TV shows. See Chapter 27.

The keyboard connection

The PC keyboard plugs into either a USB port or the special keyboard port on the console.

A wireless PC keyboard uses a wireless receiver that must be connected to the console with either a USB or standard keyboard connection. Wireless keyboards operate off batteries that must be charged so that the keyboard can work.

A typical PC keyboard

There's no such thing as a typical PC keyboard. Each manufacturer likes to customize things a tad, plus special keyboards have *even more* buttons than standard keyboards. But if there were a typical PC keyboard, it would look like the model shown in Figure 11-1.

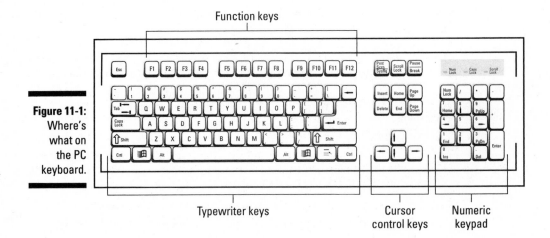

Figure 11-1: Where's what on the PC keyboard.

You can safely divide the typical PC keyboard into four areas, shown in Figure 11-1:

Function keys: These keys are positioned on the top row of the keyboard. They're labeled F1, F2, F3, and so on, up to F11 and F12. They're also called *F-keys*, where F stands for *f*unction and not anything naughty.

Typewriter keys: These keys are the same types of keys you would find on an old typewriter: letters, numbers, and punctuation symbols. They're often called *alphanumeric* keys by humans too young to remember typewriters.

TIP

"Must I learn to type to use a computer?"

The short answer: No, you don't need to learn to type to use a computer. Plenty of computer users hunt and peck. In fact, most programmers don't know how to type, but that brings up an interesting story: A computer software developer once halted all development and had his programmers learn how to touch-type. It took two whole weeks, but afterward, they all got their work done much faster and had more

time available to break away and play those all-important computer games.

As a bonus to owning a computer, you can have it teach you how to type. The Mavis Beacon Teaches Typing software package does just that. Other packages are available, but I personally enjoy saying the name Mavis Beacon.

Cursor-control keys: Also called *arrow keys,* this clutch of keys is used primarily for text editing.

Numeric keypad: Borrowing a lot from a calculator, the numeric keyboard makes entering numbers quick and easy.

These four areas are common to all PC keyboards. Again, the keyboard you use may have more keys with custom functions. Such variations are mentioned elsewhere in this chapter.

- ✔ The standard PC keyboard is known as a 104-key keyboard. Yes, 104 buttons are on that keyboard. Go ahead: Count 'em! I dare you!

- ✔ The *cursor* is the blinking goober on the screen that shows you where the characters you type appear. As though *cursor* isn't weird enough, the blinking doodad is also called an *insertion pointer.*

- ✔ See the section "Keys that are also locks," later in this chapter, for more information on how the numeric keypad can also be used for text editing.

- ✔ If you're really old — and I mean ancient — you must remember that a computer keyboard has 1 and 0 keys. Don't type a lowercase *L* to represent the numeral one or a capital letter *O* for zero.

- ✔ PC keyboards use the Enter key. Macintosh keyboards have a Return key.

- ✔ No "Any" key appears on the keyboard. When a program prompts you to "Press any key" do what I do: Press the spacebar.

Modifier keys

Four keys on the computer keyboard qualify as shift keys, though only one is named Shift. The other three are Ctrl, Alt, and Win. Rather than call them all *shift keys*, the term *modifier keys* seems more appropriate.

A modifier key works in combination with other keys: You hold down a modifier key and then press another key on the keyboard. What happens then depends on the keys you press and how the program you're using reacts to the key combination.

You use the keys like this: Press and hold down the modifier key, and then tap the key it's modifying. Release the modifier key.

For example, to use the keyboard shortcut for the Save command, you press and hold the Ctrl key and tap S. That key combination is written as Ctrl+S. To close a window on the display, you hold down the Alt key and press the F4 key, written as Alt+F4.

✔ The Shift key is used to make capital letters or to access the punctuation and other symbols on the number keys and other keys. That's how you can create the %@#^ characters that come in handy for cursing in comic strips.

✔ Ctrl is pronounced "control." It's the *control* key.

✔ Alt is the *alternate* key.

 ✔ Win is the Windows key, adorned with the Windows logo.

✔ Most of the time, pressing a modifier key by itself does nothing. However, when pressed by itself, the Win key pops up the Start button menu. Pressing the Alt key by itself activates menu bar shortcuts in some programs.

 ✔ Even though you may see Ctrl+S or Alt+S with a capital *S,* it doesn't mean that you must press Ctrl+Shift+S or Alt+Shift+S. The *S* is written in uppercase simply because Ctrl+s looks like a typesetting error.

✔ Multiple modifier keys are also used together, as in Shift+Ctrl+C and Ctrl+Alt+F6. Just remember to press and hold down both modifier keys first and then tap the other key. Release all the keys together.

 ✔ Some manuals use the notation ^Y rather than Ctrl+Y. This term means the same thing: Hold down the Ctrl key, press Y, and release the Ctrl key.

Strange keyboard abbreviations

The key caps are only so big! Therefore, some words have to be scrunched down to fit on the keyboard. Here's your guide to some of the more oddly named keys and what they mean:

Print Screen is also known as PrScr or Print Scrn.

Page Up and Page Down are written as PgUp and PgDn on the numeric keypad.

Insert and Delete appear as Ins and Del on the numeric keypad.

SysRq means System Request, and it has no purpose.

Keys that are also locks

Three keys on the PC keyboard change how certain parts of the keyboard behave. They are the Lock keys, and there are three of them:

Caps Lock: This key works like holding down the Shift key, but it works only with the letter keys. (Think *Caps* as in *cap*ital letters.) Press Caps Lock again, and the letters return to their normal, lowercase state.

Num Lock: Pressing this key makes the numeric keypad on the right side of the keyboard produce numbers. Press this key again, and you can use the numeric keypad for text editing; the numeric keypad is labeled with both numbers and arrow key symbols.

Scroll Lock: This key has no purpose. Some spreadsheets use it to reverse the function of the cursor keys (which move the spreadsheet rather than the cell highlight).

When a lock key is on, a corresponding light appears on the keyboard. The light may be on the keyboard or on the key itself. That's your clue that a lock key's feature is turned on.

✔ Caps Lock affects only the keys A through Z; it doesn't affect any other keys.

✔ If you type This Text Looks Like A Ransom Note and it appears as tHIS tEXT lOOKS lIKE a rANSOM nOTE, the Caps Lock key is inadvertently turned on. Press it once and then try typing your stuff again.

✔ If you press the Shift key while Caps Lock is on, the letter keys return to normal. (Shift kind of cancels out Caps Lock.)

Useful-key tour

Some common, handy keys are to be found on the PC's keyboard. Here are the ones worth noting:

 Two Enter keys are on the keyboard. They're duplicates, the second Enter key added to the numeric keypad simply for convenience. Normally, you press the Enter key to end a paragraph in a word processor. In Windows, pressing the Enter key is also the same as clicking the OK button in a dialog box.

 The Escape key is labeled Esc, but it means Escape. Pressing the key doesn't immediately take you to some luscious tropical locale complete with refreshing beverage. Nope, pressing the Esc key is the same as clicking Cancel in a dialog box.

 Don't bother looking on the keyboard: It has no Help key. Instead, whenever you need help in Windows, whack the F1 key. F1 equals help. Commit that to memory.

 The Tab key is used in two different ways on your computer, neither of which generates the diet cola beverage. In a word processor, you use the Tab key to indent paragraphs or line up text. In a dialog box, you use the Tab key to move between the various graphical gizmos.

- Use Tab rather than Enter when you're filling in a form in a program or dialog box or on the Internet. For example, press the Tab key to hop between the First Name and Last Name fields.

- The Tab key often has two arrows on it — one pointing to the left and the other to the right. These arrows may be in addition to the word *Tab*, or they may be on there by themselves to confuse you.

- The arrows on the Tab key go both ways because Shift+Tab is a valid key combination. For example, pressing Shift+Tab in a dialog box moves you "backward" through the options.

- The computer treats a tab as a single, separate character. When you backspace over a tab in a word processing program, the tab disappears completely in one chunk — not space by space.

Weird-key tour

The computer keyboard sports strange keys, buttons you'll probably never press. Here's the list:

The Break key shares a keycap with the Pause key. It's not used any more, which is good because it should have been spelled B-r-a-k-e in the first place.

 Some games may use the Pause key to temporarily suspend the action, but it's not a consistent thing.

 The backslash (\) leans to the left. Don't confuse it with the forward slash key, which leans to the right (/).

 The Print Screen key, also named PrtSc, takes a snapshot of the Windows desktop, saving the image in the Windows Clipboard. You can then paste that image into any program that lets you paste a graphical image.

 The AltGr, or Alt Graph, key is used on non-US keyboards to help non-English-speaking humans access characters specific to their non-English language.

 Some international keyboards sport a Euro currency symbol, often found sharing the 4 key with the dollar sign.

 The System Request key shares its roost with the Print Screen key. It does nothing.

 This booger is the Context key. It lives between the right Windows and Ctrl keys. Pressing this key displays the shortcut menu for whatever item is selected on the screen — the same as right-clicking the mouse when something is selected.

Keys for doing math

 No matter how hard you look, you won't find a × or ÷ key on the computer keyboard. That's because computer math doesn't involve multiplication or division.

Just kidding. Computers take advantage of punctuation symbols to carry out various mathematical operations. To help you remember the symbols, the keyboard designers clustered them around the numeric keypad, where most of the math stuff takes place anyway. Here's the list:

- ✔ + is for addition.
- ✔ – is for subtraction.
- ✔ * is for multiplication.
- ✔ / is for division.

 You use the asterisk (*) for multiplication, not the lowercase *x*.

Special keys on special keyboards

Any keys beyond the standard 104 keys (see Figure 11-1) on your PC's keyboard are probably custom keys, added by the keyboard manufacturer because they look cool or the manufacturer figured that you need special functions such as volume control, play/pause, start e-mail, or what-have-you. The buttons can do anything because they're nonstandard.

When you have a nonstandard keyboard, you most likely also have a special program that came with your computer. That special program controls the keyboard's special buttons, sometimes allowing you to reassign their functions. Look for the special program on the Start menu's All Programs menu or in the Control Panel.

Control the Keyboard in Windows

If you plan to write a lot of fast-paced theatrical drama on your computer, you'll probably write the word *Aaaaaaaaaaaaaaa* a lot. To do so, you press and hold the A key. After a delay, the A key repeats itself, spewing out the letter *A* like water from a fire hose. You can control both the delay and how fast the character repeats itself by using the Keyboard Properties dialog box in Windows, shown in Figure 11-2.

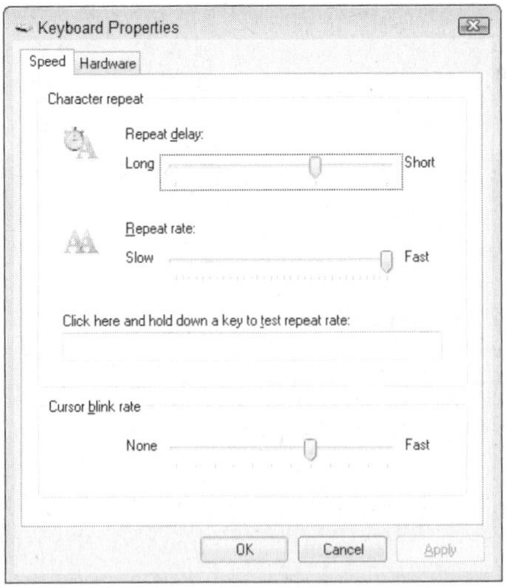

Figure 11-2:
Control the keyboard here.

To open the Keyboard Properties dialog box, follow these steps:

1. **Open the Control Panel window.**

   See Chapter 5 if you need help opening the Control Panel window.

2. **Choose Large Icons from the menu by the View By item, near the upper right corner of the window.**

3. **Click the Keyboard icon to display the Keyboard Properties dialog box.**

4. **Use the mouse to manipulate the sliders in the dialog box to set the rates, and then test out the rates in the text box that's provided.**

5. **Click the OK button only when you're happy.**

   You might want to change Control Panel view back to Category view before you close its window.

6. **Close the Control Panel window when you're done.**

Say Hello to the Mouse

Your computer's mouse is an *input* device. Although the keyboard (another input device) can do almost anything, you need a mouse in order to control graphics and graphical whatnots on the screen — especially in an operating system like Windows.

- ✔ Your PC may have come with a specific mouse, but you can always buy a better replacement.

- ✔ The plural of computer mouse is *mice*. One computer has a mouse. Two computers have mice.

Connecting the mouse

The computer mouse connects to the console using a USB port. Some older mouse models may use the specific mouse port.

The mouse usually rests to the right of the keyboard, with its tail pointing back to the computer. The flat part of the mouse goes on the bottom.

You need space to roll the mouse around, usually a swath of desktop real estate about the size of this book.

Wireless mice don't use cables. The wireless mouse communicates with a base station or another gizmo, typically attached to the console's USB or mouse port. A wireless Bluetooth mouse may not require a connector, because it uses a Bluetooth receiver internal to the console.

- ✔ See Chapter 2 for more information about where the mouse plugs into the PC console.

- ✔ You can also set the mouse on the left side of the keyboard if you're left-handed. See the section "Using the mouse left-handed," later in this chapter.

- ✔ The wireless mouse requires power, which probably comes in the form of batteries. They must be replaced or recharged occasionally, or else the mouse doesn't work.

Basic mouse parts

A typical computer mouse is shown in Figure 11-3, where the basic and important mouse features are illustrated.

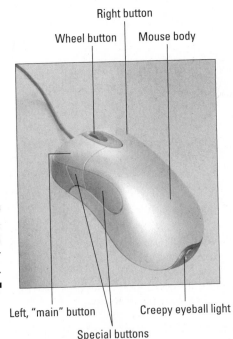

Right button

Wheel button | Mouse body

Figure 11-3:
A typical
computer
mouse.

Left, "main" button

Special buttons

Creepy eyeball light

Mouse body: The mouse is about the size of a bar of soap. You rest your palm on its body and use your fingers to manipulate the mouse buttons.

Left (main) button: The left button, which falls under your right hand's index finger, is the *main* button. That's the button you click the most.

Wheel button: The center, or wheel, button can be pressed like the left and right buttons, and it can be rolled back and forth. Some wheels can even be tilted from side to side.

Right button: The right button is used for special operations, although right-clicking mostly pops up a shortcut menu.

Special buttons: Some mice come with special buttons, which can be used for Internet navigation or assigned specific functions by using special software (see "Control the Mouse in Windows," later in this chapter).

On the mouse's belly, you find its method of motion detection, which is either a light on an optical mouse or a hard rubber rolly-ball on a mechanical mouse. Of the two types, optical mice are better. They last longer and are easier to clean. Also, optical mice don't need a mouse pad, which is necessary for a mechanical mouse's ball to gain proper traction. An optical mouse can work on any nonreflective surface.

Other mouse species

The variety of computer mice seems endless. They have different styles and shapes, special buttons, and unique features designed to drive the mildest of nerds into a technogeek frenzy.

The most common mouse variation is the multibutton mouse. This mouse type can come adorned with more than the traditional left-right wheel buttons. The largest number of buttons I've ever seen on a computer mouse is 57. (I kid you not.)

A popular mouse variation is the *trackball,* which is like an upside-down mouse. Rather than roll the mouse around, you use your thumb or index finger to roll a ball on top of the mouse. The whole contraption stays stationary, so it doesn't need nearly as much room and its cord never gets tangled. This type of mouse is preferred by graphical artists because it's often more precise than the traditional "soap-on-a-rope" mouse.

Another mouse mutation enjoyed by the artistic type is the *stylus* mouse, which looks like a pen and draws on a special pad. This mouse is also pressure sensitive, which is wonderful for use in painting and graphics applications.

Finally, those *cordless 3-D* mice can be pointed at the computer screen like a TV remote. Those things give me the willies.

Mouse Maneuvers

 The computer's mouse controls a graphical mouse pointer or mouse cursor on the screen, shown in the margin. Roll the mouse around on your desktop, and the pointer on the screen moves in a similar manner: Roll the mouse left, and the pointer moves left; roll it in circles, and the pointer mimics that action. Tickle the mouse, the pointer laughs.

Moving the mouse, and clicking the buttons, is how the mouse works with the computer. Specific names are given to those actions. Here's a list:

Point: When you're told to "point the mouse," you move the mouse on the desktop, which moves the mouse pointer on the screen to point at something interesting (or not).

Click: A *click* is a press of the main (left) mouse button — press and release. It makes a clicking sound (if you lean in to the mouse closely enough).

Right-click: This action is the same as a click, although the right mouse button is used.

Double-click: A double-click is two clicks of the mouse in a row without moving the mouse. The clicks don't need to be *really* fast, and you can adjust the click time, as covered later in this chapter; see the section "Fixing the double-click."

Drag: The drag operation is a common and multistep process: Point the mouse at the thing you want to drag, a graphical object or an icon. Press and hold the mouse's button, and then move the mouse to move the object on the screen. Keep the mouse button down until you're done moving the mouse. Release the mouse button to "drop" whatever you moved.

Right-drag: This action is the same as a drag, but the mouse's right button is used instead.

Ctrl+drag: This action is the same as a drag, though you also press the Ctrl key on the keyboard while you drag around a graphical doodad.

Shift+drag: Just like a Ctrl+drag, but the Shift key is used instead.

 The best way to learn how to use a computer mouse is to play a computer card game, such as Solitaire or FreeCell (both of which come with Windows). You should have the mouse mastered in only a few frustrating hours.

Control the Mouse in Windows

In Windows, the mouse is controlled, manipulated, and teased by using the Mouse Properties dialog box, shown in Figure 11-4.

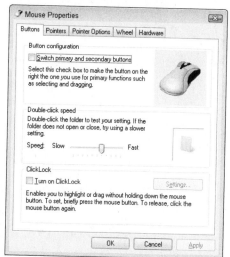

To display the dialog box, open the Control Panel and choose the Hardware and Sound category. In that category, beneath the Devices and Printers heading, click the Mouse link to see the Mouse Properties dialog box.

The Mouse Properties dialog box you see on your PC may look different from the one shown in Figure 11-4. Some custom mice feature their own tabs and options in the dialog box, such as controls for assigning functions to any special mouse buttons.

Making the pointer easier to find

To help you locate a wayward mouse pointer, use the Pointer Options tab in the Mouse Properties, shown in Figure 11-5. The options in the Visibility area, near the bottom of the dialog box, can come in handy, especially on larger displays or when the screen is particularly busy.

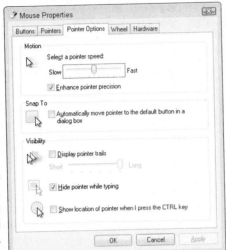

Figure 11-5:
Ways to find
a wayward
mouse.

✔ The Display Pointer Trails option spawns a comet trail of mouse pointers as you move the mouse about. Jiggling or circling the mouse makes lots of visual racket, which allows you to quickly locate the mouse pointer.

✔ The Ctrl key location option allows you to find the mouse pointer by tapping either Ctrl key on the keyboard. This action makes a radar-like circle appear, by zeroing in on the cursor's location.

✔ You can also employ the Snap To option, which specifically jumps the mouse pointer to the main button in any dialog box that appears. (I find this option annoying.)

Another way to make the pointer more visible is to choose a more visible mouse pointer: Click the Pointers tab in the Mouse Properties dialog box. Use the options there to choose a different look or size for the mouse pointer.

Fixing the double-click

If you can't seem to double-click, one of two things is happening: You're moving the mouse pointer a little between clicks or the double-click *rate* is set too fast for human fingers to manage.

The *double-click rate* is set in the Mouse Properties dialog box, on the Buttons tab in the Double-Click Speed area. (See Figure 11-4.) Practice your double-clicking on the tiny folder icon off to the right. Use the Slow-Fast slider to adjust the double-click speed to better match your click-click timing.

Using the mouse left-handed

In Windows, you can adjust the mouse for southpaw use on the Buttons tab, as shown in Figure 11-4. Put a check mark by the box labeled Switch Primary and Secondary Buttons. That way, the main mouse button is under your left index finger.

    ✔ This book and all computer documentation assume that the left mouse button is the main button. *Right-clicks* are clicks of the right mouse button. If you tell Windows to use the left-handed mouse, these buttons are reversed. A right click is then a left click.

    ✔ Left-handed mice are available, designed to fit your left hand better than all those biased, right-hand-oriented mice on the market.

The Fun Input Gizmos

In the original IBM PC, the joystick connected to something called the analog-to-digital port, which made using a joystick on a computer sound all scientific and important. Joysticks are now referred to as *gamepads* or *game controllers*, but they're still input devices, worthy of note in this chapter.

Most PC games don't require a joystick, er, gamepad for their operation. I know because I scientifically tested dozens of games in the name of research for this book. You can get by just fine by using a combination of the keyboard and mouse to perform the required actions (flying, driving, killing aliens) in nearly all computer games. That doesn't lessen the impact of the game controller, of course.

To add a game controller to your PC, simply plug it in. All the controllers are USB, so they plug into the standard USB port. The PC instantly recognizes the game controller.

Unless the game you're playing (or scientific research you're doing) specifically requires a gamepad, you have to configure the thing to work with your game. The gamepad should come with a translation program, which allows you to assign the device's buttons and controls to various keyboard commands for the games you play. You need to configure that program before using the gamepad with your game.

✔ Yes, configuring a joystick or gamepad to work with a game that doesn't specifically require a joystick or gamepad isn't a fun thing to do.

✔ Be sure to read the game's manual to see which gamepads are recommended for the game. When the game doesn't mention a gamepad, you probably don't need one.

✔ Some elaborate game pads are out there, especially for the flight simulator and car simulator games. Some people go nuts with the whole simulator thing.

Chapter 12

P Is for Printer

Computers and their printers have a shared lineage. The first computer terminals were often teletype machines, a type of noisy keyboard-printer-phone thing. That history explains why computers on TV and in film make noise when they display characters on the screen, though it could be just another manifestation of Hollywood's lack of touch with reality.

Eventually the teletype morphed into three unique computer peripherals: the keyboard, the monitor, and the printer. All three gizmos are still considered part of the basic computer system. Although you might not purchase a printer when you buy your PC, it's still something worth looking into, and definitely something worth having. This chapter covers things associated with PC printers and printing.

The Printer, the Paper, the Document Maker

You need a printer attached to your computer system because dragging the PC around and showing everyone what's on the screen is just too much of a chore. No, it's much better to *print* your stuff on paper, to create a *hard copy* of your data, documents, and doodles. The printer makes all that possible.

Types of computer printers

Computer printers are categorized by how the ink gets thrown onto the paper as well as by any special printer features or options. You can pick from one of three general types of printers:

Inkjet: The inkjet printer creates its image by spewing tiny balls of ink directly on the paper. It's that jet-of-ink action that gives this printer category its name. The inkjet printer is the most common type of computer printer.

Laser: Laser printers are found primarily in the office environment, where they can handle the high workloads. The printer uses a laser beam to create the image. The result is crisp and fast output, but at a premium price over the standard inkjet type of printer.

Impact: Impact printers are few and far between these days, although once they were the dominant type of computer printer. These printers are slower and noisier than the other types of printers. They use a ribbon and a device that physically bangs the ribbon on the paper. Because of that, impact printers are primarily used now for printing invoices or multicopy forms. They're not practical for home use.

Two additional types of printers use the inkjet method of lobbing ink onto paper: photo printers and all-in-one printers.

A *photo printer* is specifically designed to print photographs. Generally, a photo printer has a wider variety of inks available for better-quality color printing.

An all-in-one printer combines a basic inkjet or photo printer with a fax machine, scanner, and copier. This type of printer is popular in home and small offices. It does everything.

✔ Inkjet printers are by no means messy. The ink is dry on the paper by the time the paper comes flopping out of the printer.

✔ A laser printer that can print in color is known as a *color* laser printer. The regular (monochrome) laser printer uses only one color of ink — usually, black.

✔ High-priced printers offer a higher-quality output, faster speed, more printing options, the ability to print on larger sheets of paper, and other amazing options.

The basic printer tour

Take a moment to examine the PC's printer and look for some handy items, as labeled in Figure 12-1:

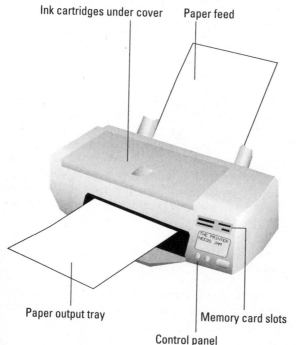

Ink cartridges under cover   Paper feed

THE PRINTER NEEDS JAM

Figure 12-1:
Notable
places on
the printer.

Paper output tray

Control panel

Memory card slots

Paper feed: The paper feed is where you store the paper that the printer eventually prints on. For more information, see the section "The printer eats paper," later in this chapter.

Manual/envelope feeder: The printer may have a special slot, tray, or foldout-thing used to manually feed special papers or envelopes. It may be hidden on your printer, and it's not shown in Figure 12-1, so look around a bit to see whether your printer has such a deal.

Ink/toner replacement: Printers don't go on printing forever. At some point, you need to feed the thing more ink. Be sure that you know how to open the printer to find where the ink goes. Also see the section "The printer drinks ink," later in this chapter.

Control panel: Refer to the next subsection for the details.

Memory card reader: Many photo printers have a place where you can directly plug in your digital camera's memory card.

Paper output tray: The printed paper comes out and is stacked up in the output tray. If the paper comes out face up, be sure to see the section "Printing in reverse order," later in this chapter.

The printer's control panel

Every printer has a control panel somewhere on its body. The fancy models have LCD screens that display text or preview and select photos for printing. Less fancy printers may have only a couple of buttons or lights. Either way, two important buttons to find or features to access on the printer's control panel are the On-line or Select button and the Cancel button.

The purpose of On-Line or Select is to tell your printer whether to ignore the computer. When the printer is offline or deselected, the computer can't print. The printer is still on, which is good because you may need to access features, unjam the printer, or do things that you otherwise cannot do while the thing is printing.

The Cancel button helps you stop printing. It's useful because today's printers are so fast that you often don't have time to cancel printing in Windows. See the section "Stopping a printer run amok," later in this chapter.

- ✔ The computer can print only when the printer is online or selected.

- ✔ If your printer seems to lack a control panel, it's probably controlled by using a software control panel in Windows. This feature is the printer's and isn't a part of Windows, so refer to the printer's manual for details.

- ✔ Printers with LCD control panels often use menu buttons to help you choose the online or form-feed options.

✔ All-in-one printers have additional buttons on their control panels — for example, buttons for making copies and scanning. A companion program in Windows probably allows for even greater control over the printer's abilities. Note that such programs are specific to your printer and aren't a part of Windows itself.

✔ Keep your printer's manual handy. For example, I put my printer's manual right beneath the printer, where I can always find it. You may never read the manual, but if your printer suddenly pops up and displays `Error 34`, you can look up `Error 34` and read how to fix it. (The voice of experience is talking here.)

The printer drinks ink

The Chinese invented ink over 3,000 years ago, but it's still basically the same stuff you use to print stuff on paper with your computer printer. The type of ink and how it's stored depend on which type of printer you're using.

Inkjet printers, which include photo and all-in-one models, use *ink cartridges.* Laser printers use *toner,* a powdery ink substance that also comes in a cartridge.

All printers use black ink or toner. Color printers also use black, plus three other inks or toners: magenta, cyan, and yellow. Photo printers add two more colors: another flavor each of magenta and cyan.

Replacing the ink in your printer works differently for each printer manufacturer. Instructions are usually found on the inside of the lid or compartment where the ink cartridges reside. Overall advice: Be careful! Spill the ink and you've got a serious mess.

✔ Yes, they make money by selling you ink. That's why the printer is cheap. It's the old "Give away the razor and sell them the blade" concept all over again.

✔ Some manufacturers sell their cartridges with return envelopes so that you can send the old cartridge back to the factory for recycling or proper disposal.

✔ Make sure that you don't breathe in the dust from a laser toner cartridge or else you'll die.

✔ Sometimes, the colors in an inkjet printer come three to a cartridge. Yes, it's true: If only one color of ink goes dry, you must replace the entire cartridge even though the other two colors are still available.

- Make a note of which type of inkjet cartridges your printer uses. Keep the catalog number somewhere handy, such as taped to your printer's case, so that you can always reorder the proper cartridge.

- Always follow carefully the instructions for changing cartridges. Old cartridges can leak and spread messy ink all over. Buy rubber gloves (or those cheap plastic gloves that make you look like Batman) and use them when changing an ink or toner cartridge. I also suggest having a paper towel handy.

- When the laser printer first warns you that `Toner [is] low`, you can squeeze a few more pages from it by gently rocking the toner cartridge: Remove the cartridge and rock it back and forth the short way (not from end to end), which helps redistribute the toner dust.

- Rather than buy new cartridges, consider getting ink cartridge refills or toner cartridges recharged. Be sure that you deal with a reputable company; not every type of ink or toner cartridge can be reused successfully.

- Never let your printer cartridges go dry. You may think that squeezing every last drop of ink saves you money, but it's not good for the printer.

The printer eats paper

Next to consuming ink, printers eat paper. Fortunately, paper isn't as expensive as ink, so it doesn't bankrupt you to churn through a ream or two. The only issue is where to feed in the paper. Like feeding a baby, there's a right end and a wrong end.

The paper goes into a feeder tray either near the printer's bottom or sticking out the top.

Some laser printers require you to fill a cartridge with paper, similar to the way a copy machine works. Slide the cartridge all the way into the printer after it's loaded up.

Confirm that you're putting the paper in the proper way, either face down or face up. Note which side is the top. Most printers have little pictures on them that tell you how the paper goes into the printer. Here's how those symbols translate into English:

- The paper goes in face down, top side up.

- The paper goes in face down, top side down.

✔ The paper goes in face up, top side up.

✔ The paper goes in face up, top side down.

Knowing the proper paper orientation helps when you're printing on both sides of a sheet of paper or loading items such as checks for use with personal finance software. If the printer doesn't tell you which way is up, write *Top* on a sheet of paper and run it through the printer. Then draw your own icon, similar to those just shown, to help orient the pages you manually insert into the printer.

Always make sure that you have enough printer paper. Buying too much isn't a sin.

Types of paper

There's really no such thing as a typical sheet of paper. Paper comes in different sizes, weights (degrees of thickness), colors, styles, textures, and, I assume, flavors.

The best general-purpose paper to get is standard photocopier paper. If you want better results from your inkjet printer, getting specific inkjet paper works best, although you pay more for that paper. The higher-quality (and spendy) inkjet paper is good for printing colors; the paper is specially designed to absorb the ink.

At the high end of the spectrum are specialty papers, such as photographic papers that come in smooth or glossy finishes, transparencies, and iron-on T-shirt transfers. Just ensure that the paper you get is made for your type of printer, ink jet or laser.

✔ Some printers are capable of handling larger-size paper, such as legal or tabloid sizes. If so, make sure that you load the paper properly and tell your application that you're using a sheet of paper that's a different size. See the later section "Basic Printer Operation" for more information.

✔ Avoid thick papers because they get jammed inside the printer. (Thicker paper stock can't turn corners well.)

✔ Avoid using erasable bond and other fancy dusted papers in your printer. These papers have a talcum powder coating that gums up the works.

✔ Don't let the expensive paper ads fool you: Your inkjet printer can print on just about any type of paper. Even so, the pricey paper *does* produce a better image.

Printer Setup

As with all other computer peripherals, a courting stage occurs between the PC console and the printer. It involves an introduction, some dating, and, finally, a full-on-marriage. You'll be grateful that the entire operation is much faster and far more successful than human courtship and bonding.

Connecting the printer

After liberating the printer from its box, and from various pieces of tape and evil Styrofoam, locate the printer's power cable. Then locate the printer cable, the one that connects the printer to the console.

Aha! The printer didn't come with a printer-to-console cable, did it? It never does. You have to buy the printer cable separately. It's just a standard USB cable with A and B ends. Refer to Chapter 3 for information on plugging things in.

Before jumping the gun, read the printer's instruction sheet to see whether you need to install software before turning the printer on. If not, turn the printer on. A USB printer is instantly recognized and configured by Windows. Life is good.

Most printers, like computers, can be left on all the time. The printer automatically slips into a low-power sleep mode when it's no longer needed. However, if you don't print often (at least every day), it's perfectly fine to turn off the printer.

✔ Some printers demand to be directly connected to the computer, not plugged into a USB hub.

✔ You can connect a number of printers to a single computer. In fact, most PCs on a network have access to multiple printers, though you can also connect two printers to a single PC using USB cables.

Finding the printer in Windows

Windows 7 lists printers, as well as all other gizmos connected to your PC, in one handy place. It's the Devices and Printers window, shown in Figure 12-2. To view the Devices and Printers window, choose Devices and Printers from the Start button menu.

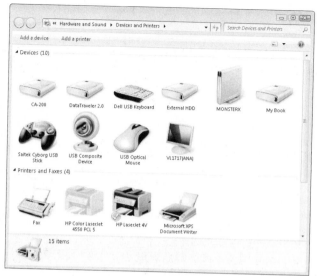

Figure 12-2:
Printers in
the Devices
and Printers
window.

Icons shown in the Devices and Printers window represent various gizmos connected to your PC, including the monitor, keyboard, external storage, Webcams, and gamepads (refer to Figure 12-2).

Printers have a separate category in the Devices and Printers window. It lists the printers attached to or available to your PC on a computer network. Those are all the printers you can use in your programs to print things.

One printer in the list is known as the *default* printer. That doesn't mean it's broken. Instead, the default printer is identified as your computer's primary printer. It's the printer you want to use most of the time. That's a handy thing to have, especially when your PC has multiple printers and you don't want to spend extra time choosing one every time you print.

To print a document in Windows, you need to use the Print command in your application. For more information, see the section "Basic Printer Operation," later in this chapter.

✔ The default printer has a green checkmark by its icon.

✔ You can select or change the default printer at any time. See the section "Setting the default printer," later in this chapter.

✔ Refer to Chapter 5 for more information on the Control Panel in Windows.

✔ Previous versions of Windows showed printers in the Printers window. You get to that window by choosing Printers (or Printers and Faxes) from the Start button menu.

Manually adding a printer

When you can't find your PC's printer in the Devices and Printers window (refer to Figure 12-2), you have to manually add the printer, in one of two ways.

First, you follow the directions that came with your PC's printer. A disc may be included, which you can use to help set things up. Keep in mind that you may need to install the software *before* you connect the printer.

Second, you click the Add a Printer button on the toolbar in the Devices and Printers window (refer to Figure 12-2). When you click the Add a Printer toolbar button, you run the Add Printer Wizard, which quizzes you about the type of printer you're adding. Follow the wizard's directions to locate and set up the printer.

Definitely print a test page to ensure that the printer is working.

When the printer is connected properly and everything is up to snuff, you see that gratifying test page print. You can then start using that printer. Its icon appears in the Devices and Printers window.

✔ Let the network administrator worry about connecting network printers.

✔ If you have an older printer using the old-style printer cable, the name of the printer port is LPT1.

Setting the default printer

To ensure that Windows uses your favorite printer whenever you do a quick-print, choose that favorite by making it the default. Follow these steps:

1. **Choose Devices and Printers from the Start button menu.**

   The Devices and Printers window appears.

2. **Right-click the printer you plan to use most often.**

3. **Choose Set As Default Printer from the pop-up menu.**

   The tiny check mark on the printer's icon confirms that you've specified the default printer.

4. **Close the Devices and Printers window.**

You can change the default printer at any time by repeating these steps.

Basic Printer Operation

Under Windows, printing is a snap. All applications support the same Print command: Choose File⇨Print from the menu, or press Ctrl+P, to see the Print dialog box, depicted in Figure 12-3.

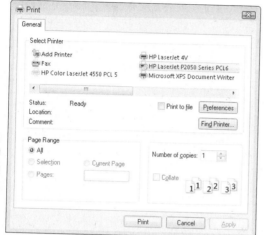

The Print dialog box shown in this figure is typical for most programs. To print the entire document, just click the Print button. Otherwise, you can use the settings in the dialog box to change what and how you print.

For example, you can choose another printer from the list of available printers to print on that printer rather than on the default.

Place a value other than 1 by Number of Copies to print several copies of your work.

Set the number of pages to print (Page Range) to print specific pages from the document. For example, type **2** to print only page 2, or type **3-9** to print pages 3 through 9.

Click the Print button after making your choices to print your document. Or, you can click Cancel and not print anything.

✔ Other printer options, such as paper size and orientation, are set in something called the Page Setup dialog box. See the next section.

✔ Use the Print command only *once*. When the printer seems slow, just wait a while before thinking that you goofed up and choosing the Print command again. Otherwise, you print one copy of the document for every time you use the Print command.

✔ The common keyboard shortcut for the Print command is Ctrl+P.

✔ Rather than waste paper, consider using the File➪Print Preview command instead. It displays a sneak peek of what's to be printed so that you can examine the printer's output before wasting a sheet of paper.

✔ In many newer applications, the printing commands are kept on a button menu because there's no File menu. Look for the button in the upper left corner of the window. Click that button to display its menu.

✔ Many applications sport a Print toolbar icon. If so, you can click that button to quickly print your document by using the default printer.

Setting the margins

The Print dialog box is concerned only with printing, not with formatting. Setting margins, paper size, and other aspects of what is to be printed is handled elsewhere in a program, usually in a Page Setup dialog box, as shown in Figure 12-4.

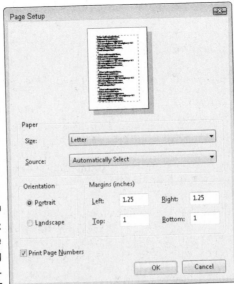

Figure 12-4:
The Page
Setup dialog
box.

To access the Page Setup dialog box, choose File⇨Page Setup from the menu. When the program lacks a menu, click the button in the upper left corner of the window and choose the Page Setup command from that menu. The Page Setup command might also be found on the Print submenu.

Change the settings in the Page Setup dialog box, as you can see in the figure.

Choose a different paper size from the Size button, though keep in mind that your printer must accept the size you select.

Choose portrait (tall) or landscape (wide) orientation for the document.

Set margins as necessary.

Click the OK button to save your changes. You need to print the document to see your work, though the preview window in the Page Setup dialog box shows you sort of what your document will look like when printed.

✔ As with the Print dialog box, each application's Page Setup dialog box is different, with commands not always in the same location.

✔ The Page Setup dialog box is where you set things like margins and paper size — not in the Print dialog box.

✔ Computer printers cannot print on an entire sheet of paper. There's usually a small margin around the sheet or just on one end of the paper, where no printing can take place. That part of the page is held by the printer's paper-feeding mechanism, and its size and location vary from printer to printer.

Printing in reverse order

Some printers cough out pages face up. What that means is that everything you print is in reverse order, with the last page printed on top. You can fix that problem by directing the program to print your stuff in reverse order, last page first. That's a job for the Printer's Properties dialog box.

To see the Printer's Properties dialog box, press Ctrl+P to summon the standard Print dialog box (refer to Figure 12-3). In that dialog box, click the Properties, Preferences, or Options button.

After you're in the Printer's Properties dialog box (which may not be called Printer's Properties), you can search for an option to print in reverse order or print from back to front. After choosing that option, click the OK button. Proceed to print your document, which then spews out of the printer properly.

Printing in reverse order isn't a printer feature; it's part of the program you use. Some programs have that feature, and others don't.

Stopping a printer run amok

The most frustrating printer experience you can have is wanting the dumb thing to stop printing. It happens. Often.

The easiest way to stop printing is to look on the printer's control panel for a Cancel button. Press that button, and all printing stops. Oh, a few more pages may pop out of the printer, but that's it.

If you have an older printer (or just a cheap one) without a Cancel button, do this:

1. **Open the Devices and Printers window.**

   In older versions of Windows, open the Printers window by choosing Printers from the Start button menu.

2. **Open your printer's icon.**

   The printer's window is displayed, similar to the one shown in Figure 12-5.

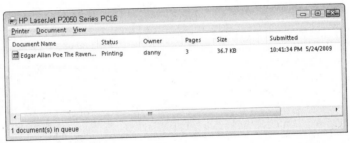

Figure 12-5:
A printer's window.

3. **Click to select the document you want to cancel.**

4. **Choose Document⇨Cancel from the menu.**

   Or, if you want to cancel all pending documents, choose Printer⇨Cancel All Documents.

5. **Click the Yes button to confirm that you want to cancel the document.**

6. **Wait.**

7. **Close the printer's window when you're done.**

It may take a few moments for the last bit of text to print. But, seriously, if the printer continues to spew pages at this point, just turn off the printer. Wait a few seconds, and then turn it back on again.

Chapter 13

PC Audio Abilities

*O*riginally, the computer's audio was a simple bell. *Ding!* When the first microcomputers came out in the 1970s, they had small, tinny speakers to emulate the bell. But computer hobbyists wanted their machines to do more than just go "beep."

Today's PCs have complex audio abilities. You'll find, built into the chipset on the motherboard, specialized sound circuitry, including a complete music synthesizer. The computer can talk, sing, play a symphony, and yes, even ding like a bell. This chapter explains all about your computer's sound system.

The Noisy PC

All PCs include sound-generation hardware on the motherboard. This hardware can process and play digitally recorded sounds, play music from a CD, generate music using the onboard synthesizer, and record sounds. That's a lot of capability, yet it's so common on a PC that the manufacturers seldom boast about it.

✔ When you're really into audio, you can add more advanced sound hardware to your PC by using an expansion card. This type of upgrade is necessary only for diehard audiophiles, people who are composing their own music, or professionals who use their PCs as the heart of an audio studio.

✔ If your PC lacks expansion slots or you have a laptop, you can upgrade your audio by adding an external, USB sound device, such as the Sound Blaster Audigy system.

Speakers hither and thither

The PC console has always come with an awful, internal speaker. It still does, but in addition, your PC most likely came with a standard set of stereo (left-right) speakers. That's fine for basic sound, but the PC is capable of so much more.

The next step up from the basic speaker set is to add a *subwoofer*. It's a speaker box designed for low-frequency sounds, which gives oomph to the bass in music or adds emphasis to the sounds in games.

Typically, the subwoofer sits on the floor beneath your PC. It plugs directly into the PC's sound-out jack (see Chapter 3), and the stereo speakers plug into the subwoofer.

The final step up the audio ladder is to go with surround sound, similar to the sound setup for a home theater. In that configuration, you can have multiple speakers located around the computer, depending on the implementation of surround sound hardware you're using.

Figure 13-1 illustrates all possible locations for speakers in a surround sound setup. You'd be nuts to have *all* those speakers connected at one time, but it's possible. Table 13-1 lists the options for surround sound.

Table 13-1	Surround Sound Speaker Options
Surround Sound Version	*Speakers Used*
3.0	Left, Right, Back Surround
4.0	Left, Right, Surround Left, Surround Right
4.1	Left, Right, Surround Left, Surround Right, Subwoofer
5.1	Left, Right, Center, Surround Left, Surround Right, Subwoofer
6.1	Left, Right, Center, Side Left, Side Right, Back Surround, Subwoofer
7.1	Left, Right, Center, Side Left, Side Right, Surround Left, Surround Right, Subwoofer

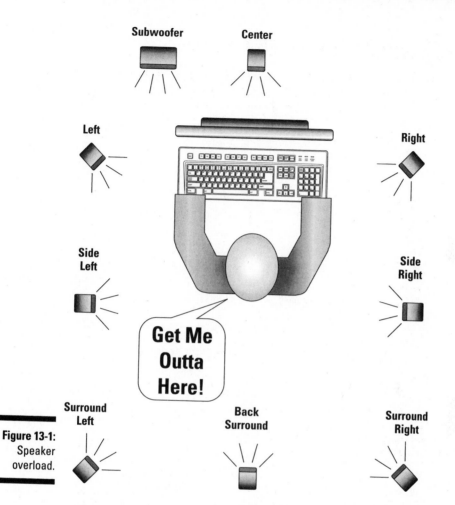

Figure 13-1:
Speaker
overload.

✔ Left and right speakers are positioned on the left and right sides of the monitor as you're facing it.

✔ I recommend getting speakers that have a volume control, either on the left or right speaker. Another bonus: a mute button on the speaker. Note that some high-end speaker systems have a control (wired or remote) that has the volume and mute buttons on it.

✔ The *.x* part of a surround sound specification refers to the presence of a subwoofer: .0 means no subwoofer; .1 means one subwoofer; .2 means two subwoofers.

✔ If you have an audio expansion card on your PC, be sure to plug the speakers into that card.

✔ Refer to my book *Troubleshooting Your PC For Dummies* (Wiley) if you're having trouble hearing sounds from your PC.

In your own world with headphones

Rather than startle everyone in the room when you launch aerial artillery in a computer game, consider using headphones with your PC instead of an external sound system. A good set of headphones can truly emulate a sound environment beyond what the traditional stereo speakers offer. In fact, some high-end gaming headphones can cost more than the standard home theater surround sound system. They're worth it.

Good headphones come with a volume control and maybe even a mute button on the same wire that connects the headphones to the PC. Better headphones come with a built-in microphone for online communications as well as game playing. This type of headphone is often referred to as a *headset*. Headphones (or headsets) plug into the console's headphone jack.

 ✔ Headphones plug into the computer's speaker jacks. Use the jacks on the front of the console.

 ✔ Headsets have two audio jacks: One goes into the speaker jack; the other, into the microphone jack. They're color-coded to help you plug them into the proper holes.

 ✔ Look for headphones that are comfy on your ears, with big, puffy "cans."

 ✔ I don't recommend a nonstereo headset. It has only one earpiece, which is okay for online communications but lousy for game-playing.

Microphone options

Any cheesy microphone works on a PC. If sound quality is important to you and you're using your PC as a digital audio studio, you have to spend money on microphones and mixers and all that. But if that's not you, any old microphone does the trick.

 ✔ Two popular types of microphones are used on a PC: condenser and dynamic. Either one works with a PC, though if your PC's sound equipment isn't up to snuff, I recommend getting a sound mixer to use as a preamp.

 ✔ If you plan to use voice over the Internet or dictation, get a headset. See the preceding section.

Sound Control in Windows

The Sound dialog box, beautifully illustrated in Figure 13-2, is the main place to visit in Windows for software control over your PC's sound hardware. That's where you set up and configure all the sound hardware on your PC, from the speakers to the microphone to the sounds that play as Windows does its thing.

Figure 13-2:
Sound
control
happens
here.

To view the Sound dialog box, follow these steps:

1. **Open the Control Panel.**

2. **Choose Hardware and Sound.**

3. **Click the main Sound heading.**

   The Sound dialog box appears.

Later sections in this chapter discuss various things you can do with the Sound dialog box.

Windows also features a second location for controlling PC audio. In the notification area on the taskbar, you find a tiny volume control. Using that control is covered later in this chapter, in the section "Adjusting the volume."

Configuring the speakers

To adjust the PC's speakers in Windows, follow these steps:

1. **Summon the Sounds dialog box.**

   Refer to the steps in the preceding section.

2. **If necessary, click the Playback tab in the Sounds dialog box.**

3. **Choose the playback device.**

   For example, click Speakers (refer to Figure 13-2).

4. **Click the Configure button.**

   If the Configure button is unavailable (dimmed), there's nothing to configure; you're done.

5. **Work through the Speaker Setup Wizard to ensure that your speakers are set up properly and that everything is working.**

6. **Close the Sounds dialog box when you're done; click OK.**

Configuring the microphone

To set up your PC's microphone, follow these steps:

1. **Open the Control Panel.**

2. **Choose Ease of Access.**

3. **Choose Set Up a Microphone from beneath the Speech Recognition heading.**

4. **Work through the Microphone Setup Wizard to properly configure the microphone attached to your PC.**

Adjusting the volume

To make the PC louder or quieter or just to shut it up, you can use the Volume Control icon in the notification area. Click that icon once to display the volume control slider, as shown in Figure 13-3. Use the mouse to slide the gizmo up for louder or down for quieter, or click the Mute button to turn off the sound.

Switch between headphones and speakers

Your PC can have both speakers and head-phones attached, but you can hear sounds from only one of those items at a time. To switch between them, right-click the Volume icon in the notification area and choose Playback Devices from the pop-up menu. In the Sound dialog box, on the Playback tab, choose the device you want to use: speakers or headphones. Click the Set Default button to confirm your choice, and then click OK.

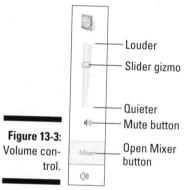

— Louder

— Slider gizmo

— Quieter

— Mute button

— Open Mixer button

Figure 13-3:
Volume con-
trol.

✔ You can also adjust the volume on your PC's speakers, if they come with a volume control knob or remote control.

✔ Choosing Mixer from the volume control pop-up (refer to Figure 13-3) displays a more complex volume setting window, where you can set the volume for various noise-producing gizmos and activities in Windows.

Windows Goes Bleep

Sounds are part of the entire Windows interface. It's a mutual thing. The computer goes bonkers and produces a "bzzt!" sound. Then you, the human, say @#$%&*! Or something similar. Truly, sound and music are what make the biological and electronic life forms dwell in harmonious friendship.

Though you can spend a lifetime configuring yourself not to say @#$%&*, it takes only a few moments to configure Windows to go "bleep." This section explains how.

✔ See Chapter 27 for information on listening to music in Windows.

✔ Also see Chapter 27 for information on making Windows talk — and listen.

Setting event sounds

Windows plays sounds at various times, sounds triggered by certain events that happen in your PC. To control which sounds play, or to disable some sounds from playing, follow these steps:

1. **Right-click the speaker icon in the notification area.**

2. **Choose the Sounds command from the pop-up menu.**

   The Sounds dialog box appears with the Sounds tab front and center, as shown in Figure 13-4. The scrolling list highlights various events in Windows. The speaker icon next to an event means that a sound is associated with that event.

Figure 13-4:
Assigning
sounds to
events.

For example, the Critical Stop event — a bad one in Windows — is high-lighted in Figure 13-4. The sound associated with that event appears on the Sounds drop-down list as `Windows Critical Stop`. That's the sound file that plays when Windows stops critically.

3. **Select an event to assign a sound to.**

   For example, select New Mail Notification, which is the sound that plays when Windows Mail picks up new e-mail.

4. **Click the Test button to hear the current sound.**

   Not every event has a sound, so the Test button is disabled when there's no sound to preview.

5. **Choose a new sound from the Sounds menu button.**

6. **Click the Test button to preview the sound you selected.**

7. **Click the OK button when you're done assigning sounds.**

You can use any sound found on your computer for an event. To do so, choose the event (Step 5) and click the Browse button. You can then use the Browse button to search for sound files on your PC. That's not as easy as it sounds, especially if you're unfamiliar with how files and folders work. (In that case, see Part IV of this book.)

✔ To remove a sound from an event, choose (None) from the top of the Sounds drop-down list.

✔ The best source for sounds is the Internet, where you can find Web page libraries full of sound samples. To find them, go to Google (`www.google.com`) and search for *Windows WAV file sounds*.

✔ You can also use sounds that you record yourself, assigning them to specific events in Windows. See the next section.

Recording your own sounds

For simple sound recording, you can use the Sound Recorder program that comes with Windows. The program sports a straightforward interface, as shown in Figure 13-5.

Figure 13-5:
The Sound
Recorder.

Assuming that a microphone is already connected to your PC and set up for use in Windows (see the earlier section "Configuring the microphone"), sound recording works like this:

1. **Pop up the Start button menu.**

2. **Choose All Programs⬦Accessories⬦Sound Recorder.**

   The Sound Recorder program appears (refer to Figure 13-5).

3. **Click the Start Recording button.**

4. **Talk: "blah blah blah."**

5. **Click the Stop Recording button when you're done.**

6. **Use the Save As dialog box to save your audio recording to permanent storage.**

7. **Close the Sound Recorder window when you're done.**

You can use the Sound Recorder to capture audio from any sound-producing gizmo attached to your PC, such as a turntable or VCR. Simply connect the gizmo to the proper Line In audio jack on the console, and then follow the same steps for recording your voice.

✔ If you need something better than the Sound Recorder program, I recommend Audacity, which is free and available on the Internet at `http://audacity.sourceforge.net`.

✔ The Windows Media Player is used to play the sounds you record. See Chapter 27 for more information.

Chapter 14

PC Leftovers

I'm a big fan of leftovers. For some reason, my mom's goulash was much better the second night. And who doesn't live for the remnants of Thanksgiving Day dinner? Well, maybe not after three days, but you have to admit that there's good value in having leftovers.

The PC has a lot of hardware guts, most of which you can merrily skip over in your efforts to become comfortable with a computer. Two items among those digital leftovers are worth a good look. The first is the PC's Power Management system, and the second is the dialup modem. Both hardware goodies are covered in this chapter.

Manage the PC's Power

I'm certain that somewhere down deep in its core, your computer secretly wants to control the world. But that's not the type of power this chapter is talking about. Nope, it's the power that the computer consumes, and literally sucks from the wall socket. Electricity. Juice. You must properly manage that power so that your computer doesn't waste energy.

✔ *Power management* is a general term used to describe the ability of computers and other appliances, such as television sets and teleportation pods, to become energy-smart.

✔ It's power management hardware that enables a computer to turn itself off.

✔ Power management also gives your PC the ability to sleep or hibernate. Refer to Chapter 4.

✔ If you're really into saving the planet, be sure to properly dispose of old computer parts. Never just toss out a PC, a monitor, or especially a battery. Try to find a place that recycles old technology. (There be gold in them thar consoles!)

✔ The current power management standard is the Advanced Configuration and Power Interface (ACPI). It specifies various ways the PC can reduce power consumption, including placing the microprocessor in low-power mode, disabling the monitor, halting the hard drives (which normally spin all the time), managing battery power in a laptop, as well as other more technical and trivial methods.

Choosing a power-management plan

Windows hides its power management settings in the Power Options window, shown in Figure 14-1. To display that window, open the Control Panel, click the Hardware and Sound heading, and then click the Power Options heading.

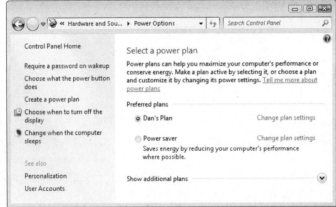

Figure 14-1:
The Power
Options
window.

The Power Options window features various plans for managing the power in your PC, as listed in Table 14-1. You can see more plans by clicking the downward-pointing arrow button to the right of the text Show Additional Plans.

Each plan controls two parts of the computer's power management scheme:

✔ The amount of time to wait before Windows automatically turns off the monitor

✔ The amount of time to wait before Windows puts the computer to sleep

Time is tracked based on your input. So when you don't type on the keyboard or move the mouse for the given length of time, Windows turns off the monitor or puts the computer to sleep. That saves energy.

To choose a plan, select the radio button next to the plan name. The Power Saver option is just fine for most folks. Close the Power Options window and you're done.

You can also customize any plan, or create your own plan by clicking the link Create a Power Plan on the left side of the Power Options window. Follow the directions on the screen. Be sure to give your power plan a clever name, such as *Dan's Plan*, which is ideal when your name happens to be Dan.

> ✔ Power management doesn't turn off the monitor; it merely suspends the video signal to the monitor. An energy-smart monitor detects the lack of signal and then automatically enters a low-power state. This state is often indicated by the monitor's power lamp, which dims, glows another color, or blinks while the monitor is in power-saving mode.

> ✔ See Chapter 4 for more information on Sleep mode.

Adding a hibernation option

Windows has never put the option to hibernate your PC in an obvious place. Because of that, my advice for putting the computer into Hibernation mode is to assign the hibernation command to the console's power button. Here's what to do:

1. **Open the Control Panel.**

2. **Choose Hardware and Sound.**

3. **Beneath the Power Options heading, choose the line Change What the Power Buttons Do.**

4. **From the menu button by the option titled When I Press the Power Button, choose Hibernate.**

5. **Click the Save Changes button.**

6. **Close the Control Panel window.**

After following these steps, pressing the console's power button hibernates the computer.

See Chapter 4 for more information on the PC hibernation.

Power-saving options for battery-powered PCs

If you have a laptop or are using a desktop PC with a UPS (uninterruptible power supply) and the UPS is connected to the PC by a USB cable, the power-plan settings information you see in the Edit Plan Settings window sports *two* columns of options rather than one: The first column is labeled On Battery; the second is labeled Plugged In.

You set the options for the On Battery column for when your laptop is being powered by its batteries or when a desktop PC is powered by a UPS during a power outage.

You set the options for the Plugged In column for when the computer is using power from the wall socket. That's the only power settings column that appears (untitled) when you have a PC that doesn't have a battery or battery-backed-up power source.

Obviously, you want more power savings when your PC is running on batteries. For a laptop, changing the display and sleep values to something quick, but not too short, makes sense. For a PC running on a UPS, my advice is to "sleep" the computer as soon as possible: Set the timeout values to 1 or 2 minutes.

✔ When your desktop PC is running "on battery," the power is off and the only thing running the PC is the UPS. That doesn't mean you can still work; it means that you should turn off the PC immediately. By setting the PC sleep time to less than a few minutes, you help your computer survive the power outage.

✔ Also see Chapter 4 for more information on UPSs.

✔ For more information on using your laptop and managing its battery life, see my book *Laptops For Dummies* (Wiley).

Merry Modems

Modem is a combination of two technical and cumbersome words, *mo*dulator and *dem*odulator. Beyond that, what a modem does is way too technical for me to bore you with now. Suffice it to say, modems are all about communications, primarily between your own PC and a remote computer or the Internet.

✔ There are two main types of computer modem: the fast broadband modem and the traditional, slow dialup modem.

✔ See Chapter 15 for information on broadband modems, which are part of the bigger arena of computer networking.

Modem speed

The gauge used to judge a modem is its speed, measured in *kilobits per second* (Kbps), or thousands of bits per second. A typical dialup modem runs at about 55 Kbps, which is fast enough to transmit a page of text in less than a second.

Broadband modems operate much faster than dialup modems. Their speeds are measured in Kbps and also in Mbps, which is millions of bits per second. For example, a DSL broadband modem running at 768 Kbps can display all the text from one of Shakespeare's plays in less than a second. A 2 Mbps modem allows you to receive, in a few seconds, everything Shakespeare ever wrote.

- ✔ Modem speed is relative; the advertised speed for a modem doesn't guarantee that all communications take place at that speed.

- ✔ Some broadband Internet companies may offer minimum speed guarantees — at a premium price.

- ✔ You can gauge your modem speed online by visiting a site such as www. dslreports.com/stest.

The dialup modem

The traditional PC modem is the dialup modem, which uses the telephone system for communications. Essentially, a dialup modem serves as your computer's phone, though the phone calls are made to other computers (and fax machines), not to people.

The modem connects to a standard telephone jack, just like a regular phone. Indeed, with a modem in your computer, you're using the telephone system to place calls, though noisy data is being sent, not the dulcet tones of human communication.

If your PC has a modem, it shows up as a device in Windows. Choose the command Devices and Printers from the Start button menu to see its icon. If you don't see a modem icon in that window, your PC doesn't have a dialup modem installed or attached.

- ✔ Most PCs sold today don't come with modems, even as part of the chipset. You can add a modem internally with an expansion card, or externally with a USB modem. Even then, unless your area utterly lacks a broadband Internet connection, there's no need to have a dialup modem in your PC.

- ✔ Well, there's one exception: Dialup modems can be used on your PC to send faxes.

✔ The main reason that dialup modems aren't as popular as they once were: They're slow. 'Nuff said.

✔ As with a phone, you must hang up a dialup modem when you finish making the call.

✔ There's no extra cost for using a modem on a standard phone line. When the modem makes a long distance call, you pay the same rates as for a voice call.

✔ You can't use your phone while your modem is talking. In fact, if somebody picks up another extension on that line, it garbles the signal and may lose your connection — not to mention that the human hears a horrid screeching sound.

Part III

Communications, Sharing, Networking

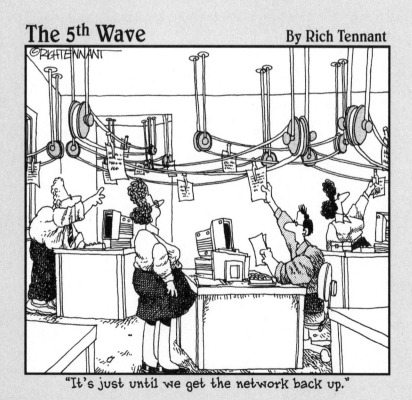

The 5th Wave   By Rich Tennant

"It's just until we get the network back up."

In this part . . .

For years, networking was supposed to be the Next Big Thing for the PC. It was coming! Watch out! Oddly enough, networking never really took hold until the Internet gained popularity, and even then it took the high-speed, or broadband, Internet to bring computer networking to full Next Big Thing status. That process took only about 20 years.

Computer networking can be a daunting and fear-laden topic, intimidating even. Thanks to the popularity of home networking and the domination of the Internet, computer networking is now something that even a mortal computer user such as yourself must deal with. Fortunately, beneath its terrible, tortuous terminology, computer networking is about the simple, friendly concepts of sharing and communications. It's useful stuff. This part of the book explains what you need to know.

Chapter 15

Necessary Networking Things

Computer networking is about sharing and communications, but that's where the similarity between it and kindergarten ends. Before you can share and communicate, you need to understand the big networking picture, which means that some hardware and software orientation must take place. It helps to know the players and the game. After all, you want to enter the network arena prepared and well armed. This chapter helps you by introducing you to necessary networking things.

The Network Arena

The bottom line with computer networking is the concept of sharing *resources* between several computers. Obviously, to understand how sharing resources works, it first helps to know what the heck a resource is.

A *resource* is something a computer uses to get work done, such as memory or processor power. For your own networking purposes, several types of resources are shared among computers connected to a network:

Mass storage: You can access information stored on other computers on the network, and those other computers can access information stored on your computer (well, information that you allow to be shared).

Printers: All computers on a network can use one or more printers connected to or shared on the network. So Serge can share his color printer with everyone (whether he likes it or not).

Internet access: Only one connection to the Internet is necessary when you have a network. All computers on the network share that connection.

Media player: Windows lets you share media files (video, audio, and pictures) among computers, as well as with any Xbox game consoles attached to the computer network.

Like everything else in computerdom, the network is a combination of hardware and software.

On the hardware side, you have the physical connection between each computer. Yes, that connection is hardware even when it's wireless.

On the software side is Windows, which contains all the necessary networking stuff you need to make the communications, the sharing, and — yes — the *love* happen on the network.

TECHNICAL STUFF

Network terms you can avoid

Here are some important network terms you should avoid:

802.11: Neither a Dewey decimal number nor Abe Lincoln's hat size on Mount Rushmore, the number 802.11 refers to the current wireless networking standard. The 11 is followed by a letter: such as *g* or *n,* which describes the specific standard and how compatible two wireless networking gizmos can be.

Ad hoc: On this type of network, wireless computers are connected to each other but not necessarily through a router or central access point.

Ethernet: This term refers to the standards and protocols used by Windows for networking. Ethernet is the most popular personal networking standard, and it's a standard for communications on the Internet as well (which is why networking is closely tied to the Internet). The specifics of Ethernet aren't important to understanding the whole networking ball of wax. Just be sure that you say it properly: "EETH-er-net."

LAN: When you connect a group of computers to form a network, you make a *local area network*, or LAN. You pronounce LAN like *land* without the *d* at the end, like how Aunt Minnie pronounced "land sakes!"

Peer-to-peer network: A network that simply connects computers is known as a *peer-to-peer network*. In that scheme, no single computer is in charge; each computer is "on the network," just like any other computer. Peer-to-peer contrasts with another scheme, *client-server.* In that setup, there's one main computer, the *server* (or a computer that merely runs special server software). Servers aren't typically found on peer-to-peer networks, and this book doesn't cover using servers or installing server software.

Network Hardware

Networking hardware involves these pieces:

The networking adapter: The hardware interface between your computer and the network. This device is required in order to connect your PC with the network.

The cables: These items are necessary to connect the PC's networking adapter to a central location, or hub. Well, cables are necessary unless you're using a wireless network.

The router: The central location where all wires are connected, or where the wireless signals converge, to complete the network.

The broadband modem: Connects the computers on your network to the Internet. Though a broadband modem isn't necessary for networking, nearly all home and small office networks feature one to round out the networking hardware picture.

Figure 15-1 illustrates a typical network layout. At the center of the network is a combination wireless base station and router. Two PCs are on the network, one connected with a wire (Dad's computer) and the other two connected wirelessly (Judy's computer and Mom's laptop).

The router in Figure 15-1 is connected to a broadband modem, which is connected to the Internet. The router is also connected to a printer, which is shared with all PCs on the network.

The network setup illustrated in Figure 15-1 is typical but not standard. The network you create may look similar, be all wireless, be all wired, have more or fewer components, or be better illustrated. This news is all good news because the network can be configured to your needs. It's very flexible.

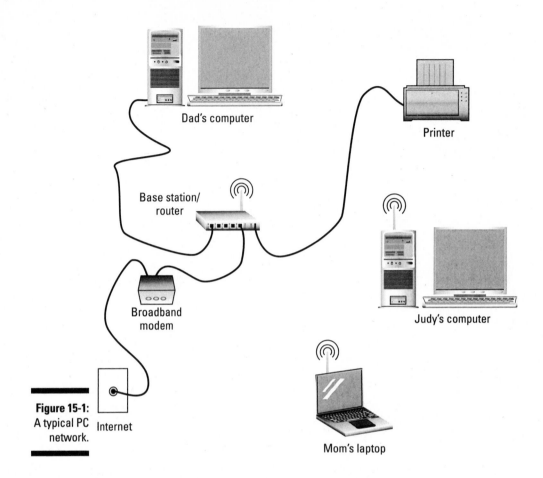

Figure 15-1:
A typical PC
network.

Dad's computer

Printer

Base station/
router

Broadband
modem

Judy's computer

Internet

Mom's laptop

Saint NIC

To let you chat it up on the network, your PC requires a *network information card,* or *NIC.* It may also be known as an Ethernet card or a network adapter. The circuitry is most often part of the chipset on the motherboard.

There are two types of NICs: The traditional one, which uses the RJ-45 adapter (refer to Chapter 2 for identification), and a *wireless* NIC, which may or may not be visible as a tiny antenna sticking out the back of your PC. A wireless NIC can also be added by using a special USB adapter.

- ✔ The standard NIC is measured by its speed in Mbps, or megabits per second: 10 Mbps is too slow, 100 Mbps is faster, and 1000 Mbps (1 *gigabit*) is the fastest and bestest.

- ✔ If you choose to go wireless, ensure that all wireless gizmos in your network adhere to the same wireless networking standard. For example, if you settle on the 802.11n standard, get all 802.11n wireless network adapters as well as an 802.11n router, as described later in this chapter.

- ✔ Yes, you can have both wireless and standard NICs inside your PC.

Network hoses

Unless you go totally wireless, you need wires to connect the computers, thus creating the network. The wire you use is a cable known as Cat 5, or Category 5, networking cable. One end of the cable plugs into your computer, into the NIC, and the other plugs into a central location, or *hub* (covered in the next section).

- ✔ Cat 5 cable comes in a variety of lengths and in several bright and cheerful colors.

- ✔ You can get creative in wiring your home or office with networking cable. I crawled under my house to wire it all up, and I used the attic and outside walls. You can also buy raceways and connectors and boxes if you don't want to tear up your walls. (Unless you're into such things, though, I recommend having an electrician do it for you.)

- ✔ If you don't want to go through all the networking wire mess, simply opt for a network setup that's all wireless. See the next section.

Not network hoses

When you have a wireless network, you don't need to buy network cables to connect your computers to the network. Instead, you use a wireless hub to get all the PCs talking. That's the easy part.

The difficult part is that configuring a wireless network takes more time and effort than setting up a wired network. Not only that, the signals for a wireless network aren't as strong as the manufacturer claims. Though you can use wireless networking in one room, the signals may not be strong enough for your entire home or office.

✔ Despite having a wireless network, you will still need a Cat 5 cable to connect the wireless hub to a broadband modem.

✔ One solution to help broadcast a wireless network beyond a single room is to set up multiple wireless hubs in a WDS network. WDS stands for Wireless Distribution System. It's a complex thing to do (like all wireless networking), but it helps stretch the signal farther. Have someone else set it up for you.

The router

At the center of the computer network is the *router*. It's the location where all the network wires (or no wires) connect.

The router's job is to coordinate local network activity and to communicate with a larger network, the Internet. It may also provide firewall support, which helps prevent bad guys on the Internet from accessing the computers on the local network.

Routers can be wired or wireless. Most wireless routers have connectors for adding computers on the network that use network cables, in case you need them.

✔ A wireless router is often called a *base station*.

✔ The wireless router's protocol (that 802.11-thing) must match or be compatible with the wireless NICs used by your computers.

✔ When you need more network connections on your router, you buy something called a *switch*. It's basically just a gang of Ethernet ports, which let you add more network computers, printers, and other gizmos to the network. The switch helps you to expand your computer network.

✔ Many routers also have USB ports for adding a printer or networked hard drive. That's a plus.

✔ Normally, there's no need to do heavy configuration of the router; most of them come ready-to-wear right out of the box. Even so, I recommend that you assign the router a new password as part of its setup. Refer to the router's manual for information on how to access the router and set the new password, or just have someone else do it for you.

✔ There's no need to turn off the router after the computer network is set up.

✔ Technically, the router you use on a small computer network isn't even a router. Nope, it's a *gateway*. That knowledge may not help you completely understand computer networking, but it might win you a bar bet.

What is Bluetooth?

Bluetooth is the name of a wireless gizmo standard, which can be confused with wireless networking, although the only similarity between the two is the wireless part.

The Bluetooth standard allows for various PC peripherals to wirelessly communicate with each other over short distances. For example, you can buy a Bluetooth expansion card and allow your PC to talk wirelessly with a Bluetooth keyboard, a mouse, a printer, or even a monitor. Theoretically, you could use a Bluetooth MP3 music player with your PC and then take it into your Bluetooth-enabled car and hear the music in the car by using Bluetooth-enabled headphones.

All Bluetooth devices sport the Bluetooth symbol, which I would illustrate in this book if the Bluetooth people weren't so uptight about their trademarks.

The modem

Having a modem is a natural part of a computer network. The modem allows the computers on your network to access the Big World Network, also known as the Internet.

Officially, the modem attached to the computer network is a *broadband* modem. The term *broadband* is the techno-magical way to say "high speed." There are three types of broadband modems:

Cable: This type of modem is the fastest you can have. Its only downside is that when more of your neighbors begin using their cable modems, the overall speed decreases. But at 2 a.m., your cable modem *smokes!*

DSL: This type of modem gives you fast access by taking advantage of unused frequencies in existing phone lines. The speed is limited by how far away your location is from the phone company's home office. Also, regular phones used on the same line as the DSL modem require special filters. But otherwise, next to cable, DSL gives you the fastest connection speeds.

Satellite: Combined with an outdoor antenna and a subscription to the satellite service, this modem option is one of the fastest available. Try to get a satellite modem that provides both sending and receiving abilities. Avoid satellite service that is "download only."

In all cases, the modem connects directly with the router in the computer network setup (refer to Figure 15-1). There's a special hole on the router for the modem; the hole might be labeled Modem or WAN for wide-area network. That's the Internet.

- ✔ You should leave the broadband modem on all the time.

- ✔ By having a broadband modem attached to your computer network, you allow all computers on the network to have fast Internet access.

- ✔ You can buy your own broadband modem or rent one from your Internet provider. I recommend buying the modem, especially when you know that you'll be in the same location and using the same service for at least a year.

- ✔ Broadband is synonymous with high-speed Internet access.

- ✔ DSL stands for Digital Subscriber Line. It has variations, such as ADSL and other *something*-DSL options. Your phone company knows more about this matter than I do. Basically, everyone calls it DSL, no matter what.

Network Software

Windows is quite adept at handling the software setup of your PC's networking abilities. In fact, there's really very little to do any more, unlike in days of old, where setting up a network required many steps, plenty of confusing terms, and the assistance of a fourth-grader. Those days are gone for good!

Getting to Network Central

The main location for nearly all networking items in Windows is the Network and Sharing Center, shown in Figure 15-2. That window displays your PC's current network status as well as the Internet connection status.

To display the Network and Sharing Center, heed these steps:

1. **Open the Control Panel window.**

   Choose Control Panel from the Start button menu.

2. **Click the heading Network and Internet.**

3. **Click the heading Network and Sharing Center.**

In addition to displaying information about the network and Internet connection, the Network and Sharing Center features links and options that let
you control various networking stuff. Later sections in this chapter tell you
what's useful and how it works.

Windows XP lacks a Network and Sharing Center. Instead, a Network
Connections window is used, which is accessed through the Network
Connections icon in the Control Panel. Sadly, it's not as friendly a place
as the Network and Sharing Center, which is why Windows XP has been
replaced. Twice.

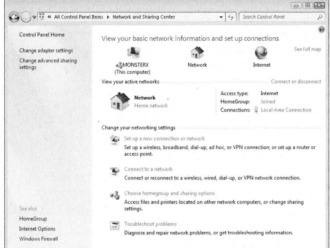

Figure 15-2:
The
Network
and Sharing
Center.

Connecting to a wired network

Windows automatically finds any network you plug into. So, by turning on
your computer and having that network hose connected, you're more or less
done with network configuration.

This book assumes that the network your PC is plugged into is already configured. If not, open the Network and Sharing Center and choose the task Set Up
a New Connection or Network. From the list of options presented, choose Set
Up a New Network and follow the directions on the screen, or just have someone else do it for you.

Connecting to a wireless network

To connect your PC to a wireless network, follow these steps in Windows 7:

1. **Ensure that the PC's wireless networking adapter is turned on.**

   A switch found on some laptop computers must be in the On position before you can access a wireless network.

2. **Click the network icon found in the notification area on the taskbar.**

   A pop-up window appears, as shown in Figure 15-3. Available wireless networks are listed, along with their signal strength.

Figure 15-3:
Choosing
a wireless
network.

3. **Choose a wireless network from the list.**

4. **Click the Connect button.**

5. **If prompted, type the network's security key.**

6. **Press the Enter key.**

   Windows attempts to connect you with the wireless network. After the connection is successful, you see the Network icon in the notification area turn into a set of signal bars, as shown in the margin.

Eventually, sometime after connecting, Windows prompts you to identify the type of wireless network you're connected to: Home Network, Work Network, or Public Network. Choose the one that's most appropriate for wherever you are.

✔ You can use the Network and Sharing Center to connect to a wireless network in Windows Vista. Choose the task Connect to a Network on the left side of the window to see a list of available wireless networks.

✔ Choose the Public Network whenever you're using your computer (laptop) at a wireless hot spot or other remote location. The Public Network option offers the most security.

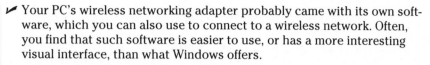

✔ Your PC's wireless networking adapter probably came with its own software, which you can also use to connect to a wireless network. Often, you find that such software is easier to use, or has a more interesting visual interface, than what Windows offers.

✔ The only time that connecting to a wireless network can be a bother is when the network doesn't display its name. In that case, you have to manually connect to the network: Open the Network and Sharing Center and select Set Up a New Connection or Network. Choose the option Manually Connect to a Wireless Network. Click the Next button and then heed the directions on the screen. You need information from the network's administrator, which is why I flagged this bullet point with one of those Technical Stuff icons.

Disconnecting from a network

There's no need to disconnect from a wired network. Just leave the cable plugged in all the time and you'll be fine.

You can manually disconnect from a wireless network by turning off the PC or simply moving out of range.

To manually disconnect from a wireless network in Windows 7, click the Network icon in the notification area and choose the wireless network from the pop-up window. Click the Disconnect button.

In Windows Vista, you manually disconnect from a wireless network by using the Network and Sharing Center; click the link titled Disconnect, to the left of the wireless network name.

Chapter 16

Basic Networking Stuff

. . . .

. . . .

*A*fter you get the hardware side of the network all connected and operating (divulged in Chapter 15), it's time to share and communicate using your computer network. The sharing is about using resources from other computers made available on the network. Those resources include printers, storage devices, and media players. Accessing all that networking goodness is this chapter's topic.

Network Fun in Windows

The main networking folder window thing in Windows is named, surprisingly, Network. Access it by opening the Network icon on the desktop, choosing Network from the Start button menu, or from a number of other places too numerous and confusing to list here. A typical Network window is shown in Figure 16-1.

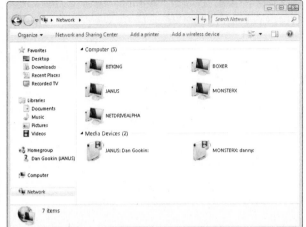

Figure 16-1:
The
Network
window.

The Network window lists various gizmos available on your computer's network. Specifically, you should see icons presenting other computers on the network. You might also see a network hard drive (if you have one) and perhaps other network stuff.

✔ The computers you see in the Network window form a *workgroup*. That term refers to the computers connected to the type of peer-to-peer networks found in most homes and small offices.

✔ In Windows Vista, network printers also show up in the Network window. In Windows 7, you find network printers in the Devices and Printers window. See Chapter 12 for information on printers, though printing on the network is covered elsewhere in this chapter.

✔ Windows Vista may also display the network's gateway, or router, in the Network window.

✔ If you don't see any icons in the Network window and you *know* that you have everything properly set up, you may not have activated "network discovery." See the section "Turning on network discovery," later in this chapter.

✔ You can refresh the Network window by pressing the F5 key, which shows any new computers that have joined the network.

✔ The Network window is named My Network Places in Windows XP.

Browsing the network

The Network window is the main location from which you can browse for shared resources on the computer network. The act of browsing involves visiting other computers on the network to discover which folders they're sharing and, optionally, opening or saving files on those computers.

To see which resources are shared by a computer on the network, open that computer's icon in the Network window. You see any shared resources listed in that network computer's window.

 The most common thing you find in a network computer's window is the shared-folder icon, shown in the margin. The icon indicates that a folder on the network computer's storage system is available for access; you can look at the folder's contents, open files, or save files to the folder, depending on the permissions of the folder. (*Permissions* are security settings that allow or restrict access to a network folder.)

✔ Make the sharing of information between networked Windows 7 computers easy by using the HomeGroup. See the section "HomeGroup Sharing," elsewhere in this chapter.

✔ Browsing through the network works just like browsing through folders on your own computer. Indeed, you most often browse for stuff on the network as you hunt for files to open or search for a location to save new files.

✔ See Chapter 21 for more information on file organization in Windows.

✔ Folders displayed in a network computer's window are *shared* folders, available for access by others on the network.

✔ Some shared folders require password access or that you have an account set up on the computer that's sharing the folders.

✔ Older versions of Windows also display any shared printers in a network computer's window. The network printer appears as an icon in the window, along with the folder icons. (In Windows 7, network printers appear in the Devices and Printers window; see Chapter 12.)

Turning on network discovery

To ensure that your PC is fully able and willing to go out slumming it on the network, you must activate network discovery. Here's what to do:

1. **Open the Network and Sharing Center window.**

   To get there, you can click the Network and Sharing Center toolbar button in the Network window; refer to Chapter 15 for specific directions.

2. **From the left side of the window, choose the task Change Advanced Sharing Settings.**

   In Windows Vista, you might need to click the downward-pointing arrow to reveal the Network Discovery area of the window.

3. **Choose Turn On Network Discovery, if it isn't on already.**

4. **Click the Save Changes button.**

   In Windows Vista, click the Apply button. Further, you must enter the administrator password or click the Continue button to proceed.

Viewing the network map

Windows enables you to view a graphical image of your computer network — a map. To do so, open the Network and Sharing Center window and click the See Full Map link near the upper right corner. (The link is titled View Full Map in Windows Vista.)

The graphical network map, similar to the one shown in Figure 16-2, illustrates various gizmos attached to the network. Older Windows computers, as well as some network-independent devices (hard drives and printers), may not show up on the map, but appear at the bottom, similar to JANUS and NETDRIVEALPHA in Figure 16-2.

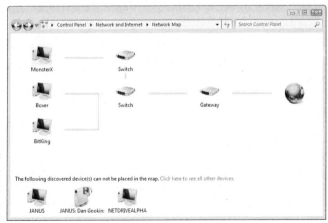

Figure 16-2:
The network
map.

When your PC has more than one way to access the network, you can choose the network to map from a menu button found at the top of the Network Map window.

HomeGroup Sharing

Windows 7 makes it easy to share documents, media files, and printers across a network by using something called a HomeGroup. All computers that belong to the same *HomeGroup* can quickly access and share their resources.

You have a choice in Windows whether to create your own HomeGroup or join an existing HomeGroup. This section explains how it all works.

✔ The HomeGroup feature is available only in Windows 7.

✔ Your PC must be configured to allow HomeGroup connections: Follow the steps in the later section "Configuring Windows to share" to confirm that the HomeGroup Connections option is turned on.

✔ You don't need to mess with the HomeGroup concept, if you don't want to. Windows still uses the more traditional method of file and printer sharing, described elsewhere in this chapter.

Creating a HomeGroup

To create your own HomeGroup, follow these steps:

1. **Open the Control Panel.**

2. **Choose the link Choose HomeGroup and Sharing Options, found beneath the Network and Internet heading.**

   The HomeGroup window appears.

3. **Click the Create a HomeGroup button.**

   If you see instead a button titled Join Now, you don't need to create your own HomeGroup. Instead, you can join an existing HomeGroup; see the next section.

   If you don't see the Create a HomeGroup button, the HomeGroup is already set up on your computer; go to Step 7.

4. **Choose the resources you want to share with other computers using the same HomeGroup.**

   Check everything.

5. **Click the Next button.**

   Windows thinks for a spell, and then it displays the HomeGroup password. You can write down that password or print it, but you can easily enough recall it on the screen later when you need it.

6. **Click the Finish button.**

7. **Close the HomeGroup window.**

Other Windows 7 computers on the network can now access and join the HomeGroup you created. See the later section "Using the HomeGroup" to find out what to do next.

Joining a HomeGroup

To join an existing HomeGroup and share files and printers with existing Windows 7 computers on the network, follow these steps:

1. **Open the HomeGroup window.**

   Refer to Steps 1 and 2 from the preceding section.

2. **Click the Join Now button.**

   If you don't see the Join Now button, either no existing HomeGroup is on the network or you're already joined to a HomeGroup.

3. **Choose the items from your PC that you want to share with the HomeGroup.**

   Check everything.

4. **Click the Next button.**

5. **Enter the HomeGroup's password.**

   The password was created with the HomeGroup, and it can be redisplayed on the main HomeGroup PC: On that computer, open the HomeGroup window and click the link View or Print the HomeGroup Password.

6. **Click the Next button.**

7. **Click the Finish button.**

8. **Close the HomeGroup window.**

Read the next section to find what you can do with a HomeGroup in Windows 7.

Using the HomeGroup

You access the resources shared in the HomeGroup just as you access any file stored on your computer's mass storage system. The key is to open a HomeGroup library in a Windows Explorer window. Here's one way to do that:

1. **Press the Win+E key combination to summon a Windows Explorer window.**

2. **From the list of locations on the left side of the window, choose HomeGroup.**

3. **Open a HomeGroup computer from the list.**

   Double-click the computer's icon to open it. You see a list of the libraries shared by that computer: documents, music, pictures, video, and perhaps others.

4. **Open a library to see shared documents.**

At this point, you can browse files and folders just as you would on your own PC, but you're really looking at information stored on another computer on the network.

✔ It helps to understand the concept of files and folders to get the most benefit from a HomeGroup. See Chapter 20 for information on files; Chapter 21 discusses the concept of folders.

✔ Chapter 21 also discusses the concept of *libraries*, which can be shared with other computers in the HomeGroup.

✔ If you don't want to share a resource on your computer with the HomeGroup, open the HomeGroup window from the Control Panel and deselect the check box next to the resource you no longer want to share. Click the Save Changes button.

Disconnecting from a HomeGroup

You don't need to disconnect from the HomeGroup as a regular activity. Only if you desire to no longer share your stuff or access shared stuff in the HomeGroup is it necessary. If so, follow these steps:

1. **Open the HomeGroup window.**

   Refer to the steps from the earlier section "Creating a HomeGroup."

2. **Choose the link Leave the HomeGroup.**

3. **Click the option Leave the HomeGroup.**

4. **Click the Finish button.**

5. **Close the HomeGroup window.**

Traditional Network Sharing

Before the concept of the HomeGroup as introduced in Windows 7, sharing was done between PCs on a network by making certain folders (and printers) available to other users on the network. By sharing those resources, you can let others on the network access your stuff, as well as access files and printers shared by others. This section explains how it works.

Configuring Windows to share

You need to confirm that everything is set up nice and tidy to enable sharing between your PC and others on the network. Follow these steps:

1. **Open the Network and Sharing Center window.**

   See Chapter 15 for specific directions.

2. **From the left side of the window, choose Change Advanced Sharing Settings.**

   In Windows Vista, the settings are found at the bottom of the Network and Sharing Center window.

3. **Review my recommended settings from Table 16-1.**

   In Windows Vista, you may need to click the Show More button to display the on–off settings.

4. **You turn each option on or off by choosing the appropriate button beneath the option's heading and description.**

   My suggestions for setting the various options are shown in Table 16-1.

5. **Click the Save Changes button when you're done.**

   In Windows Vista, you must click the Apply button after making each individual setting change.

Table 16-1	Settings That Control Sharing on the Network	
Option	*Recommended Setting*	*Effect of Enabling*
Network Discovery	On	Your PC can see other computers on the network and other computers can see your PC.

Option	Recommended Setting	Effect of Enabling
File and Printer Sharing	On	Other computers on the network can access shared folders on your PC as well as any printers attached to your PC.
Public Folder Sharing	On	You control access to the Public folder on your PC.
Media Sharing	On	Other network users can access your PC's music and media files by using Windows Media Center across the network.
File Sharing Connections	128-bits	You can set the level of encryption for file sharing.
Password Protected Sharing	Off for home offices and On at work	You control who has access to shared files and printers on your PC.
HomeGroup Connections	On (Allow)	You specify whether Windows manages shared files as a HomeGroup or whether you do so manually by logging into each PC on the network.

Here are some sharing issues worthy of note:

✔ File and printer sharing are two separate categories in Windows Vista.

✔ The File Sharing Connections and Home Groups Connections categories are available only in Windows 7.

✔ The *Public folder* is a location in Windows where you can share files between multiple users on a single PC. You can also share files with folks on the network, if you allow Public folder sharing as described in this section.

✔ The Password Protected Sharing option limits access to your PC and its files to only those who have a password-protected account on your PC. This option is a bother for home networks and wherever security isn't an issue. I turn off the option in my office but recommend turning it on in just about any situation except for the most secure ones.

✔ Media Sharing allows you to use Windows Media Center to play or access media files on another PC in the network.

✔ All these sharing options and configuration aren't necessary when you use HomeGroup sharing in Windows 7, described earlier in this chapter.

Sharing a folder

If you want other people on the network to have access to a folder on your computer, you *share* the folder. This concept makes the folder — and its contents (all files and subfolders) — available to all other computers on the network. Here's how to share a folder:

1. **Ensure that Network Discovery and File Sharing are enabled on your PC.**

   Refer to the previous section.

2. **Right-click the folder you want to share.**

3. **Choose Properties from the pop-up menu.**

   The folder's Properties dialog box appears.

4. **Click the Sharing tab.**

5. **Click the Advanced Sharing button.**

   In Windows Vista, enter the administrator password or click the Continue button.

6. **Click to put a check mark by the option labeled Share This Folder.**

   You can set a Share name, which helps to better identify the folder on the network.

7. **Click OK.**

   The folder is now shared.

8. **Click the Close button to dismiss the folder's Properties dialog box.**

Other PCs can now access the folder on the network. See the next section.

   ✔ See Chapter 21 for more information on the concept of a folder.

   ✔ In Windows Vista, shared-folder icons appear with the graphical "sharing friends" flag beneath them, as shown in the margin.

   ✔ To unshare a folder, repeat the steps in this section, but in Step 6 remove the check mark.

   ✔ Don't share an entire disk drive. It's a security risk; Windows warns you when you try to do so.

Accessing a network folder

You access a folder elsewhere on the network just as you would access any folder on your PC's disk system. The difference is that you need to browse to the folder from the Network window.

After opening the Network window, as discussed earlier in this chapter, you can then open any computer to see which folders it's sharing. Open a folder icon to reveal its contents.

You may be required to log in to another computer to access its folders. Logging in, or not, depends on the folder's permissions as set by whoever shared the folder.

Chapter 17

The Internet Quick and Dirty

*T*he Internet. It's a network, and possibly part of your PC's computer network. It's also everywhere. The Internet is unavoidable. Thankfully, it's also been around a while, so most of the Internet basics are widely known. Still, I feel the need to provide you with an Internet roundup and review, just to ensure that you could run the Internet category in a round of Double Jeopardy.

What Is the Internet?

The *Internet* is composed of hundreds of thousands of computers all over the world. The computers send information, they receive information, and — most important — they store information. That's the Internet.

✔ The Internet consists of all the computers connected to the Internet. Whenever your computer is "on" the Internet, it's part of the Internet.

✔ No one owns the Internet, just as no one owns the oceans. The company you pay for Internet access is merely providing you with the access, not with the Internet's content.

How to Access the Internet

Windows is geared to use the Internet. In fact, Windows prefers that you have a broadband Internet connection and that your PC is *always* connected to the Internet. But before sating Windows's online lusts, you have a few things to attend to, as covered in this section.

Choosing an ISP

You need five items to access the Internet:

- ✔ A computer
- ✔ A modem
- ✔ Internet software
- ✔ Money
- ✔ An Internet service provider, or ISP

The first three items you should already have. The fourth item, money, is needed to pay for the fifth item, which is the outfit that provides you with Internet access.

Your ISP can be your telephone company or cable company, both of which compete to provide you with broadband DSL or cable Internet access.

For satellite Internet access, you have to check the yellow pages, which is also what you do for plain old dialup Internet access. ISPs are listed under *Internet* in any yellow pages book or phone directory.

The ISP provides you with the Internet access. It may configure your broadband modem for you or provide information on how to set things up yourself. In addition, it may also give you these items:

- ✔ For a dialup modem, the phone number to call
- ✔ For a broadband modem, the modem's IP address, the DNS address, and, possibly, a gateway address
- ✔ Your ISP's domain name — the `blorf.com` or `yaddi.org` part
- ✔ Your Internet login ID and password
- ✔ Your Internet e-mail name, address, and password (if it's different from your login ID and password)

✔ The name of your ISP's e-mail server, which involves the acronyms POP3 and SMTP

✔ A phone number to call for help (very important)

Finally, the ISP bills you for Internet access. The prices can be cheap, sometimes less than $10 per month for dialup access. You pay more for faster connections, with some high-speed broadband connections costing upward of $50 per month. Be sure to compare prices when choosing an ISP.

✔ The S in ISP stands for *service*. You pay a fee, and the ISP provides you with Internet access *and* service. That means technical support: someone you can phone for help, classes, software — you name it.

✔ In some situations, you may not need any of the five items on my Internet access list. For example, if you work for a large company, it may already give you Internet access through the network at your office. Ditto for universities and government installations. And, you can always find free Internet access at a community library near you.

Configuring Windows for the Internet

Windows is automatically set up to use the Internet. Merely by connecting a broadband modem to your PC or to the PC's network, you suddenly and instantly have Internet access. Windows sees it. You're all set.

Things work differently when you have dialup access. In that case, you must create a network connection for the modem to use. Directions for this task should come from your ISP. It gives you a phone number to dial, plus perhaps other options to set, such as configuring your e-mail program.

Connecting to the Internet

There's no need to fuss over connecting to the Internet when you use a broadband modem; the connection is always on. Internet programs start up quickly and access the Internet just as fast.

Dialup connections are active only when you use the Internet. When you run an Internet program, or when any software attempts to access the Internet, Windows directs the PC's modem to dial into your ISP. After making the connection, you're "on" the Internet and can use Internet software.

✔ To test the Internet connection, run the Internet Explorer program. When you run Internet Explorer, or any program that accesses the Internet, your computer attempts to make an Internet connection. When the connection works, you see a Web page displayed in Internet Explorer. Otherwise, you see an error message. If so, contact your ISP for assistance.

✔ As long as you have an Internet connection, you can run any program that accesses information on the Internet: Web browser or e-mail or any complex program that would stun you with foreboding technology.

✔ You should hang up, or *disconnect,* from the dialup connection when you're done using the Internet. The directions that came from your dialup ISP explain how to do that.

✔ For other Internet connection problems, woes, and worries, refer to my book *Troubleshooting Your PC For Dummies* (Wiley), available worldwide in bookstores with good-looking employees.

✔ To cancel a dialup connection, click the Cancel button when you see it dialing.

✔ Why is your dialup modem connecting to the Internet? Most likely, it's because some program or Windows itself is requesting information. Canceling that request isn't a problem, nor does it mess things up. Programs can wait until *you* want to connect to the Internet to conduct their business. Dammit! You're in charge!

It's a World Wide Web We Weave

The Internet lived an unpopular and nerdy existence before the World Wide Web — or "the Web" — came about. The Web introduced pretty graphics and formatted text to the Internet, which made it safe for normal people. This section offers some helpful Web information.

Browsing tips

The Web is pretty cinchy, so rather than bore you with what you already know, I thought I'd offer you a raft of useful Web browsing tips. Note that many of these are specific to Internet Explorer (IE) version 8, the current version of the Microsoft Web browser included with Windows.

✔ If you prefer to see a real, live menu bar in Internet Explorer, press the F10 key on the keyboard. To keep that menu bar on all the time, choose View➪Toolbars➪Menu Bar from the menu.

 ✔ In the lower right corner of the IE window, you find a Zoom menu. Use it to help make Web pages with small text more visible.

 ✔ You can easily recall previously typed Web page addresses from the address bar: Click the down-arrow button to the right of the address bar.

✔ To remove all previously typed Web page addresses, click the Safety button on the toolbar and choose Delete Browsing History. In the dialog box that appears, click the Delete button.

✔ The easiest way to set a home page is to visit the Web page you want as your home page. After you're there, click the menu button by the Home icon on the toolbar. Choose Add or Change Home Page from the menu. In the dialog box that appears, choose Use This Webpage As Your Only Home Page, and click the Yes button.

 ✔ If a Web page doesn't load, try again! The Web can be busy, and often when it is, you see an error message. Reload a Web page by clicking the Refresh button (shown in the margin) on the Address bar.

✔ Clicking the Refresh button is one quick way to fix the "missing picture" problem.

✔ When a Web page isn't found, you probably didn't type the Web page address properly. Try again.

✔ You can type a Web page address without the `http://` part, but if you don't get to where you want to go, try again with the `http://` part.

✔ Not all Web page links are text. Quite a few links are graphical. The only way to know for certain is to point the mouse pointer at what you believe may be a link. If the pointer changes to a pointing hand, you know that it's a link you can click to see something else.

✔ A tiny menu button lives to the right of the Forward button in IE. Use that menu button to recall recent Web pages you visited.

✔ When you accidentally click a link and change your mind, click the Stop button. The Internet then stops sending you information. (You may need to click the Back button to return to where you were.)

✔ Press Ctrl+D to add any Web page you're viewing to your Favorites. Don't be shy about it! It's better to add it now and delete it later than to regret not adding it in the first place.

Printing Web pages

To print any Web page, click the Printer button on the toolbar. That's pretty much it.

Sadly, some Web pages don't print right. Some are too wide. Some show white text on a black background, which doesn't print well. My advice is to use the Print Preview command, found on the Print toolbar button's menu, to look at what will print before you print it. If you still have trouble, try one of these solutions:

✔ Consider saving the Web page to disk. Choose Save As from the Page toolbar button's menu. Ensure that you choose from the Save As Type drop-down list the option labeled Web Page, Complete. Then you can open the Web page file in Microsoft Word or Excel or any Web page editing program and edit or print it from there.

✔ Use the Page Setup command, found on the Print toolbar button's menu, to select landscape orientation for printing wider-than-normal Web pages.

✔ Use the Properties button in the Print dialog box to adjust the printer. Press Ctrl+P to see the Print dialog box. The Properties settings depend on the printer itself, but I have seen printers that can reduce the output to 75 or 50 percent, which ensures that the entire Web page prints on a single sheet of paper. Other options may let you print in shades of gray (*grayscale*) or black and white.

Searching-the-Web tips

The Web is full of information, and some of it might even be accurate! The issue is getting to the information you want. The following are my Web-page-searching tips:

✔ My main search engine these days is Google, at www.google.com, but I can also recommend the Microsoft search engine Bing, at www.bing.com.

✔ Web search engines ignore the smaller words in the English language. Words such as *is, to, the, for, are,* and others aren't included in the search. Therefore:

✔ Use only key words when searching. For example, to look for *The Declaration of Independence,* typing *declaration independence* is good enough.

✔ Word order matters. If you want to find out the name of that red bug with six legs, try all combinations: *bug red six legs*, *red bug six legs*, or even *six legs red bug*. Each variation yields different results.

✔ When words *must* be found together, enclose them in double quotes, such as *"Beverly Hillbillies" theme* or *"Weber barbecue"* setup. A quoted search finds only Web pages that list the words *Weber barbecue* together in that order.

✔ If the results — the matching or found Web pages — are too numerous, click the link (near the bottom of the page) that says Search within results. That way, you can further refine your search. For example, if you found several hundred pages on Walt Disney World but are specifically looking for a map of the Animal Kingdom, you can search for *"Animal Kingdom map"* within the results you found for Walt Disney World.

E-Mail Call!

Nothing perks up your Internet day like receiving fresh e-mail. It means that people care. It means that someone is thinking of you — even if they just want you to buy cheap C1AL1S (whatever that is). Welcome to this chapter's brief and tip-packed e-mail tip section.

Downloading an e-mail program

Windows 7 doesn't come with an e-mail program. You have to download, or copy from the Internet, the Windows Mail program. To do so, visit this Web page:

```
http://download.live.com
```

On that page, click the link for Mail, found under the IM and E-Mail heading. On the next page, click the big Download button. At that point, you begin to download the Mail program; see the section in Chapter 18 about downloading a program to find out what to do next.

✔ Windows Vista comes with the Windows Mail e-mail program already installed. It's essentially an upgraded and better version of the old Outlook Express mail program.

✔ You can also use other e-mail programs, including Web-based e-mail such as Gmail, Windows Live, and Yahoo! Mail, or full-on e-mail programs such as Mozilla Thunderbird or Eudora. Use Google or Bing to search for these programs, available for free on the Internet.

Getting the most from e-mail

Here are some general e-mail tips and suggestions for using e-mail:

✔ Don't put spaces in an e-mail address. If you think that it's a space, it's probably an underline or a period.

✔ You must enter the full e-mail address, such as `zorgon@wambooli.com`, for the message to be properly sent.

✔ You can type more than one address in the To field. If so, separate each one with a semicolon or comma, as in

`president@whitehouse.gov, first.lady@whitehouse.gov`

✔ When you're done composing your e-epistle, check your spelling by clicking the Spelling button. It's normally found on the e-mail program's toolbar, usually with the ABC or check mark graphic on the button.

✔ Many e-mail programs offer a Read Receipt option, which promises to alert you when the recipient reads your missive. My advice: Don't bother. The read receipt is no guarantee that the recipient actually reads the message. Often, it just annoys people.

✔ When you don't want to send the message, close the New Message window. You're asked whether you want to save the message. Click Yes to save it in the Drafts folder. If you click No, the message is destroyed.

✔ When you type the wrong e-mail address, the message *bounces* back to you. It isn't a bad thing; just try again with the proper address.

✔ Please don't type in ALL CAPS. To most people, all caps reads like YOU'RE SHOUTING AT THEM!

✔ Be careful what you write. E-mail messages are often casually written, and they can easily be misinterpreted. Remember to keep your messages light in tone.

✔ Don't expect a quick reply from e-mail, especially from folks in the computer industry (which is ironic).

✔ To send a message you have shoved off to the Drafts folder, open the Drafts folder. Then double-click the message to open it. The original New Message window is then redisplayed. From there, you can edit the message and click the Send button to finally send it.

✔ When you have trouble seeing the text in an e-mail message, choose View➪Text Size from the menu and choose a larger or smaller size from the submenu.

✔ Also see Chapter 18, which covers e-mail file attachments.

Chapter 18

Flinging Files

*N*etworking is all about communications and sharing. It has its roots way, way back in the early steam-powered computing era. The idea wasn't to "tweet" personal thoughts, send photographs from telephones, or even play *Call of Duty*. Nope, the idea was to get information in the form of a *file* from one computer into another without anyone having to lift anything or walk anywhere. That was the goal in those days, and it's still something useful that your computer and its network are more than capable of handling today.

✔ See Chapter 20 for important information on the concept of a computer file.

✔ Copying a file to your computer is known as *downloading*. When someone sends you a file over the Internet, you *download* it. (Think of the other computer as being on top of a hill; it may not be, but it helps to think of it that way.)

✔ Sending a file to another computer is known as *uploading*.

Get Stuff from a Web Page

The text and pictures you see on a Web page can easily be copied from that Web page and saved on your own computer. Well, actually, the information you see on the display *is* already on your computer: The text, images, and other stuff you see are sent from the Internet and stored temporarily somewhere in your computer while you're viewing that Web page. This section explains how to save some of that information permanently.

Saving an image from a Web page

To save an image from a Web page to your PC's hard drive, right-click the image and choose Save Picture As from the pop-up menu. Use the Save Picture dialog box to find a happy home for the picture on your hard drive.

✔ Windows 7 prefers to store images in the Pictures Library. Older versions of Windows use the Pictures or My Pictures folder. See Chapter 21 for more information on libraries and folders.

✔ Nearly all images on the Web are copyrighted. Although you can save a copy to your hard drive, you're not free to duplicate, sell, or distribute the image without the consent of the copyright holder.

✔ To set the image as the Windows desktop wallpaper, choose Set As Background from the pop-up menu after right-clicking the image.

Grabbing text from a Web page

You can copy text from a Web page and save it for later or paste that text into another document or e-mail message. Here's how:

1. **Select the text you want to copy.**

   Drag the mouse over the text, which highlights the text on the Web page. The text is now selected.

2. **Press Ctrl+C on the keyboard to copy the text.**

3. **Start your word processor or e-mail program.**

   Or, start any program into which text can be pasted.

4. **Paste the text into a document or e-mail message.**

   Press Ctrl+V on the keyboard or choose Edit➪Paste from the menu.

5. **Print. Save. Whatever.**

   Use the proper commands to save or print or edit the text.

Free Software on the Internet

The Internet is the world's largest software store. That's great. What's even better is that most of the software is free. Using your computer and Web browser program, you can search for free programs and then install and use them until you grow old or bored.

Finding programs on the Web

The key to unlocking all those free programs on the Internet is to find them first. For downloading demo and preview programs, visit the manufacturer's Web page. Almost all the big program names have those freebie or trial copies you can use for a while at no cost.

You can also use Google, Bing, or any Web search engine to help you locate programs. For example, type **free word processor** and then peruse the results.

- ✔ Microsoft keeps, on its Windows Live Web site, a slew of programs that once came free with Windows: `http://downloads.live.com`.

- ✔ For general software, I can recommend the SourceForge Web page: `www.sourceforge.net`.

- ✔ Avoid visiting Web pages that offer free screen savers, desktop backgrounds, or device drivers. Those programs are most likely not legitimate, and if you download them, you will regret it.

- ✔ If you search for hacker tools or free movies, music, books, or other illegal material, odds are good that you'll end up at an illegitimate Web site. The result may be a virus or another infection on your PC, not the software you wanted.

- ✔ The Web can be a scary place; stick to the manufacturer's Web sites wherever possible.

- ✔ See Chapter 19 for more information on Web security.

Downloading a program

Obtaining a program, or any file, from the Internet is called *downloading*. It's done by following these steps:

1. **Visit the Web page that contains the download link.**

   The link may be text, or it may be a big, fun graphical button. Sometimes, the link takes you to another page. Eventually, you'll find the download link or button.

2. **Click the link or graphical image that begins the download.**

3. **Mind the security warning.**

Most Web browsers alert you whenever software attempts to flow into your computer. You must grant permission; otherwise, who-knows-what might be downloaded into your PC.

4. Click the Save button.

In Internet Explorer version 8, click the Save button to save the file you're downloading. In older versions of Internet Explorer, you must first click a special warning bar that appears above the window. Either way, click the Save button to save the file.

5. Click the Save button in the Save As dialog box.

Generally speaking, the filename and location are fine. The filename may be cryptic, but it's the name of the program you're downloading, plus perhaps a version number. The file's location is the Downloads folder in your personal account area, which is perfect.

6. Sit and watch as the file is copied from the Internet to your computer.

Figure 18-1 illustrates the download progress, albeit in a static manner.

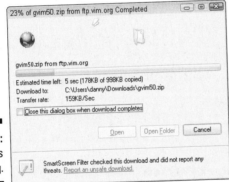

Figure 18-1:
A file is
downloading.

7. To install the program, click the Open button.

8. If you're greeted with a security warning, click the Allow button.

9. Obey the directions on the screen to finish the installation.

The directions are specific to whatever it is you're installing. If you're installing a program from a Compressed Folder or Zip file, see the next section.

After installing the program, you can run it or do anything you would normally do with any software installed on your computer. See Chapter 23 for more information on installing software.

✔ Downloading a program and installing it works just like installing software you bought from the store. The only difference is that rather than use an optical disc, you use a file you download from the Internet to install.

✔ For more information on the program, look for a README file among the files that are installed or downloaded.

✔ Downloading the file is free. If the file is shareware, however, you're expected to pay for it if you use it. Don't worry: The program will remind you. Often.

✔ Even though the file was downloaded, if you don't want it, you have to uninstall it as you would uninstall any program (refer to Chapter 23).

Installing from a Compressed Folder

When you download software that comes in a Compressed Folder, you need to complete a few more steps to finish the download. Here's what you need to do, as continued from Step 9 in the preceding section:

10. **Open the compressed folder you just downloaded; press the Enter key.**

11. **Click the Extract All Files toolbar button.**

    The Extract Compressed (Zipped) Folders Wizard appears.

12. **Click the Extract button.**

    Windows creates a folder with the same name as the compressed folder and copies all files from the compressed folder into the new folder. That new folder then opens, appearing on the screen.

13. **Locate the Setup or Install program.**

    If the program doesn't appear in the window, open the only folder in the window, or open the BIN folder.

14. **Open the Setup or Install program's icon.**

15. **Follow the steps on the screen to continue installing the software.**

If the whole Compressed Folder download thing bothers you, search for a version of the download that uses a self-extracting format rather than Zip. Those files end with the EXE filename extension. If such an option is available, choose it.

E-Mail File Attachments

The ability to send and receive files along with your e-mail is just one of the things that makes e-mail so incredibly popular. Not only can you send pictures back and forth, but e-mailing documents has also nearly put the post office out of business. In fact, it has been decades since I last sent in a printed manuscript of a book. Just about all file transfers between individuals are now done by sending e-mail attachments.

All e-mail programs have the ability to send and receive attachments. The following sections are written generally, though emphasis is on the Microsoft Mail and Windows Live Mail programs, which are popular with Windows.

Receiving an e-mail attachment

Most e-mail programs alert you to the presence of an e-mail file attachment by flagging the message with a teensy paperclip icon. The icon is your clue that the message contains an attachment.

To save the attachment in most e-mail programs, choose File⇨Save Attachment(s) from the menu. Use the Browse button to find a proper folder for the attachment; click the Save button.

In some e-mail programs, such as those that lack a menu bar, you can either double-click the attachment to view it or right-click the attachment and choose a Save command from the pop-up menu to save the thing to a folder. I recommend saving the file to a folder first and then opening it later. By saving the file in a folder, you make it easier to find — and manage — later.

- ✔ Don't open attachments you weren't expecting, especially program files — even if they're from people you know. Just delete the message.

- ✔ Your PC's antivirus program may alert you to the presence of a nasty e-mail file attachment even before you open the e-mail. See Chapter 19 for more information on antivirus programs.

- ✔ At some point, you may receive a file that your PC cannot digest — a file of an unknown format. If so, Windows displays one of those "Windows cannot open this file" type of dialog boxes. My advice? Click the Cancel button. Respond to the e-mail and tell the person that you can't open the file and need to have it resent in another format.

Sending an e-mail attachment

To attach a file to an outgoing message, follow these beloved steps:

1. **Compose the message as you normally would: Enter the name, subject, and message content.**

   Some people wait to write the message content *after* they attach the file. That way, they don't forget to send the attachment.

2. **Click the Attach button on the toolbar.**

   Sometimes, the button appears as a paper clip icon, as shown in the margin. It might also be named Attach File to Message.

3. **Use the Open dialog box to locate the file you want to attach.**

   Refer to Chapter 21 for information on using the Open dialog box.

4. **Select the file in the Open dialog box.**

5. **Click the Open button.**

6. **(Optional) To add another attachment, repeat Steps 2 through 5.**

7. **Click the Send button to send the message.**

Sending a message with a file attached takes longer than sending a regular, text-only message.

✔ Be careful with the size of the file attachments you send! Some folks cannot receive large files. The limit might be 5MB, or as low as 1MB. The alternative? Burn an optical disc and send the files by snail (regular) mail. See Chapter 24.

✔ Look for an Add Photos or Attach Pictures button to quickly send properly formatted images to your e-mail buddies.

✔ Send JPEG or PNG pictures. Any other picture format is usually too large and makes the recipient wait a long time to receive the message. See Chapter 25 for more information on picture file formats.

✔ Don't send file shortcuts; send only originals. If you send a shortcut, the people receiving the file don't receive the original. Instead, they get the teensy shortcut, which doesn't do them any good.

✔ Not everyone you send e-mail to has the same PC setup as you do. For example, some folks may have WordPerfect rather than Word. When you send them a file they cannot read, they'll be disappointed or frustrated or both. How do you know? Ask first.

Part IV
Basic Computing

The 5th Wave · By Rich Tennant

"Well, she's fast on the keyboard and knows how to load the printer, but she just sort of plays with the mouse."

In this part . . .

A computer is a technological marvel, but it's not a piece of art. The PC shouldn't sit in a museum, being ogled or gathering dust. You have a computer — you should use it! To do so, you go beyond the basics of PC hardware and software and actually employ some computing skills, including creating things, managing your stuff, and working with programs. This part of the book introduces you to those activities.

Chapter 19

Be Safe Out There

Many PC users harbor fears. There is the fear that the computer will get angry with you. There is the fear that you will suddenly, unpredictably, and irrevocably lose all your stuff. Then there is the fear that the bad guys are lurking around every corner on the Internet, waiting to steal from you. It makes you wonder why anyone ever bothers to turn on the computer.

The PC will never be angry with you. You might lose your stuff, but it's possible to get that stuff back. That last fear, though, is real: The bad guys *are* out there. You can do a lot to help fend off their attacks, starting by reading the good information in this chapter.

✔ To help save your stuff, see Chapter 22 for information on computer backup.

✔ For more information on PC security, refer to my books *Troubleshooting Your PC For Dummies* and its larger, more encompassing big brother, *Troubleshooting & Maintaining Your PC All-In-One For Dummies* (both from Wiley Publishing, Inc.).

Fight the Bad Guys

The PC bad guys have a host of names as rich and colorful as any comic book (see the following sidebar, "PC super-villain roundup"). Knowing the names is important only when you also know the names of the superheroes who help you thwart the plans of the evil ones. Windows has many such superheroes:

Internet Explorer: Microsoft's Web browser, Internet Explorer, comes with a rich set of features for keeping your computer safe. These include ample warnings when software tries to install itself in your PC from the Internet as well as ways to protect you from visiting phony Web sites.

Windows Defender: The Windows Defender program helps you scan for and remove a clutch of bad guys, especially insidious start-up programs and spyware.

Windows Firewall: The firewall helps to close the windows and bar the doors that bad guys use to infect PCs.

Windows Update: Keeping your PC's software up-to-date is important because the bad guys like a target that stands still.

Backup: To keep your stuff safe, I recommend that you back it up. The backup procedure creates a safety copy of all files on your PC so that if disaster strikes — naturally created or motivated by evil — you can recover your stuff.

Antivirus: Your PC needs a good antivirus program to fight infections that fly in from the Internet or arrive on rogue media. Windows doesn't come with a specific antivirus program, but you can easily obtain a free program. See the section "Antivirus protection," later in this chapter.

Bottom line: Use these tools to help keep your PC safe and its owner happy.

✔ See Chapter 22 for information on using Backup to protect your PC's files.

✔ See Chapter 23 for information on using Windows Update.

✔ You can avoid many nasty programs by simply using common sense. In fact, the most successful computer viruses have propagated simply because of human nature. It's that *human engineering* the bad guys count on, or your ability to be tricked into doing something you wouldn't do otherwise, such as open a questionable e-mail attachment or click a Web page link because you're fooled into thinking, "Your PC is at risk!"

✔ Your ISP can be of great help in dealing with nasty programs on the Internet. Don't forget to use their assistance, especially when you first try fixing things on your own and it doesn't help.

PC supervillain roundup

As with most things about computers, malicious software, or *malware,* is named in either a technical or silly manner. Neither name helps: The technical name is confusing, and the silly name is clever for only people who would otherwise understand the technical names. Regardless, here's your handy guide:

phishing: Pronounced "fishing," this term applies to a Web page or an e-mail designed to fool you into thinking that it's something else, such as your bank's Web page. The idea is to *fish* for information, such as account numbers and passwords. The Web page or e-mail tricks you into providing that information because it looks legitimate. It isn't.

pop-up: A pop-up isn't a nasty program, but it can be annoying — especially when you're assaulted by several pop-ups all at once. How any legitimate marketing person would believe that multiple, annoying pop-up windows would entice anyone to buy something is beyond me, but it happens and you can stop it.

spyware: A rather broad category, *spyware* refers to a program that monitors, or spies on,

what you do on the Internet. The reasoning is advertising: By knowing where you go and what you do on the Internet, information obtained about you can be sold to advertisers who then target ads your way.

Trojan: A program is labeled a *Trojan* (horse) whenever it claims to do one thing but does another. For example, a common Trojan is a special screen saver that saves the screen but also uses your PC on the Internet to relay pornographic images.

virus: A *virus* is a nasty program that resides in your PC without your knowledge and infects the computer. The program may be triggered at any time, where it may take over the computer, redirect Internet traffic, use your computer to flood out spam messages, or do any of a number of nasty and inconvenient things.

worm: A *worm* is simply a virus that replicates itself, by sending out copies to other folks on your e-mail list, for example.

Internet Explorer Tools

Internet Explorer comes with a host of security features as well as extra bulletproofing to help keep you safe on the Internet. The feature list is vast, so for brevity I limit my discussion in the following sections to the two most annoying issues: pop-up windows and phishing.

Blocking pop-ups

To confirm that pop-ups are being blocked in Internet Explorer, follow these steps:

1. **Start Internet Explorer.**

2. **Click the Tools button on the toolbar.**

   The Tools menu appears (pops up, actually).

3. **Choose Pop-up Blocker.**

   The Pop-Up Blocker submenu is displayed.

4. **Choose Turn On Pop-Up Blocker, if necessary, and then click the Yes button to confirm.**

   Otherwise, if the menu command is Turn Off Pop-Up Blocker, you're already set.

When set in action, the pop-up blocker suppresses almost any pop-up display window. That means you miss out on all those ads! Yep.

When IE blocks a pop-up window, a warning banner is displayed just above the part of the window where you view the Web page. The banner reads "Pop-up blocked. To see this pop-up or additional options, click here." Clicking the banner displays a menu of options.

✔ Blocking pop-up windows may disable certain Web page features, such as a pop-up video window, a menu, or another informative display. In those cases, it's obviously okay to allow pop-ups for that window or Web page: Click the warning banner and choose Temporarily Allow Pop-Ups from the menu.

✔ The pop-up blocker doesn't work to block certain animated pop-up windows. So if you see that the pop-up blocker is on yet pop-up windows still appear, just accept that, lamentably, there's nothing you can do about it.

Phighting phishing

The *phishing* scam effectively fools you into doing something you would never otherwise do. The Web page looks legitimate, but it isn't. Internet Explorer automatically helps you fight this kind of scam. Confirm that everything is set up properly by following these steps:

1. **Click the Safety button on the toolbar.**

2. **Choose the InPrivate Filtering Settings command.**

3. **Click the big button, Block for Me.**

   If you don't see the big Block for Me button, InPrivate Filtering is on and instead you see a summary of how things are working; click the OK button.

InPrivate Filtering alerts you to any Web page link that, well, appears to be fishy. The link may claim that it goes to one Web page when in fact it goes to another. Or, the link may go to a Web site known for doing naughty things with people's personal information. Either way, you're warned.

Don't lower your guard just because Internet Explorer features InPrivate Filtering: It's human engineering that the bad guys count on to make their scams work. No financial institution sends vital information by e-mail. None of them! When in doubt, phone your banker and confirm the message. Oftentimes, you discover that the message is bogus. Even if it shouldn't be, it's better to be safe than to be violated by a crook.

The Action Center

The headquarters for security issues in Windows 7 is the Action Center, illustrated in Figure 19-1. The Action Center window provides a quick summary of your PC's current security state and lists any pending problems or issues with links or buttons that help you resolve those issues.

To open the Action Center, click the link Review Your Computer's Status, found beneath the System and Security heading in the Control Panel window. High-priority items are flagged in red in the window, and lower priority items are flagged in orange.

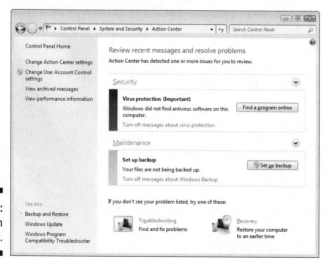

Figure 19-1:
The Action
Center.

Click the Show More button in the window to view all the details for your PC's security and maintenance conditions. When an area is expanded, you see lots of status information and updates plus links that take you to specific locations in Windows where you can change settings or deal with issues.

- ✔ Generally speaking, follow the advice in the window.

- ✔ In Figure 19-1, the PC is lacking antivirus protection. To solve that issue, click the button Find a Program Online; see the section "Antivirus protection," later in this chapter.

- ✔ Also in Figure 19-1, the PC hasn't yet had its important files backed up. See Chapter 22 for information on PC backup.

- ✔ In Windows Vista, the Action Center is named Windows Security Center. It serves the same purpose but lacks a lot of the detail of the Action Center.

Windows Firewall

In construction, a *firewall* is used to slow the advance of a fire. It's created from special slow-burning material and rated in *hours*. For example, a three-hour firewall takes, theoretically, three hours to burn through — and that helps protect a building from burning down before the fire department shows up.

On a computer with an Internet connection, a *firewall* is designed to restrict Internet access, primarily to keep unwanted guests from getting in — or out of the computer. The firewall effectively plugs holes left open when the Internet was originally designed.

Windows comes with a firewall named, coincidentally, Windows Firewall. You start it from the Control Panel: Click the heading System and Security, and then click the heading Windows Firewall. The Windows Firewall window appears, shown in Figure 19-2.

As far as you're concerned, Windows Firewall has only two settings: On and Off. To change the setting, click the link Turn Windows Firewall On or Off on the left side of the Windows Firewall window (refer to Figure 19-2).

When the firewall detects unwanted access, either to or from the Internet, you see a pop-up window alerting you to the intrusion, such as the one shown in Figure 19-3. At that point, you can choose to allow access by the named program by clicking the Allow Access button. If you want to continue blocking the program, just click Cancel.

Figure 19-2:
The
Windows
Firewall
window.

Figure 19-3:
Windows
Firewall in
action.

If you're in doubt about your PC's firewall or just want to ensure that it's doing its job, I recommend that you give it a test. Many programs available on the Internet probe your PC's firewall and look for weaknesses. One such program is ShieldsUP!, which can be found on the Gibson Research Web site:

```
http://grc.com
```

Windows Defender

Windows Defender is a single name given to a slate of tools used to protect your PC from snooping programs as well as from irritating startup programs. At its core, however, Windows Defender scans your PC for nasty programs known as spyware.

In Windows 7, the Windows Defender program runs automatically. You're alerted to any problems in the Action Center window (refer to Figure 19-1). To specifically visit the Windows Defender program window, you follow a set of tricky steps:

1. **Pop up the Start button menu.**

   Click the Start button or press the Win key on the keyboard.

2. **In the Search box, at the bottom of the menu, type** Windows Defender.

3. **Choose Windows Defender from the search results list that's displayed.**

   Just press the Enter key to open the window.

The Windows Defender main window is rather boring — well, unless you have a problem. Otherwise, it just lists a quick summary saying that your PC is running normally. You can close the window.

✔ Other anti-spyware programs are available, and most often they can be found in the various security suite programs.

✔ It's okay to run more than one anti-spyware program in your computer at a time. Well, I'd run two, if you have them: another program plus Windows Defender. There's no need to load up on anti-spyware programs.

✔ For more information on using Windows Defender, refer to my book *Troubleshooting Your PC For Dummies* or my more comprehensive title *Troubleshooting & Maintaining Your PC All-In-One For Dummies*, both published by Wiley.

Antivirus protection

Windows doesn't come with an antivirus program, though you may have such a program installed on your computer. Manufacturers include Norton AntiVirus, McAfee VirusScan, and, often, the AVG program. All of them work. You need to use one.

If your PC doesn't yet have antivirus software, you can click the button Find a Program Online, found in the Action Center window (refer to Figure 19-1). Clicking that button takes you to a Web page where you can pick and choose an antivirus program, by downloading it directly to your computer over the Internet.

After the antivirus program is installed, it works by scanning your computer for signs of infection. The program has two modes of operation:

Active Scan: In Active Scan mode, your antivirus software takes a look at every dang doodle file and program on your computer, looking for viral presence. Antivirus programs scan all the files on your PC regularly, if not daily.

Interception: In Interception mode, the antivirus program works to scan incoming e-mail and files you transfer from other computers as well as stuff that floats in from the Internet. If an infection tries to walk into your PC, it's stopped.

These names, Active Scan and Interception, are my own. The antivirus program you choose probably has its own pet names but still carries out those actions.

✔ When the antivirus program alerts you to an infection, deal with it! Quarantine or delete the infection immediately.

✔ Antivirus programs use quarantine as a way to isolate potentially infected files, preventing them from attacking your PC. Though the file has been quarantined, it hasn't been deleted, but your system is still safe. (You can delete the quarantined files later.)

✔ You can run two antivirus programs on your PC, though not at the same time. You use only one antivirus program in Interception mode, but you can scan your PC using two antivirus programs, one after the other, to ensure that whatever one misses, the other might catch.

✔ You can access the antivirus program by clicking its little icon, which appears in the taskbar's notification area.

✔ See Chapter 18 for more information on downloading software from the Internet.

✔ Viruses spread because of simple human engineering. Most folks know not to open strange or unexpected e-mail attachments. Yet viruses continue to be spread by these types of techniques. Perhaps the best antivirus tool you have is your own brain: Being thoughtful and not careless prevents viruses from being installed in the first place, making antivirus programs necessary but not vital.

User Account Control warnings

In its efforts to make Windows a more secure operating system, Microsoft has presented you (the user) with something called the *User Account Control,* or *UAC.* It displays various warning dialog boxes and pop-up windows whenever you attempt to change something in Windows, such as a computer setting or option, or when you try to download software from the Internet. A typical UAC is shown in Figure 19-4.

Figure 19-4:
A typical
UAC.

 The UACs are to be expected whenever you see a link or button flagged with the UAC shield icon, shown in the margin. It's your clue that you should expect a UAC warning to appear. If the action is expected, click the Continue button or, if prompted, type the administrator's password and then click the OK button.

If you see a UAC warning when you're not expecting one, click the Cancel button. For example, when you're on the Internet and you see a UAC warning about installing software or changing your home page, click Cancel!

Chapter 20

Know What a File Is

*T*here's a lot of stuff to absorb when it comes to computers. There's hardware. There's software. Things are given weird, technical descriptions or silly names that make no sense. Acronyms litter the landscape like leaves after a windstorm. And, to top it off, the computer is simply cold and cruel. How do some people manage to get by?

Well! I'll tell you: The secret to getting the most from any computer is to understand the basic element of computer storage, the *file*. When you can get your arms around the concept of a file, the rest of this computer nonsense begins to make sense. This chapter helps you start down that pleasant pathway.

Behold the File!

I would guess that a big percentage of folks who use a PC don't have the slightest idea what a file is. Yes, there's a File menu. You save files. You open files. That's about it.

Allow me to properly introduce you to a computer file:

A *file* is a chunk of information stored in a computer. That's it.

The word *file* is used because, in an office setting, information is traditionally stored on paper, and those papers are grouped into file folders, stored in a file cabinet. The same analogy applies to computer files, though I don't think that the comparison has been successful.

When you think of a file, don't even think of a paper file. Instead, think of a file as a container. The container can be any size: small or large. Unlike a printed sheet of paper, the file-container holds a variety of stuff: text, graphics, sounds, video, programs, and lots of other things.

The guts of a file

At its teensiest, tiniest level, all information in a file is *binary,* or just a series of ones and zeros, like this:

```
11000100011011110111001011010010110111001100111100001
```

Boring!

Computers do miraculous things with ones and zeros, however. That mysterious binary information can be organized in a way that the computer can understand. The computer can then present the information to you as a document, an audio file, a program, or any of a variety of things more useful than individual ones and zeros.

- ✔ As the human, you never need to worry about looking inside a file to see those frightening ones and zeros. The computer's operating system automatically presents the information inside a file to you the way it's supposed to look — or sound.

- ✔ All files contain ones and zeros. The difference between a video, a document, and a program file is how the file is recognized by the operating system. See the next section.

- ✔ The computer organizes the ones and zeros into groups called *bytes*. On a PC, eight bits are in a byte. So, a picture file that contains 1 megabyte of information contains about 8 million ones and zeros.

Things that describe a file

Files have descriptions, just like people do. Files have names, birthdays, and a place where they live, and, like people, files have character. Files do, however, lack personality.

When describing a file, you use the term *attribute*. The attributes identify the file as unique, keeping the file's contents from getting all sloppy and confused with other files. In Windows, five key attributes help define a file: name, size, date, type, and icon.

Name: All files have a name, or *filename*. The name is given to the file when it's created and, hopefully, the name describes the file's contents or gives you a clue to what the file is used for.

Size: The number of bytes in a file determines the file's size, or how much space it occupies in the PC's storage system (both memory and media). Some files are tiny, some can be quite large.

Date: When a file is created, the operating system slaps it just like a doctor slaps a human baby. But a file doesn't breathe, and it lacks a butt, so a *date-and-time stamp* is slapped on it. This stamp helps you organize and find files. A second date-and-time stamp is applied to a file whenever it's updated, changed, or modified. (The original creation date and time remain unchanged.)

Type: Finally, each file has a type, which depends on the file's contents. So, a file that contains graphics is identified as a picture file type, a word processing document is identified as a document type, and so on.

Icon: Closely related to the file type is the icon displayed in Windows. (Icons represent files in a graphical operating system.) File types and icons are covered in more detail in the later section "File Types and Icons."

Another file attribute is its location. That's a big deal, so the file's location is covered in the next section.

- ✔ Refer to Chapter 8 for more information on bytes.

- ✔ A file can consist of zero bytes, in which case the file exists but lacks content.

- ✔ The largest size that a file can be is *huge*. You never need to worry about a file getting too big in Windows.

- ✔ The date-and-time stamp is one reason that the PC has an internal clock. It also explains why it's important to keep the PC's clock up to date. Refer to Chapter 6 for more information on setting the clock.

- ✔ Additional attributes are used to describe files — for example, whether a file is a system, hidden, read-only, or compressed file or an archived or encrypted file or a bunch of other trivial things. The operating system keeps track of all that stuff.

Files dwell in folders

An important part of a file's description is its location. Files dwell on storage media inside the PC. Under Windows, those storage media are known by their *drive letters*. So, no matter where the file lives, it lives first on storage media identified by a letter of the alphabet, such as C: for the C drive — a popular place for files to be found.

After the drive letter, and in keeping with the computer's file cabinet metaphor, the storage media is organized using folders. All files dwell inside folders. A specific file is found on a specific drive and in a specific folder.

Folders are used to keep files separate and organized. When folders are used well, they help you find your files quickly. They also help keep your sanity: Without folders, storage media would bloat with tens of thousands of files and your head would explode trying to find anything.

See Chapter 21 for more information on folders and file organization.

Filenames

All files have a name. Just like Adam named the animals in the Garden of Eden, you (the human) get to name the files in your computer. Well, at least you get to name the files you create. It's a big responsibility, so you must be wise and creative with your filename choices. This section offers words of wisdom.

Choosing the best name

You name a file when you create it. Specifically, you create something in a computer program, or an *application.* Then you save your something. When you save, you use the Save As dialog box (covered later in this chapter) to name the file as well as to find a location for the file and, optionally, set the file type.

The best rule for naming files is to be descriptive and brief. Use letters, numbers, and spaces in the name. Here are some examples:

```
Bio
Pool Party
Speech August 8
2010 Vacation to Omaha
How to drive whilst in Canada
```

Each of these examples is a good filename, which properly explains the file's contents.

- ✔ Upper- or lowercase doesn't matter. Although capitalizing Nantucket is proper, for example, Windows recognizes that filename the same as nantucket, Nantucket, NANTUCKET, or any combination of upper- and lowercase letters.

- ✔ It's tradition in computer documentation to see filenames written in ALL CAPS. That doesn't mean that files must be named using all capital letters.

✔ Although case doesn't matter in a filename, it *does* matter when you're typing a Web page address.

✔ The file's name reminds you of what's in the file, or what it's all about — just like naming your vacation home The Money Pit tells everyone what your vacation home is all about.

✔ You can rename a file at any time after it has been created. See Chapter 22.

✔ All the rules for naming files also apply to naming folders. See Chapter 21.

Obeying the filenaming rules

This section describes the law of naming files in Windows. All this stuff is optional reading; as long as you stick with naming files using letters, numbers, and spaces, this stuff is merely trivia.

Characters: Files can be named using any combination of letters and numbers, plus a smattering of symbols.

Length: Technically, you can give a file a name that's over 200 characters long. Don't. Long filenames may be *very* descriptive, but Windows displays them in a funny way or not at all, in many situations. Better to keep things short than to abuse long-filename privileges.

Forbidden characters: Windows gets cross if you use any of these characters to name a file:

```
* / : < > ? \ | "
```

These symbols hold special meaning to Windows. Nothing bad happens if you attempt to use these characters. Windows just refuses to save the file — or a warning dialog box growls at you.

Use periods sparingly: Although you can use any number of periods in a filename, you cannot name a file with all periods. I know that it's strange, and I'm probably the only one on the planet to have tried it, but it doesn't work.

Spaces: Filenames can contain spaces, though it's common in computerland to use the underscore (or underline) character rather than a space.

Numbers are okay: Feel free to start a filename by using a number. You can even use symbols, though not the forbidden characters I just listed. I mention it because rumors are out there saying that starting a filename with a number is bad. Poppycock.

File Types and Icons

It's truly difficult to look inside a file at all those ones and zeros and try to determine what they represent. Yeah, it sounds like a job for a computer, but even a computer would balk at such a chore. So another solution was devised.

The solution used by Windows identifies a file by using the last part of the file's name, what's called the *filename extension*. That part of the name helps the operating system determine what's in a file, which icon to slap on the file, and which program to use to open or view the file's contents. This section discusses the relevant points.

What's a filename extension?

The filename *extension* is a secret bit of text that's added to a filename when the file is first created. The filename extension is applied by the program that creates the file. It tells the operating system three things:

✔ The type of file that's created — document, graphics, or sound, for example

✔ Which program created (or *owns*) the file

✔ Which icon to use to represent the file

It's the extension that offers a clue to what's inside a file, and the operating system relies heavily on that extension.

Filename extension details

The filename extension is created when the file is first saved to the PC's storage system. The extension is added automatically; there's no need to manually type it. In fact, the extension is hidden from you specifically to prevent you from messing things up. (See the next section.)

Details-wise, the filename extension appears at the end of a filename. It starts with a period and is followed by one to four characters. For example, the .txt filename extension is used to identify text files in Windows. Web page files use the .htm or .html filename extensions. Graphics files have a number of filename extensions, depending on the graphics file type: gif, jpg, png, and tiff, for example.

Gazillions of filename extensions are out there, too many to list here. If you're curious, you can visit the Web site www.filext.com to review or look up a filename extension. But don't fuss over filename extensions: In your role as computer operator, you merely need to know that the extensions exist. Beyond that, don't mess with them.

How to see or hide the filename extension

Because the filename extension is so important to Windows, it's often concealed from view. You don't see the extension when you examine files in a window, and you don't see the extension when you open or save a file. You can, however, direct Windows to display that extension for you, revealing what was once hidden. Abide by these steps:

1. **Open the Control Panel.**

   Choose the Control Panel item from the Start button menu.

2. **Click the Appearance and Personalization heading.**

3. **From beneath the Folder Options heading, click the link Show Hidden Files And Folders.**

   No, you don't show hidden files or folders, but by clicking the link, you quickly see the View tab in the Folder Options dialog box.

4. **Remove the check mark by the item on the list that says Hide Extensions for Known File Types.**

   Or, if the item is already set the way you like, you're just dandy.

5. **Click OK to close the Folder Options dialog box.**

6. **Close the Computer window.**

My advice is to show the extensions, not only because they exist but also for security reasons: When the extensions are hidden, bad guys find it easier to slip in a virus or another bad program disguised as something else. As long as you read the information in this section and understand why extensions are necessary and how they're used, you'll be okay with the extensions visible.

✔ When you elect to show the filename extensions, be careful never to change or delete the extension when you rename a file. See Chapter 22 for more information on renaming files.

✔ It's possible for a file not to have an extension in Windows. That's okay. The file then becomes an "unknown file type." Just leave it be.

Icons

Windows is a graphical operating system, and, as such, it uses *icons,* or tiny pictures, to represent files. The picture relates to the file type, which is determined by the filename extension. The picture can also be related to the program used to create or view the file.

Figure 20-1 shows a file icon. The icon represents a Microsoft Word document, and the filename appears beneath the icon. The filename extension, docx, also appears.

Figure 20-1:
A file with
an icon,
a name,
and an
extension.

Chapter 1.docx

How Files Are Born

Files are created by using programs — software. Specifically, the software that creates stuff is an *application.* For example, you use the word processing application Microsoft Word to create documents, brochures, novels, plays, and conspiracy theories.

The stuff you create in an application is built in the computer's memory, the *temporary* storage. To keep your creation for the long term, you must save that information as a file on the PC's storage system. The command that does it is the Save command.

Windows programs feature two Save commands: Save and Save As. Both exist on the File menu or, in some programs, the commands are on a button that appears in the upper left corner of the application's window.

The first time you save your stuff to disk, the Save As command is used (even if you choose File➪Save). Choosing the Save As command summons the Save As dialog box, shown in Figure 20-2. You use that dialog box to give the file a name, choose a location for the file, and, optionally, set the file type, as described in the figure.

Favorite folders and other
locations for saving files

Location where the
file will be saved

File's specific location (Address bar)

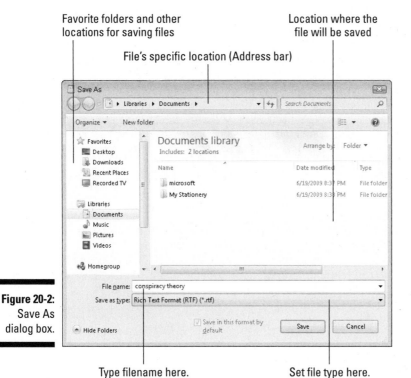

Figure 20-2:
Save As
dialog box.

Type filename here.

Set file type here.

Though the Save As command *creates* the file, the Save command is used to update, or *refresh,* the contents of the saved file. So, after initially saving, you work a little bit and then you use the Save command, File➪Save. It works this way until you're done, when you save one last time after you finish creating something or just before quitting the program.

The Save command is how you save the stuff you create in Windows, and it's how files are born.

- ✔ In Microsoft Office 2007, the Save and Save As commands are on the Office button menu.

- ✔ The Save command can also be accessed from the Save button on a toolbar or by pressing Ctrl+S on the keyboard.

- ✔ You can also use the Save As command specifically to save a file with a new name, in a new location, or as a new file type.

- ✔ Refer to the filenaming rules earlier in this chapter for information on what you can name a file. Be clever. Be descriptive. Be brief.

- ✔ Save often!

✔ After saving, the stuff you created exists as a file on the PC's storage system. There's no need to confirm this. Had there been an error, Windows would promptly inform you.

✔ After a file has been saved, the file's name appears on the title bar (at the top of the window).

✔ See Chapter 21 for information on folders, which is where files are saved on the PC's storage system. The folder display occupies a major portion of the Save As dialog box (refer to Figure 20-2).

✔ The Save As dialog box appears only the first time you save your stuff to disk; from that point on, the Save command merely resaves a file to disk.

✔ Not every Save As dialog box looks like the one shown earlier, in Figure 20-2. Some are simpler, some are more complex.

✔ The Save As Type drop-down list directs the program to save the file as a specific file type. This tool can be used to override the program's normal file type and save your stuff in a specific type. For example, you can use this option to save a graphical image in a specific file format, which is covered in Chapter 25.

Chapter 21

Organizing Files with Folders

*T*he most important thing on your PC is your stuff, the information you create or obtain and keep on the computer's storage system. That stuff dwells in containers called *files*, so understanding files is an important part of getting the most from your PC. The files themselves dwell inside their own containers, which are *folders*. If you want to build upon a happy relationship with your computer, it follows that after understanding files, you need to understand folders. Chapter 20 covers files; this chapter is all about folders.

About Folders

A *folder* is a container for files, and files are containers for data — the stuff you collect or create on the computer. Basically, folders exist to help keep your files organized. The objective: to maintain your sanity. If being sane is important to you, you need to know about folders.

More than just containing files, folders can be used to keep your stuff organized. Without folders, files would exist in one huge clump on the PC's storage media. That would be a Bad Thing.

Think about it: The typical PC hard drive stores between 10,000 and 50,000 files. Imagine finding just one file! Heck, it would take you a week to scroll through the list. I won't even go into the madness of duplicate filenames and how sluggish the computer would behave anytime you saved or opened anything on the storage system. Yech!

No, folders are the key to organizing files on your computer's storage media. Windows uses folders to keep its stuff organized. You can do the same with your stuff.

✓ A *folder* is a storage place for files.

✓ Refer to Chapter 20 for information on files. It's very important! Understanding files is the key to getting the most from your computer.

✓ Folders keep like files grouped together — the way barbed wire keeps prisoners, vicious animals, and toddlers from wandering off.

✓ Folders appear in Windows using the folder icon, as shown in the margin. When the folder is empty, it appears as shown in the margin. A folder with contents appears full, sometimes even previewing the contents in the folder icon itself.

✓ To open the folder, double-click it with the mouse. Folders open into a window that displays the folder's contents. See the section "Using Windows Explorer," later in this chapter.

✓ In addition to files, folders can hold other folders. Folders within folders! Just like those Russian matryoshka dolls. See the section "Subfolders and parent folders," elsewhere in this chapter.

✓ Folders may also be referred to as *directories*. This term is merely a throwback to the early days of computing and the Unix operating system, which was used by Julius Caesar.

Famous Folders

Folders are a necessary part of file organization, and they're used all over your computer: When Windows was first set up on your PC, it created a slew of folders, some for it and some for you. Software you install on your computer also creates folders. This section explains all that folder stuff.

The root folder

Storage media exist to store files, and files *must be* stored in folders. Therefore, all the computer's storage media are organized into folders. It all starts with one, main folder, the *root folder*. In the same way a tree trunk has many limbs branching out from it, all other folders on your hard drive branch out from that main, root folder.

The root folder doesn't have a specific icon. Instead, it uses the icon for the media that the root folder is on. So, the root folder on drive C has the same icon as drive C.

You can see the root folder icons in the Computer window: Open the Computer window by choosing the Computer command from the Start button menu. All the icons you see in that window represent the root folder for the various storage media. Opening an icon in the Computer window displays the contents of that storage media's root folder.

✔ The root folder is simply the main, or only, folder on any storage media.

✔ The root folder resembles the lobby of a grand building: It's merely a place you pass through to get to somewhere else. Where else? Why, to other folders, of course!

✔ Never add, delete, or change any files or folders in the root folder. It belongs to the operating system, not to you.

✔ While you're at it, never mess with any files or folders found in the following folders: Windows, WINNT, or Program Files. My general rule is never to mess with any file or folder on your computer that you didn't create.

✔ The root folder may also be called the *root directory*.

Subfolders and parent folders

Folders can contain both files and other folders. When one folder exists inside another, it's a *subfolder*. This term has nothing to do with underwater naval vessels or hoagie-like sandwiches.

Say you have a folder named Vacation and that folder exists inside a folder named 2010. The Vacation folder is said to be a subfolder of the 2010 folder. Conversely, the 2010 folder is said to be the *parent* folder of the Vacation folder.

A subfolder can also be called a *child* folder, but that's just a tad cheeky, now, isn't it?

✔ You can create your own folders. See the section "Creating a new folder," later in this chapter, for the details.

✔ No limit exists on the number of subfolders you can have. A folder can be inside a folder inside a folder, and so on. If you name the folders well, it all makes sense.

✔ As the topmost folder on any storage media, the root folder has no parent folder, though in the Windows hierarchy, the "parent folder" of any storage media is the Computer window, and the Computer window's parent folder is the desktop.

A place for your stuff

Humans don't use the root folder; the root folder is for the computer only. The proper place for your stuff is the User Profile folder. Yes, that's a dreadful name.

The *User Profile* folder is the main folder for storing your stuff on the computer. It's named after your account on the computer. So, if your account is named Danny, the User Profile folder is named Danny.

To see the contents of your User Profile folder, choose your account name from the left side of the Start button menu. The contents of your User Account folder are displayed in a window, similar to the one shown in Figure 21-1.

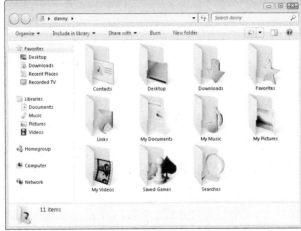

Figure 21-1:
The User
Account
folder
window.

Inside the User Account Folder window, you find about a dozen folders precreated for you, each of which helps you organize the stuff you collect or create on your computer. Table 21-1 lists the folders commonly found.

Additional subfolders may be found in your User Profile folder — folders you created yourself or folders added by programs you installed. That's all okay; the User Profile folder is your own, and it's where you're supposed to create folders to help organize your stuff.

> ✔ You can also view the contents of your User Profile folder by opening your account's icon on the desktop or by choosing your account icon in a folder window or in any of a zillion other, confusing ways that I don't mention here.

- Don't mess with any folders outside your User Profile folder.

- All applications automatically choose the User Account folder or one of its subfolders when you use the Save As dialog box to save a file.

- In Windows Vista, the My Documents, My Pictures, My Music, and My Video folders are named without the *My* prefix.

- Behind the scenes, the My Documents, My Pictures, My Music, and My Video folders in Windows 7 are named Documents, Pictures, Music, and Video. You just see the My prefix thanks to special software trickery. Don't be surprised if you occasionally see the folders minus their My prefix; they're the same folders. Yeah, it's weird, but it's Windows.

- Windows 7 adds a level of file organization to the folder concept by creating something called a *library*. Refer to the section "Working with libraries," later in this chapter.

Table 21-1	Subfolders Found in the User Profile Folder
Folder Name	*Contains*
Contacts	A database of people's names used by e-mail, list-making, or personal-information programs
Desktop	A duplicate of files and shortcuts placed on the desktop
Downloads	Files downloaded from the Internet
Favorites	Bookmarks set and used by Internet Explorer
Links	Shortcuts to popular files and folders, displayed in the Windows Explorer window
My Documents	Text documents and similar files
My Music	Audio and music files, used by Windows Media Player and other musical programs
My Pictures	Digital images, photographs, drawings, and artwork
My Videos	Films, movies, and animations
Saved Games	Information retained by games so that you can remember your spot or high score from a previously played game
Searches	A set of predefined or saved file searches (see Chapter 22)

Manage Your Folders

Folders are something you're supposed to use. Windows makes suggestions for you, giving the examples of the My Documents, My Video, My Music, and other folders. You can choose to use those folders, create your own folders, make folders within folders — all for the purpose of organizing the stuff on your computer. It's up to you to make it happen, and this section explains how.

Using Windows Explorer

One duty of an operating system is to help you organize the stuff you create. In Windows, that duty is assigned to the program Windows Explorer. It's the program that displays folder windows on the desktop and allows you to manage your folders and files.

A sample Windows Explorer folder window is shown in Figure 21-2. That window appears whenever you open a folder or storage media icon.

Navigation pane

Organize menu   Folder/window name   View menu

Address bar   Subfolders   Toolbar

Figure 21-2:
Windows
Explorer.

Libraries   Details pane   Folder contents

In Figure 21-2, Windows Explorer displays the files and folders found in the My Documents folder. You can see My Documents as the last item (on the right) on the Address bar. Also visible are the Navigation pane and the Details pane, as illustrated in the figure.

✔ Windows Explorer isn't the same program as Internet Explorer.

✔ My favorite way to start Windows Explorer is to press Win+E on the keyboard.

✔ You control what's visible in the Windows Explorer window by using the Organize toolbar button's menu. From the Layout submenu, you can choose a pane to view or summon the traditional menu bar.

✔ The size and appearance of the icons in the Windows Explorer window depend on settings you make from the View toolbar button menu.

✔ Toolbar buttons come and go in Windows Explorer, depending on what you're doing and which type of icon is selected.

Working with folders

You can manipulate folders using the Windows Explorer window. The things you can do are described in the wee li'l sections here.

Opening a folder

To open a folder, double-click its icon. The contents of that folder are then displayed in the window. You also see that folder appear in the Address bar list, at the top of the Windows Explorer window.

Returning to the parent folder

To move back to a parent folder after visiting a subfolder, you can click the Back button on the Address bar (on the far left, just like when you explore the Web). Or, you can click the parent folder's name on the Address bar. For example, in Figure 21-2, you can click the danny folder to visit the parent of the My Documents folder.

You can add commonly visited folders to the Favorites list in the Navigation pane. To do so, simply drag the folders icon over to the Favorites list. That way, you can revisit the folder quickly by choosing it from that list.

Creating a new folder

To make a new folder, click the New Folder button on the toolbar. The New Folder icon appears in the window, ready to be given a new name: Type the new folder's name immediately. Make it short and descriptive. Pressing the Enter key locks in the new folder's name.

You can use the folder immediately after creating it.

- You can also create a new folder when saving a file; a New Folder button appears in the Save As dialog box. See Chapter 20.

- Folders are created in the current folder window. The new folder becomes a *subfolder* of the current folder, so be sure that you're in the right folder window when you create a new folder.

- Folder names are the same as filenames. See Chapter 20.

- Folders can also be renamed, just like filenames. See Chapter 22.

- Sometimes, the New Folder button gets pushed off the Windows Explorer toolbar. It's still there; you just need to click the "show more" chevron at the end of the toolbar to display the New Folder button.

- In Windows Vista, the New Folder command is found on the Organize button's menu.

Working with libraries

A *library,* which is a special feature in Windows 7, contains a selection of files from multiple folders. It's a handy thing to have, especially when working with large projects or collections of files that may exist in several folders. You can do many things with libraries.

- Libraries are unique to Windows 7.

- Libraries not only organize files for you, but they also can be shared by other people who also use your computer.

- You can share libraries with users on your computer network by using a HomeGroup. See Chapter 16 for more information on HomeGroups.

- I'll admit that the concept of the library is something that may take you a while to adjust to. My advice is to understand folders first. After you appreciate how folders work, move on to working with libraries.

Viewing libraries

To display the list of libraries available on your computer, or shared between computers on the network HomeGroup, choose the Libraries heading from the Navigation panel in any Windows Explorer window. Libraries appear in their own window, as shown in Figure 21-3.

To view the contents of a library, double-click to open its icon. Libraries contain files and folders. Yet the files and folders you see are culled from various folders located throughout your PC's storage system, as well as from, possibly, the computer network.

✔ You can work with files in a library the same as you can work with files in a folder.

✔ To see which folders are included in a library, click the link located by the word *Includes* beneath the library name in the Windows Explorer window.

✔ If you create or save any files (or folders) in a library, they're created in your own account's area on your computer.

Choose libraries from here.   Click to create a new library.   Library icons

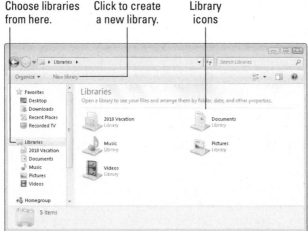

Figure 21-3:
The
Libraries
window.

Building a new library

To create a new library, obey these steps:

1. **Click the New Library button in the Library window (refer to Figure 21-3).**

2. **Immediately name the New Library icon, just as you would when creating a new folder.**

   Be descriptive and brief.

3. **Open the new library you just created.**

   The library is empty.

4. **Click the button named Include Folder.**

   Use the Include Folder dialog box to browse through your folders to find one you want to add.

5. **Select the folder you want to add.**

6. **Click the Include Folder button.**

Libraries need to have more than one folder to be useful. To add folders, click the link after the word *Includes* in the library's window. (The link is found beneath the library name.) Click the Add button in the Locations dialog box to choose another folder to add to the library.

The Open Dialog Box

As you use your computer, you often find yourself digging through folders with the Open or Browse dialog box, off to fetch a file somewhere. For example, you want to open that document you worked on yesterday, the one that contains your plans for winning the Junior Miss Avocado pageant.

The Open dialog box, depicted in Figure 21-4, is summoned by using the Open command (or Ctrl+O). Similarly, its sister the Browse dialog box appears whenever you issue a Browse command. Either way, the dialog box lets you hunt down a specific file on disk.

Places to look for files

Narrow files displayed by file type

Address bar   Folder/library   Files and folders

Figure 21-4:
The typical
Open
dialog box.

Type a specific
file to open.

Click to open the
selected file.

Yes, the Open dialog box looks and works a lot like a Windows Explorer window. It has the same panes, toolbar, and file list. The bonus information specific to opening files, however, is found near the bottom of the dialog box (refer to Figure 21-4).

The File Name text box allows you to manually enter a filename — which is a typically silly and nerdy thing to do, so I don't recommend it.

The File Type button is used to help narrow the list of files in the Open dialog box. By showing only files of a certain type, you can more easily scope out the file you want.

Finally, you click the Open button to open the selected file. Note that the Open button often has a menu button next to it. Clicking that button displays options for opening a file.

✔ Not every program can open every type of file. Programs work best on the files they create themselves.

✔ The Open dialog box's look varies subtly from program to program, but it works the same way in all of them.

✔ When you're really stuck finding a file, use the Windows Search command. See Chapter 22.

Chapter 22

Files Managed

A teensy part of using the computer is the concept of file management. It has nothing to do with going to meetings or Hawaiian Shirt Friday. *File management* is more about cleaning up the clutter, undoing some mistakes, and continuing your ongoing efforts toward organization, which directly relates to your sanity. This chapter discusses the smattering of file management tools available to you in Windows.

Files Ready for Action

Files (and folders) must be *selected* before you can abuse them. As with eating peanuts, you can select files individually or in groups.

To select a single file, click its icon once with the mouse. Click. A selected file appears highlighted onscreen, similar to the one shown in Figure 22-1. The file named REUNION is ready for action.

Figure 22-1:
The icon
(file) on
the right is
selected.

Selecting multiple files is a bit more involved. The rest of this section explains how.

- ✔ Clicking a file with the mouse *selects* that file.
- ✔ Selected files appear highlighted in the folder window.
- ✔ File manipulation commands — Copy, Move, Rename, and Delete, for example — affect only selected files.

Selecting all files in a folder

To select all files inside a folder, click the Organize button on the toolbar and choose the Select All command. This command highlights all files in the window — including any folders (and all their contents) and marks them as ready for action.

You can also use the Ctrl+A keyboard shortcut to select all files in a folder.

Selecting a random smattering of files

Suppose that you need to select four icons in a folder, similar to the ones shown in Figure 22-2.

Figure 22-2:
A random
smattering
of files is
selected.

BIO.DOC DOC File 11.0 KB	chap3.txt Text Document 852 bytes
conspiracy theory.rtf Rich Text Document 205 bytes	Edgar Allan Poe The Raven.txt Text Document 7.10 KB
EDITOR.DOC DOC File 3.56 KB	ENGLISH.DOC DOC File 14.5 KB
FIND ME.pfx Personal Information Exchange 2.49 KB	LOG File 5.07 KB

Here's how:

1. **Click to select the first file.**
2. **Press and hold the Ctrl key on the keyboard.**

   Either Ctrl (control) key works; press and hold it down.
3. **Click to select the next file.**
4. **Repeat Step 3 until you have selected all the files you want.**
5. **Release the Ctrl key when you're done selecting files.**

Now you're ready to manipulate the selected files as a group.

To deselect a file from a group, just Ctrl+click it again.

Selecting a swath of files in a row

To select a queue of files, such as those shown in Figure 22-3, pursue these steps:

1. **Choose List from the View menu button on the toolbar.**

   Refer to Figure 21-2, in Chapter 21, for the location of the View button.
2. **Click to select the first file in your group.**
3. **Press and hold the Shift key.**
4. **Click to select the last file in your group.**

   By holding down the Shift key, you select all files between the first click and the second click (refer to Figure 22-3).
5. **Release the Shift key.**

The files are now ready for action.

Name	#	Title	Contributing artists	Album
01 A Hard Day's Nigh...	1	A Hard Day's Night	The Beatles	A Hard Day's Night [UK]
02 I Should Have Kno...	2	I Should Have Known Better	The Beatles	A Hard Day's Night [UK]
03 If I Fell.wma	3	If I Fell	The Beatles	A Hard Day's Night [UK]
04 I'm Happy Just to ...	4	I'm Happy Just to Dance Wi...	The Beatles	A Hard Day's Night [UK]
05 And I Love Her.wma	5	And I Love Her	The Beatles	A Hard Day's Night [UK]
06 Tell Me Why.wma	6	Tell Me Why	The Beatles	A Hard Day's Night [UK]
07 Can't Buy Me Love...	7	Can't Buy Me Love	The Beatles	A Hard Day's Night [UK]
08 Any Time at All.wma	8	Any Time at All	The Beatles	A Hard Day's Night [UK]
09 I'll Cry Instead.wma	9	I'll Cry Instead	The Beatles	A Hard Day's Night [UK]
10 Things We Said To...	10	Things We Said Today	The Beatles	A Hard Day's Night [UK]
11 When I Get Home....	11	When I Get Home	The Beatles	A Hard Day's Night [UK]
12 You Can't Do That...	12	You Can't Do That	The Beatles	A Hard Day's Night [UK]
13 I'll Be Back.wma	13	I'll Be Back	The Beatles	A Hard Day's Night [UK]

Figure 22-3: A group of files in a row is selected.

Lassoing a group of files

Another way to select files as a group is to lasso them. Figure 22-4 illustrates how to do it by dragging over the files with the mouse.

Figure 22-4:
Lasso a
group of
files with
the mouse.

To lasso the files, start by pointing the mouse above and to the left of the icon herd you want to rope. Holding down the mouse button, drag down and to the right to create a rectangle surrounding ("lassoing") the file icons (refer to Figure 22-4). Release the mouse button, and all the files you have lassoed are selected as a group. A vocal "Yee-ha!" is considered appropriate in this circumstance.

Unselecting stuff

To unselect a file, simply click anywhere in the folder (but not on an icon). Or, you can close the folder window, in which case Windows immediately forgets about any selected files.

Stuff You Do with Files

Files can sit there all the doo-dah-day. You create them and then you can open them, edit them, print them, save them again, and so on. Anything beyond that falls under the realm of file management, which is the dawn of truly using your computer (but without becoming a computer nerd). It's necessary stuff: copying, moving, deleting, renaming, and otherwise working with files that already exist. Keep reading this section to see how it's all done.

Copying a file

When you copy a file you're creating a duplicate of that file but in a different location. For example, you copy a file from one folder to another folder or from one storage media to another.

The metaphor that Windows uses for copying files or folders is copy-and-paste: You copy a file from one folder to another using the same commands you use to copy and paste text or graphics. Here's a quick outline of how it's done:

1. **Select the files or folders you want to move or copy.**

   Directions for selecting stuff are found earlier in this chapter. (Again, selecting is required before you copy or paste text or graphics.)

2. **Press Ctrl+C on the keyboard to copy the files.**

   Nothing visually changes, but the files have been selected for copying.

3. **Open the folder where you want the files to be copied.**

   The folder can be another folder in your User Account area, a subfolder, a parent folder, or even the root folder of some removable media you just stuck into the PC.

4. **Press Ctrl+V to paste the files into the folder window.**

   The copied files appear in the window.

Copying files makes duplicates; after you copy the files, you have the original as well as the copy you just made.

- ✔ If you make a mistake, you can undo the file copy by pressing Ctrl+Z, the Undo command shortcut. You must use Ctrl+Z right after copying the files for the Undo command to be successful.

- ✔ Copying files makes exact duplicates. As an alternative, you might consider creating a *shortcut file* instead. See the later section "Creating a shortcut" for more information.

- ✔ It's possible to copy and paste a file into the same folder. When you do so, Windows makes a duplicate of the original, giving the duplicate a new name to let you know that it's a duplicate. (Two files in a folder cannot share the same name.)

- ✔ When you copy a folder, you're copying all files in that folder plus all files in any subfolders.

> ✔ You can copy a file to any removable media by simply opening that media's icon in the Computer window. When copying to an optical disc, remember that the disc must first be prepared for use. See Chapter 24.

> ✔ Copy and Paste commands can be found on the Organize button menu in the Windows Explorer window. You can use those commands rather than the keyboard shortcuts Ctrl+C and Ctrl+V, though I find the keyboard shortcuts easier to use.

> ✔ See Chapter 21 for more information on folders because understanding how they work, as well as how to navigate between folders, is an important part of copying files.

> ✔ You can also copy a file by dragging its icon from one folder window to another. It's technical, however, because you need to open both folder windows at one time and arrange them on the desktop so that you can see what you're dragging with the mouse. Also, you must press and hold the Ctrl key to ensure that the file is *copied* between folders, not moved. All those rules are why I recommend using Ctrl+C and Ctrl+V instead of dragging the files around with the mouse.

Moving a file

To move a file, you perform the same steps as outlined for copying a file in the preceding section. The difference is that the moving operation is a *cut-and-paste*, not a copy-and-paste; in Step 2 in the preceding section, press Ctrl+X for cut rather than Ctrl+C for copy.

After you paste the file, the original is deleted; the file is *moved* from its old folder into the new folder. That's the essence of cut-and-paste, similar to the way you cut a block of text in a word processor to move it elsewhere in the document.

> ✔ Use Ctrl+X to cut selected files and then Ctrl+V to paste then, which moves the files from one folder to another.

> ✔ If you elect to move a file by dragging it between two folders, you must remember to press the Shift key when dragging to ensure that the files are moved, not copied.

Creating a shortcut

A file *shortcut* is a 99 percent fat-free copy of a file. It enables you to access the original file from anywhere on the PC's mass storage system, without consuming the storage space required to duplicate the same file over and over. For example, you can create a shortcut to the Microsoft Word program and put it on the desktop for easy access. Such is the essence of the file shortcut.

You make a shortcut the same way as you copy a file, as discussed in the section "Copying a file," earlier in this chapter. The difference comes when you paste: Rather than press Ctrl+V to paste the file copy, you right-click in the folder. From the pop-up menu that appears, choose the Paste Shortcut command.

A shortcut file appears with a tiny arrow nestled in its lower left corner, as shown in the margin. That's your clue that the file is a shortcut and not a full-blown copy.

- ✔ To quickly create a shortcut on the desktop, right-click an icon and choose Send To➪Desktop (Create Shortcut) from the pop-up menu.

- ✔ Shortcuts are often named with the suffix `Shortcut`. You can edit out the `Shortcut to` part, if you like. Refer to the section "Renaming files," later in this chapter.

- ✔ Shortcuts work only on your computer. Do not e-mail them to your friends, because they receive only the stubby shortcut and not the original file.

- ✔ Have no fear when you're deleting shortcuts: Removing a shortcut icon doesn't remove the original file.

Deleting files

Every so often, it's necessary to go on a file cleaning binge. The task involves cleaning out the deadwood — removing files and folders you no longer want or need.

To kill a file, select it and press the Delete key on your keyboard. You may see a confirmation prompt; click Yes. The file is gone.

Well, not really. The files you delete aren't killed off. No, they're banished to a place called the Recycle Bin; see the next section.

- ✔ You can also delete a file by dragging its icon from the folder window to the Recycle Bin icon on the desktop (if the Recycle Bin icon is visible).

- ✔ You can delete folders just like you delete files, but keep in mind that you delete the folder's contents — which can consist of dozens of icons, files, folders, jewelry, small children, widows, and refugees. Better be careful with that one.

- ✔ Never delete any file or folder unless you created it yourself.

- ✔ Programs aren't deleted in Windows; they're uninstalled. See Chapter 23.

Bringing dead files back to life

If you just deleted a file — and I mean *just* deleted it — you can use the Undo command to get it back: Press Ctrl+Z on the keyboard.

When Undo doesn't do it, or undo it (or whatever), take these steps:

1. **Open the Recycle Bin on the desktop.**

   If the Recycle Bin icon isn't visible on the desktop, press Win+E to summon a Windows Explorer window. Then on the Address Bar, click the triangle to the left of the word *Computer* to display a menu. Choose Recycle Bin from that menu.

2. **Select the file you want recovered.**

3. **Click the Restore This Item button on the toolbar.**

   The file is magically removed from Recycle Bin limbo and restored afresh to the folder and disk from which it was so brutally seized.

4. **Close the Recycle Bin window.**

Renaming files

Windows lets you rename the files and folders you create. You may want to do this to give the folder a better, more descriptive name, or you may have any number of reasons to dub a new name upon the file. Here's how it's done:

1. **Click the icon once to select it.**

2. **Press the F2 key, the keyboard shortcut for the Rename command.**

   Yeah, it's difficult to remember that F2 is the Rename command keyboard shortcut. Dog-ear this page.

   After pressing F2, the file's current name is highlighted or selected — just like selected text in a word processor.

3. **Type a new name or edit the current name.**

4. **Press the Enter key to lock in the new name.**

You must still adhere to the filenaming rules, laid down in Chapter 20. Also, you cannot give the file (or folder) the name of a file that already exists in that folder.

✔ You can undo the name change by pressing the Ctrl+Z key combination. You must do it *immediately* after the booboo occurs in order for it to work.

✔ When you forget that F2 is the keyboard shortcut for the Rename command (and you've loaned this book to a friend who should have bought their own copy anyway), you can choose the Rename command from the Organize toolbar button's menu.

✔ Windows lets you rename a group of icons all at one time. It works the same as renaming a single icon, except that when the operation is completed, all selected icons have the same new name — plus a number suffix. For example, you select a group of icons and press the F2 key. When you type Picture as the group filename, each file in the group is given the name Picture (2), Picture (3), and so on, to the last file in the group — Picture (24), for instance.

Finding Lost Files

Losing track of your files in Windows is no big deal. Unlike losing your glasses or car keys, Windows sports a powerful Search command. Lost files are found almost instantly. Even the Amazing Kreskin couldn't find things faster!

Windows is littered with Search boxes. You'll find one on the Start button menu and in the upper right corner of any folder window. Just type the name of the file you're looking for and Press Enter. Quickly, you see a list of matching files, even files that contain the text you typed into the Search box. It's quite amazing.

Here are some searching tips:

✔ Start in a parent folder, such as your User Account folder or the Computer folder window. The search progresses "downward" through the folders.

✔ You can press Win+F to quickly summon a Search window.

✔ When you find yourself searching for the same stuff over and over, you can save the search. Click the Save Search button in the Search Results window. You can then redo the search by opening the saved search icon in the Saved Searches folder, found in your User Profile folder.

✔ This book's wee companion, *PC For Dummies Quick Reference* (Wiley) contains many more Search window options and variations for finding just about any file based on its type, size, or date.

That All-Important Safety Copy

The most precious things on your computer are your files: the things you create, your music, video, and pictures. Computers are subject to the same breakdowns and malfunctions as anything else made by man. (Though keep in mind that computers don't explode.) As such, it makes sense to keep a safety copy of your files. To do so, you employ a program called *Backup*.

Windows comes with a Backup program. To start it, open the Control Panel and choose the link Back Up Your Computer, found beneath the System and Security heading. Use the Backup and Restore window to configure and then run a backup for your computer.

Setting up Backup is pretty easy, though if you need more information, refer to my book *Troubleshooting Your PC For Dummies* (Wiley), which has more detailed instructions than I have room for here.

One of the best ways to use Backup is to get an external hard drive for your PC. It's cheap — often just $100 for a 500GB or larger-capacity drive. Use that external drive as your backup drive.

Chapter 23

Software Installed, Uninstalled, and Upgraded

● ●

In This Chapter

▶ Adding programs to your PC

▶ Starting programs

▶ Pinning programs

▶ Creating desktop shortcuts

▶ Removing software

▶ Updating and upgrading software

▶ Using Windows Update

● ●

A computer system is a thing to behold, but it's not worth a darn unless it has software inside the thing that actually gets something done. Those programs are the things that make the computer useful to you, make you productive, keep you entertained, or distract you to the point of obsession. This chapter covers the topic of computer programs.

Installing Software

Computer programs don't magically jump from the (mostly empty) software box into your PC. Nope, all software in your computer must be properly granted entry. The process, called *install* or *setup*, is something you'll do often as you use your computer and explore its possibilities.

Here are some generic steps for installing computer programs. These steps assume that you purchased a software program at the store or had it shipped to you. For information on installing software you download from the Internet, refer to Chapter 18.

1. **Open the software box.**

   This step may seem obvious, but I recommend that you try not to rip up the box. You should keep it intact, either for long-term storage or in case the store lets you return the software.

2. **Savor the industrial epoxy odor of the box's insides.**

3. **Scour the box for printed information.**

   Specifically, you want to find a Read Me sheet or *Getting Started* booklet.

   You may have a manual in the box. The manual is a joke. Gone are the days when computer software came with manuals. The manual is now "on the disc," in the form of a Help file, which isn't very helpful.

   If installation instructions are in the box, follow them.

4. **Locate the installation disc or discs.**

   When you have more than one disc, note in which order they're used; the discs should be numbered, and you start with the first disc.

5. **Insert the installation disc into the PC's optical drive.**

6. **Run the installation program.**

   If you're lucky, the installation program runs automatically when you insert the disc. Or, you see the AutoPlay dialog box, from which you can choose the Install or Setup command. Otherwise, obey these substeps:

   A. Open the Computer window.

   B. Right-click the optical drive's icon.

   C. Choose from the menu the command Install or Run Program from Your Media. If that command isn't available, choose the AutoPlay command.

7. **Obey the instructions on the screen.**

   Read the information carefully; sometimes they slip something important in there. My friend Jerry (his real name) just kept clicking the Next button rather than read the screen. He missed an important notice saying that an older version of the program would be erased. Uh-oh! Poor Jerry never got his old program back.

   You may also be hit with a User Account Control (UAC) warning here. If so, type the administrator password or click the Yes or Continue button to proceed.

   You have to agree to abide by the software license.

   The software may ask for a serial number. It can be found somewhere inside the box, in the manual or on a piece of paper.

   If asked to, replace one disc with another. This process may go on for some time.

8. **Eventually, you're done.**

   Wait for the Installation program to end. You see a message telling you whether the installation was successful.

9. **Close the Installation program window.**

10. **If prompted, restart Windows.**

11. **Start using the program!**

Put the installation discs back into the software box, and store the software box somewhere for long-term keeping.

See the next section for information on running your newly installed program.

 It takes time to learn new software: There's a learning curve — even for computer games. It's natural to be frustrated at first. That's okay; you're only human. Just keep trying and eventually you'll learn the program. Of course, buying a good book about the software is an excellent idea!

 ✔ You may find, in addition to the installation disc, other discs in the software box, bonus programs, supplements, and libraries of clip art. You don't need to install that stuff, if you don't want to.

 ✔ Many applications require some form of validation or registration, which means that you need to connect to the Internet to complete the installation process. For folks without an Internet connection, a phone number might be provided to help activate the product the old-fashioned, human way.

Running a Program

After the software gets into your PC, the next thing you do is Run That Program. As with other tasks in Windows, you have many different ways to run your programs, some of them actually useful. The following sections describe the necessary methods.

The Start button menu

All programs installed on your computer can be found on the Start button menu; specifically, in the All Programs submenu. To start the program hunt, click the All Programs button on the Start menu and then start sifting through the list, plus any submenus, to find your program.

The Start button menu also lists recently used programs on the left side of the menu, shown in Figure 23-1.

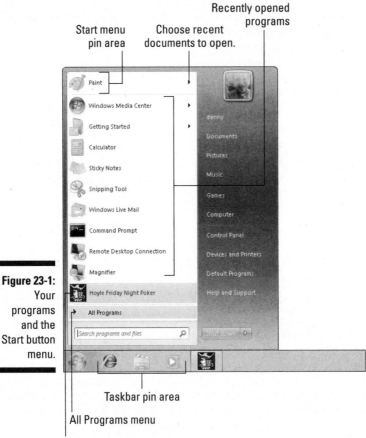

Start menu pin area

Choose recent documents to open.

Recently opened programs

Taskbar pin area

All Programs menu

Recently installed program

Figure 23-1: Your programs and the Start button menu.

New applications you install appear highlighted on the Start button menu (refer to Figure 23-1). You may even see the program's icon displayed at the bottom of the Start button menu, ready for action.

- ✔ Recently used programs appear on the Start button menu as you use those programs. You typically have to open a program twice for it to show up in that list.

- ✔ The triangle to the left of a recently used program can be clicked to display a submenu of recently opened files. To start the program and open a file, choose it from the submenu displayed.

The pin areas

It's handy to have a program always available right on the Start menu, such as the Paint program (refer to Figure 23-1). Programs that you want to quickly access can be *pinned* to the Start menu and then they'll always appear on the top of the list. Likewise, programs can be pinned to the taskbar. Either way, one click starts the program.

To add any program to the pin-on area, right-click the program's icon and choose the Pin to Start Menu command from the pop-up menu. For example, you can right-click any icon displayed on the Start button menu or on the All Programs menu.

Programs can also be pinned to the taskbar, such as the three icons shown earlier, in Figure 23-1. To pin a program to the taskbar, right-click the program's icon and choose the command Pin to Taskbar. (In older versions of Windows, the programs pinned to the taskbar were said to be part of the Quick Launch toolbar.)

The desktop shortcut icon

Another handy way to start a program is to open its icon on the desktop. The icon isn't the full-blown program. No, it's a *shortcut* icon, which references the real program. Still, by double-clicking the program's shortcut icon on the desktop, you start the program. It can be handy.

To place a shortcut icon to a program on the desktop, right-click the program's icon and choose the Send To⇨Desktop (Create Shortcut) command from the pop-up menu. The shortcut file is created, and its icon appears on the desktop. For example, you can right-click any program found on the All Programs menu to place a shortcut copy of that program's icon on the desktop.

Uninstalling Software

Programs installed on your computer must be properly uninstalled. You can't just delete the program or its folder. Fortunately, the uninstall procedure isn't complex. In fact, all computer applications anticipate being uninstalled someday, so an easy uninstall procedure is available. Here's how it works:

1. **Open the Control Panel.**

2. **Click the link Uninstall a Program, found beneath the Programs heading.**

   The Programs and Features window appears. It lists all software installed on your PC.

3. **Select the program you want to uninstall.**

4. **Click the Uninstall/Change button on the toolbar.**

5. **If prompted by a User Account Control, type the administrator password or click the Continue button.**

6. **Continue reading instructions on the screen to uninstall the program.**

   The uninstall directions vary from program to program, but eventually the program is removed.

Updating and Upgrading

It's a common saying in the computer industry that software is never done. In fact, if it weren't for managers, the programmers would never finish. Even when they do finish, things called bugs need to be fixed and people demand new features, which are added. The result is the *software update* or, more drastic, *software upgrade*.

What's the difference between an update and an upgrade? *Updates* are gradual and tiny. They repair, or *patch,* software you've already purchased. For example, an update may fix a bug or problem. An update can fine-tune some features. And, generally speaking, updates are free.

Upgrades, however, are complete revisions of programs. An upgrade presents a new release of the software, along with a version number. For example, the latest version of Microsoft Office is an upgrade, not an update. Also, upgrades cost money.

My advice: Update frequently. If the manufacturer offers a patch or a fix, install it as recommended. On the other hand, updates are necessary only when you desperately need the new features or modifications or when the upgrade addresses security issues.

- ✔ *Update:* A minor fix to some software you own. A patch. No charge.

- ✔ *Upgrade:* A new version of the program. You pay for it.

- ✔ Here's something else to keep in mind: If you're still using DoodleWriter 4.2 and everybody else is using DoodleWriter 6.1, you may have difficulty exchanging documents. After a while, newer versions of programs become incompatible with their older models. If so, you need to upgrade.

- ✔ In an office setting, everybody should be using the same software version. (Everybody doesn't have to be using the *latest* version, just the *same* version.)

Windows Update

I highly recommend that you keep your PC's operating system updated. This task requires regular communications between your computer and the Microsoft mothership. No need to fret: The scheduling happens automatically. If any new updates, or *patches,* are needed, they're automatically installed on your computer. You need to do nothing.

Well, you do need to ensure that you configured your PC to accept automatic updates by using the Windows Update service. Here's how:

1. **Open the Control Panel window.**

2. **Click the System and Security heading.**

3. **Click the link Turn Automatic Updating On or Off, beneath the Windows Update heading.**

   Ensure that updates are being checked regularly, on a schedule.

4. **Click the OK button if you made any changes.**

   You may need to type the administrator's password or click the Continue button to confirm your choice.

5. **Close the window.**

Windows updates your PC regularly. Occasionally, you may see a pop-up message from the notification area, shown in Figure 23-2, telling you about pending updates or informing you of updates that have just been installed.

Figure 23-2: Windows updates will be installed.

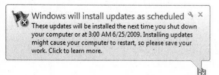

Windows will install updates as scheduled ⚑ ✕
These updates will be installed the next time you shut down your computer or at 3:00 AM 6/25/2009. Installing updates might cause your computer to restart, so please save your work. Click to learn more.

When you leave your PC on all the time, you may notice that Windows has restarted in the middle of the night, just after an update. That's okay: it's part of the update process.

"Should I upgrade Windows?"

Microsoft produces a new version of Windows about once every few years. As with previous Windows upgrades, the newer version offers better features and a different way of doing things than did the previous version. Even so, you don't have to upgrade to the newer version of Windows. In fact, I strongly recommend against it.

Windows is your PC's operating system. It's closely geared to the hardware in your computer. In fact, it has been so customized that replicating that specific customization, especially with a newer version of the operating system, is *very* difficult. That's why upgrading Windows causes lots of people problems, compatibility issues, and unnecessary headaches.

If you really want the new version of Windows, my advice is to buy a new computer with the new version of Windows preinstalled. That's the best way to do it.

Part V
Your Digital Life

The 5th Wave   By Rich Tennant

"Drive carefully, remember your lunch,
and always make a backup of your
directory tree before modifying
your hard disk partition file."

In this part . . .

Welcome to the digital life. Digital clocks quietly began the revolution years ago. Now, everything is digital: The pictures you take are digital. The movies you watch were made with digital cameras and watched on digital screens. Your music is stored digitally. You use digital phones. The games you play are digital. It's a digital world.

At the center of your digital life is the computer. It's the hub of all things digital, much of the basic stuff you do in life. The computer lets you manage your photos, watch or create movies, listen to your music, and basically run your 21st century life. This part of the book explains how it's done.

Chapter 24

Your Personal Disc Factory

. . . .

. . . .

*B*ehold the optical disc! It's your PC's removable media of choice. The computer eats optical discs, consuming them for their data, music, or video. Better still, your PC has the ability to create discs. Indeed, armed with a stack of recordable discs, you and your computer can become your own personal disc factory. This chapter tells you how.

✔ Creating an optical disc on your computer is known as *burning* a disc. It has nothing to do with fire.

✔ For information on creating a music CD, refer to Chapter 27.

✔ See Chapter 26 for information on creating a video DVD.

Disc Creation Overview

Making optical discs on your PC is super cinchy. You need an optical drive that can write to recordable optical media, which is pretty much standard PC hardware these days. Then you need Windows; the operating system has all the tools you need to burn an optical disc.

First, ensure that your PC came equipped with a recordable optical drive. You can tell by looking at the stickers or "tattoos" on the drive's faceplate. Or, you may see any of the abbreviations listed in Table 24-1.

If you need help identifying your PC's optical drive, see Chapter 9.

Second, you need software. That software is Windows, which recognizes blank optical media inserted into the recordable optical drive. Later sections in this chapter tell you what to do when Windows identifies a recordable optical disc.

Your PC may have also come with a third-party disc creation tool, such as the popular Nero program. You can use that program instead of Windows (it's easier to use), but this book covers only the Windows method of burning a disc.

Third, you need a recordable optical disc. This disc creation saga is perhaps the most confusing part. Thanks to the slow evolution of disc-burning technology, you can find a host of different recordable optical disc formats. Table 24-1 sorts things out for you.

Table 24-1	Recordable Optical Disc Formats
Format	*Description*
CD-R	The standard recordable CD format
CD-RW	A format in which the disc can be recorded just like a CD-R, though it can be completely erased and used again
DVD-R	The most popular DVD recordable format, compatible with computers and home movie DVD players
DVD+R	A DVD recordable format that records much faster than DVD-R but isn't as compatible with home movie DVD players
DVD-RW	The erasable version of the DVD-R format, where the disc can be completely erased and used again
DVD+RW	The erasable version of the DVD+R format
DVD R DL	A *dual-layer* version of the DVD-R format that holds twice as much data but can be read only in dual-layer optical drives
DVD RAM	Also known as RAM2; can be recorded to and erased similarly to the RW format but isn't as commonly used

The good news is that most optical drives support all the recordable disc formats. Only if you have an older PC does your optical drive not support some formats. Even then, you can easily add to the computer system an external optical drive that supports those formats. See Chapter 9.

- ✔ An optical drive with the Multi label on it can pretty much record *all* the various optical disc formats.

- ✔ Discs are cheap! I recommend buying them in 25-, 50-, or 100-disc packs.

- ✔ You may not think that the discs are cheap, but when CD-Rs first came out, they were about $5 a pop. Recordable DVDs were originally $15 each!

- ✔ Some CD-Rs are labeled specifically for music. These music CD-Rs are of a lower quality than data CD-Rs because music doesn't have the same accuracy demands as data storage.

- ✔ The RW format discs are more expensive than the other, write-once disc formats.

Make a Data Disc

As long as you have the proper optical drive in your PC, plenty of recordable discs, and Windows, you can make your own data discs. This section tells you how.

What to put on the disc?

The burning burning-question is "What kind of data should I put on an optical disc?" Obviously, you don't want to use an optical disc, such as a removable hard drive. That's because information can be written to the disc only once. When it's full, it's done! An RW disk can be erased and you can start over, but that's not a practical replacement for hard drive storage. Therefore, I recommend using optical discs for archiving and data transfer.

Archiving is just a fancy word for storage. For example, when I'm done writing a book, I archive all the text documents, figures, pictures, — even

my contract — on a disc. Even if the files don't fill up the disc, that's okay; archiving isn't about maximizing storage potential. With the files safely saved on the disc, I have a secondary backup copy that I can use if I need to. The duplicate files are always there, handy on the archive disc.

Discs are also excellent for transferring information between computers, which is why new software comes on a disc. I use discs to send files in the mail that are too big to send by e-mail. (How big? Anything larger than 10MB is too big for e-mail.)

Preparing the disc for use

As with all removable media, you begin your disc creation journey with a recordable disc in one hand and your computer at the ready. Start here:

1. **Put the recordable disc into the drive.**

   Windows is smart enough to recognize the disc and asks you what to do with it by using the AutoPlay dialog box, as shown in Figure 24-1.

Figure 24-1: A blank disc is detected.

If you don't see anything displayed, the disc may be defective. Fetch another. If you still don't see anything, your PC may not have a record-able optical drive.

2. **Select the option Burn Files to Disc.**

   The Burn a Disc dialog box shows up.

3. **Type a name for the disc.**

   Name the disc based on its contents. Or, you can just accept the current date, which is already shown in the dialog box.

4. **Choose a formatting option.**

   In Windows Vista, you'll need to first click the Show Formatting Options button to reveal the formatting option choices. Two formats are used by Windows:

   Like a USB Flash Drive, or Live File System: In this format, information is written to the disc immediately. You can eject the disc, use it in another computer, and then reinsert the disc and keep adding files to it. You can use the disc until it's full.

With A CD/DVD Player, or Mastered: This format collects files to be written to the disc, storing them on the PC's hard drive. All waiting files are written to the disc at one time. Then the disc is *closed*, and further writing to the disc is prevented.

Of the two formats, the Mastered format is more compatible with other optical drives, and it makes the most efficient use of disc space. The USB Flash Drive/Live File System, however, works more like traditional removable media in a PC.

5. **Click the Next button.**

For the USB Flash Drive/Live File System, Windows formats the disc, preparing it for use.

The CD/DVD Player/Mastered format doesn't require preparation at this time; the disc isn't officially prepared for use until you eject it.

6. **Start using the disc.**

The disc is *mounted* into your PC's permanent storage system. Windows may display an AutoPlay dialog box for the disc, or it might automatically open the disc's root folder window. The optical drive's icon now appears in the Computer window. The disc is ready for use.

Working with a USB Flash Drive/ Live File Format disc

After setting up a USB Flash Drive/Live File Format recordable disc, discussed in the preceding section, you can work with it just like you work with any storage media: Copy files to the disc's window, create folders, and manage files as you normally do. For a disc, information is written to the disc as soon as you copy it over. That's why it's the *Live* File System — your interaction with the disc is pretty much real-time.

When you're ready, you can eject the disc. Windows alerts you that the disc is being prepared so that other PCs can access the information. Then the disc is ejected. You can then use the disc on another PC or reinsert it into your computer. You can continue to burn files to the disc until it's full.

You can erase, rename, or move a file after it has been burned to a USB Flash Drive/Live File System disc, but doing so wastes disc space. If possible, try to do your file manipulations *before* you copy the files to the disc.

Working with a CD/DVD Player/Mastered disc

You work with a CD/DVD Player, or Mastered, disc just as you would work with any media in Windows. Files can be copied, folders can be created, and so on. The only difference you see is that the files you put on the disc appear with a download flag on their icon, as shown in the margin. The icon also appears "ghostly" or faint.

The reason for the faint download icons is that nothing is actually written until the disc is ejected. Feel free to manage the icons at any time with no fear of it's affecting anything on the disc.

When you're ready to burn the disc, follow these steps:

1. **Open the Computer window.**

2. **Open the optical drive's icon.**

   You see the files and folders waiting to be burned to the disc.

3. **Click the Burn to Disc toolbar button.**

   The Burn to Disc dialog box appears.

4. **Enter a name for the disc.**

5. **Set a recording speed.**

   The recording speed preselected for you is, doubtless, okay — though one school of thought says that choosing the *slowest* recording speed ensures a reliable disc-writing session. Who knows?

6. **Click the Next button.**

   The files are burned to the disc.

   The disc is ejected automatically when it's done.

7. **Remove the disc from the drive.**

8. **Click the Finish button to close the Burn To Disc dialog box.**

With a Mastered disc, you cannot write any additional information to the disc after it's been burned.

Using the Burn button

Burn

Folder windows sport a Burn toolbar button, which can be used to quickly burn the folder's contents to an optical disc. After clicking the Burn button, the PC pops open the optical drive and a dialog box prompts you to insert a writable disc into the drive. Do so.

After inserting the disc, you see the Burn a Disc dialog box, described in the section "Preparing the disc for use," earlier in this chapter. Choose a disc file format. Windows automatically copies the files from the folder (the one where you clicked the Burn button) to the disc.

If you choose the CD/DVD Player or Mastered format, you must obey the directions from the preceding section to close and burn the disc, making it ready for use.

Erasing an RW disc

RW discs are prepared and worked with just like regular recordable discs. All information in this chapter applies to both formats. The main difference is the addition of a toolbar button that lets you reformat the RW disc and start over.

| Erase this disc | To reformat the RW disc, open the Computer window and click to select the optical drive. The Erase This Disc toolbar button appears; click that button. Follow the directions on the screen to completely erase the disc and start over.

- ✔ RW discs are different from other recordable discs. It says *RW* on the label, and the disc is more expensive, which is most obvious when you try to taste it.

- ✔ RW discs may not be readable in all optical drives. If you want to create a CD with the widest possible use, burn a CD-R rather than a CD-RW disc. For a DVD, use the DVD-R format.

- ✔ It's often said that RW discs are best used for backing up data because they can be reused over and over. However, on a disc-per-disc basis, it's cheaper to use non-RW discs instead. And, for the sake of convenience, I recommend using an external hard drive rather than optical discs to backup your stuff. See Chapter 22.

Labeling the disc

I highly recommend labeling all removable media, from recordable discs to memory cards. Even if you name things only A or B, that's fine because it helps you keep track of the discs.

- ✔ Label your disc *after* it's been written to. That way, you don't waste time labeling what could potentially be a bad disc (one that you would throw away).

✔ I use a Sharpie to write on the disc. Write on the label side; the other side is the one containing your important data. You don't want to write on that.

✔ Do not use a sticky label on your recordable optical disc. Only if the label specifically says that it's chemically safe for a recordable disc should you use it. Otherwise, the chemicals in the sticky label may damage the disc and render the information that's written to it unreadable after only a few months.

Disposing of a disc

Sure, you can just toss a disc into the trash. That's okay — in most places. Some communities classify an optical disc as hazardous, and it must be properly disposed of or sent off for recycling.

If you don't want anyone else to read the disc, you probably don't want to throw it away intact. The best solution is to destroy the disc by getting a paper shredder that can also handle crunching optical discs.

Some folks say that you can effectively erase a disc by putting it in a microwave oven for a few seconds. I don't know whether I trust or recommend that method. And, don't burn a disc; its fumes are toxic.

Chapter 25

The Whole Digital Photography Thing

*B*ack up! Move left! Move right! Roger, you're not smiling! Okay, every-one, say "Cheese!" Such is the ritual of taking the traditional photo-graph. Captured on film and developed using a chimerical process, the picture would take a while to return to you from "the developer." Only then would you discover that, once more, Grandma had cut off the top of Uncle Ed's head in the picture. But never mind: It was a memory.

Today's images are captured digitally. After the shutter clicks, a quick check of the camera confirms whether the image looks okay. If not, you can delete that image and instantly snap another one. The outfit known as "the developer" has been replaced by the personal computer, which stores, organizes, and prints your photos and lets you fling them far and wide by using e-mail or a social net-working Web site. Welcome to the 21st century version of photography.

The Digital Camera

Snapping digital pictures is easy. A digital camera is as simple to operate as the Brownie cameras of a century ago. No, the problem with a digital camera is how to move those images from the camera into the PC. After they're in the computer, you can store the pictures, edit, print, or send them off hither and thither on the Internet. But before all that happens, the images must get inside the PC. This section explains how that's done.

Connecting a digital camera

The pictures you take with a digital camera are stored on a mass storage device, exactly the same way as information is stored on your computer. To move those images from the camera into the computer, you have to make both the camera and the computer talk with each other. You have two ways to do that:

 ✔ Connect the camera to the PC with a cable. The cable came with your digital camera.

 ✔ Remove the media card from the camera and plug it into the PC's console.

Either way, the result is that the storage media in the camera, where the digital images are stored, becomes part of the PC's storage system. That makes it easy for you to copy the pictures from the camera's media to the PC's media.

 ✔ You don't have to use the PC to print digital images. Many photo printers can read memory cards from digital cameras and print the images directly. See Chapter 12 for more information on printers.

 ✔ Another non-PC option is to drop off the digital camera's memory card at "the developer." These days, the developer prints the pictures for you "in about an hour" and probably gives you an optical disc copy of the images to sweeten the deal.

 ✔ See Chapter 9 for more information on the media cards used by digital cameras.

Importing images

When you connect a digital camera, or insert its media card into your PC console, you might see an AutoPlay dialog box, similar to the one shown in Figure 25-1. The AutoPlay dialog box is designed to assist you with importing the images from the camera into the PC.

Figure 25-1:
Importing images from a memory card.

If you don't see the AutoPlay dialog box, follow these steps:

1. **Open the Computer window.**

   Choose the Computer command from the Start button menu. (It's My Computer in Windows XP.)

2. **Right-click the icon representing the digital camera's media card.**

3. **Choose the Open AutoPlay command from the pop-up menu.**

The AutoPlay dialog box lists several options for dealing with the digital camera's images. My advice is to choose the option Import Pictures and Videos. Follow these steps:

1. **From the AutoPlay dialog box, choose the option Import Pictures and Videos.**

   A dialog box appears in the lower right corner of the screen, monitoring the input progress.

2. **Type a *tag* to identify the images.**

   The tag can be a name, an event, a place, or the subject matter of the images. Tags help you organize your images.

3. **Click the Import button.**

When the import is complete, a window appears and shows you the pictures, which are now saved on your PC's mass storage system. You can now view, edit, print, or share the images.

> ✔ For older versions of Windows, choose the command Import Pictures Using Windows. The pictures are imported using the Windows Photo Gallery program, which is a handy tool for managing digital images.

> ✔ If you've installed a photo management program on your PC, choose that program's option from the AutoPlay dialog box rather than the Import Pictures and Videos option.

> ✔ The imported images are stored on the main hard drive, in the Pictures or My Pictures folder. See the section "Storing pictures in Windows" for information on the Pictures folder.

> ✔ After you import the images, feel free to remove the originals from the digital camera's media card. Erase or reformat the media card using the digital camera's control panel. That way, you have plenty of room to store a new batch of pictures.

The Scanner

Your prehistoric, paper photographs and slides aren't barred from entering the digital realm. You can use a gizmo called a *scanner* to take those flat pictures and transform them into digital images, stored right inside your PC. This section explains how it works.

Introducing the scanner

A scanner works like a combination photocopier and digital camera. You place something flat, like a photograph or transparency, in the scanner — just like it's a photocopier. Press a button or run a program and the image is scanned and then beamed into the computer, ready for you to save, edit, print, or store.

Figure 25-2 illustrates the typical computer scanner, not because you may be unfamiliar with what it looks like, but more because I really like the illustration.

Most scanners are thin (like the model in the picture), use the USB interface, and have handy function buttons that let you immediately scan, copy, fax, e-mail, or read text from whatever item is placed on the scanner glass.

> ✔ The scanner must have something called a *transparency adapter* to be able to scan slides and film negatives.

> ✔ The scanner appears in the Devices and Printers window in Windows 7, along with other gizmos attached to your PC. Choose Devices and Printers from the Start button menu to see the scanner's icon.

✔ Those buttons on the scanner can be handy. For instance, I use the Copy button all the time to make quick copies. (My office doesn't have a photocopier.) The only reservation I have about the buttons is that the tiny icons by the buttons are confusing; if need be, use a Sharpie and write down the button's function in English.

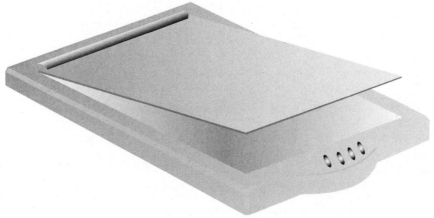

Figure 25-2:
A typical
scanner.

Scanning an image

Scanners come with special software that helps you scan an image and transfer it into the PC. The scanner might also come with some primitive form of image editing software as well. My advice is to use the software that came with the scanner, which is often your best choice.

If you don't have any scanner software, you can use Windows to scan an image. Follow these steps:

1. **Turn the scanner on, if necessary.**

2. **Choose Devices and Printers from the Start button menu to display the Devices and Printers window.**

3. **Open the scanner's icon in the Devices and Printers window.**

   Double-click the scanner's icon to open it. A New Scan dialog box appears, looking similar to the one shown in Figure 25-3.

4. **Place the material to be scanned into the scanner, just as though you were using a photocopier.**

Set resolution

Set file type

Portion of image to scan

Preview area

Drag here to resize scan area.

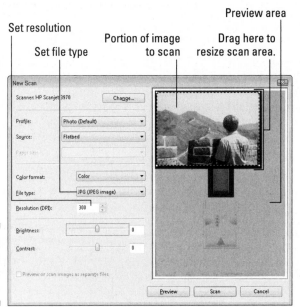

Figure 25-3:
Making a
real picture
digital.

5. **Click the Preview button.**

The scanner warms up and shows you a preview of the pictures in the scanner, as shown in Figure 25-3.

6. **Adjust the scanning rectangle so that it encloses only the part of the image you want scanned.**

Drag the corners of the rectangle by using the mouse to resize it. Only the portion of the preview inside the rectangle is scanned as an image and stored on the computer.

7. **Click the Scan button.**

The scanner reads the image, turning it into digital information to be stored in your PC.

8. **Type a tag for the images.**

The *tag* is a general description for all the images. Use short, descriptive text, such as Summer 2010 Vacation, Meteorite Hit, or Chiam's Bris.

9. **Click the Import button.**

The image is saved to the PC's storage system and displayed in a folder window.

10. **Close the folder window.**

11. **Repeat steps 4 through 10 to scan additional images.**

Scanners that read documents

One of the software packages that came with the scanner is probably OCR software, where OCR stands for *optical character recognition*. This type of program scans a text document (printed material) and turns the scanned image into editable text.

The OCR scan procedure works just like scanning an image: You place the document in the scanner and then run the OCR software to start a new scan. The OCR software "reads" the document being scanned and saves the information as a text file. You can then edit the text file, print it, and so on. It's not perfect, but using OCR software is better than having to sit and type text.

After you become comfortable with scanning, you can add some extra steps. For example, you can set the image resolution, brightness, and contrast options, and even choose another source for scanning, such as the scanner's transparency adapter.

✔ When you have lots of images to scan, such as a lifetime of vacation slides, consider sending the slides to a scanning service. No, this option isn't cheap, but consider what your time is worth and how much you need to digitize your pictures.

✔ Information about graphics file types and image resolution is found elsewhere in this chapter. Bone up on that stuff to help you make the best scans possible.

✔ See Chapter 21 for more information on folders.

Picture Files

After an image makes the journey from your digital camera to the computer, it becomes a *file* on your PC's mass storage system. Specifically, it becomes a *picture* file. Windows allows you to do quite a few things with picture files, and you should know a few picture-file concepts if you plan to get the most from your PC as the center of your digital photography universe. This section explains that stuff.

✔ To work with picture files, you need an image editing program, something like Photoshop Elements or another program whose name I can't think of now. Those programs let you perform image editing, tasks such as cropping, resizing, rotating, removing red-eye, and other fancy tricks.

> ✔ A good photo management program to start with is Windows Photo Gallery. It comes prepackaged with Windows Vista. To download a free copy for other versions of Windows, visit this Web page:
>
> `http://download.live.com/photogallery`
>
> ✔ See Chapter 20 for more information on the topic of computer files.

Storing pictures in Windows

Windows organizes your pictures into the Pictures folder. Any images you import or scan into the PC using Windows eventually end up in that location.

To view the Pictures folder, choose the Pictures command from the Start button menu. The Pictures folder window appears, shown in Figure 25-4. You see icons there representing images stored on your PC, including folder icons that are used to organize the pictures by date.

Images (large icons)

Folders containing more images

Quick link to Pictures folder

View button menu thing

Figure 25-4: Images stored in the Pictures folder.

See the next section for what you can do with pictures in the Pictures folder or any other folder window.

> ✔ The Pictures folder is also referred to as My Pictures in some versions of Windows.
>
> ✔ Also see Chapter 21 for more information on how folders are used to organize your stuff in Windows.

Picture file formats

Just as there are different flavors of ice cream, there are different flavors of picture files on your PC. Not that you should care: Your computer can open, display, and even edit just about any old picture file format. The problem comes when you deal with someone who isn't as PC-flexible as you. In that case, it helps to know a modicum of information about the PC picture file formats.

A file format is known by its filename extension, which is the very last part of a filename. The filename extension doesn't show up in Windows unless you recajigger Windows to make it show up. See Chapter 20. (I recommend that you configure Windows to display the extensions.)

Here are the popular picture file formats:

JPG: Pronounced "jay peg," this common image file format is used by just about every digital camera and all over the Internet. JPG is also written as JPEG.

PNG: Pronounced "ping," this picture format is also quite common, but not as popular as JPG.

TIFF: This picture file format is good for keeping detailed images, such as photos you want to edit or enlarge, or images you want to put in documents. It isn't a good format for e-mail or the Internet because, unlike JPG and PNG, the TIFF picture files are very large. TIFF can also be written TIF.

BMP: The Windows Bitmap file format is used primarily in Windows — specifically, in the Paint program. BMP files are too large for e-mail or the Internet and, honestly, aren't good for storing digital photographs.

CRW: Camera Raw format is used in an uncompressed, unmodified image taken at high resolutions in certain high-end digital cameras. It's preferred for professional photographers and people who need the purest, rawest images possible. Unless you're doing professional work, you can avoid this format.

GIF: Pronounced "jif," this older, simple format is for storing simple color images. It was (and still is) popular on the Internet because the file size is small, but the files don't contain enough information to make them worthy of modern digital imaging.

Many, many other graphics file formats are out there, including those specific to various photo editing programs. If I were to give you a bottom line bit of advice, it would be to keep and save all your digital images in either the JPG or PNG file format.

Viewing pictures in Windows

Images are viewed automatically in Windows simply by setting the proper icon size. In a folder window, use the View menu to choose Large Icons or Extra Large Icons. Refer to Figure 25-4 to see where to find the View menu. In that Figure, icons are shown using Large Icons view.

A second way to view a picture icon is to preview it: Click once to select the icon, and then click the Preview button that appears on the toolbar.

✔ In Windows Vista, the View menu is titled Views and found on the left side of the menu bar.

✔ You can select more than one image icon to preview several icons at a time in a special preview window. Click the left- or right-arrow buttons in that window to page through your images.

✔ To view all files in a folder, click the Slide Show button on the toolbar. That runs the Slideshow program and displays the images one after another.

✔ You can also select a specific picture folder to use as a screen saver. The image files in that folder appear on the display whenever the screen saver is activated. See Chapter 10 for more information on screen savers. The name of the Picture Folder screen saver is Photos.

✔ Windows XP doesn't have an icon preview function: Double-click a picture icon to open and view it.

Changing picture file formats

Occasionally, you need to convert an image from one picture file type to another. For example, you may have been silly and saved your digital camera images as TIFF files. Although that file format has its purposes, and TIFF images are by no means shoddy, they're just *too freakin' huge* to send as e-mail attachments. Instead, you're better off converting the TIFF image to JPG. Here's how I do it:

1. **Open the folder window containing the image file icon.**

   See Chapter 21 for information on folders.

2. **Click to select the image icon.**

3. **Click the menu button to the right of the Preview button on the toolbar.**

   The menu button looks like a downward-pointing triangle.

4. **Choose Paint from the Preview button's menu.**

   The image opens in the Paint program. That's where you use the Save As command to save the image using a new file type.

   The Paint program in Windows 7 is different from previous versions of Windows, so accessing the menus is done differently. Rather than struggle to describe the things you see on the screen, I have you use keyboard shortcuts.

5. **Press the F10 key to activate the menu shortcuts.**

6. **Press F and then V to access the file types submenu.**

7. **Press P to save the image as a PNG file or J to save it as a JPG.**

   A Save As dialog box appears, where you can give the file a new name or save it in a new location on the PC's storage system.

8. **Type a new filename (optional).**

9. **Click the Save button.**

   The image is now saved with a new picture file format.

10. **Close the Paint program's window.**

If you have a more sophisticated graphics program, like Photoshop Elements, you can use it, rather than Paint, to make the conversion. Or, you can use any popular image conversion program, none of which I can name off the top of my head.

In older versions of Windows Paint, choose the File⇨Save As command to summon the Save As dialog box. Then use the Save as Type drop-down list to choose the picture file type.

Image Resolution

When you deal with digital images, the topic of resolution rears its ugly head. It isn't an area you need to know about, but by understanding it, you can better deal with issues such as big images on the screen or images that look ugly when they're enlarged.

Resolution deals with dots — specifically, the number of *dots per inch*, or *dpi*. Each dot represents the smallest part of an image, a teeny splotch of color. It comes into play in two areas: when an image is created and when an image is reproduced.

Setting resolution

An image's resolution is set when that image is created. You set resolution when you set up your digital camera, when you scan an image, or when you create an image from scratch using a painting program.

Resolution determines how much detail, or visual information, the image contains. So, an image set at 400 dpi has four times the detail of an image created at 100 dpi. More dots per inch means greater resolution, more information, more detail.

Though it might seem that setting the highest possible resolution is always best, that's not always the case. Keep reading in the next section.

Choosing the best resolution

Resolution plays its most important role when an image is output. Images can end up on the computer monitor or on a printer or simply stored for future use. To set the proper resolution, it helps to know where the image ends up.

For example, a PC monitor has a resolution of 96 dpi. If you scan a 4 x 6 photograph at 100 dpi and then display that image on the PC's monitor, it appears at nearly exactly its original size and detail. That's because the input and output resolutions are nearly identical.

If you were to scan the same photograph (4 x 6) at 200 dpi, it would contain twice the information and detail as the same image scanned at 100 dpi. When displayed on a computer monitor, the image would appear twice as large. That's because the image's 200 dpi is more than twice the 96 dpi of the monitor.

A printer's resolution can often be 300 dpi or 600 dpi. An image created at 100 dpi prints at one-third its original size when the printer uses 300 dpi output resolution. To properly render an image at its "real" size on a printer, it helps to create that image at the printer's output resolution, 300 dpi or 600 dpi — or even higher.

Bottom line: Low resolutions are fine for the Internet. For printing your digital photographs, choose a higher resolution. For enlarging photographs, choose the highest resolution possible.

✔ To produce the best results, you must set an image's *original* resolution based on its eventual output.

✔ Though you can resize an image to make its resolution higher, the result isn't as good as setting it when the image is created; the image becomes jagged and boxy looking. Bottom line: You cannot create more detail where none exists.

✔ The 100 dpi resolution is also known as *Web resolution* in many graphics applications and as a setting on various digital cameras.

Chapter 26

Video on the PC

*I*t's not that odd to consider that a computer can be used to watch videos or television. Way back in the early days, prehistoric computers traditionally used TV sets as their monitors. I remember programming for hours watching a TV set hooked up to a Commodore 64, and then all the money I spent on "artificial tears" to service my dried, fuzzed-out eyeballs. Man, those were the days.

Watching video on your PC today isn't that unusual. As part of its job as the hub of your 21st century digital life, the computer is home to the videos you watch on the Internet, videos you create, and even good old-fashioned television. It's called video on the PC, the subject of this chapter.

PC Movies

Forget jamming that Super 8 cartridge into the camera or hanging a pale bed sheet on a wall: Today's home movies are all digital. They begin their life in a digital camera, are stored on digital media cards, and eventually wind up on the computer. They're shared via the Internet. Doing all that stuff is as easy as ever, thanks to the power of the computer and the information in this section.

Storing video in Windows

A special place exists in your PC's storage system for video. It's the Videos or My Videos folder. That's the location where any videos you add to the computer are saved. Here's how to display the contents of that folder:

1. **Click the Start button to pop up the Start button menu.**

2. **Choose your account name from the Start button menu.**

   The account name should be the top item on the right side of the Start button menu. Choosing your account name displays your account's home folder, which is given the nerdy name User Profile.

3. **Double-click to open the folder named either My Videos or Videos.**

   The contents of the folder are displayed.

The folder lists video files available on your computer's storage system. The files are shown as icons, and even more video files may be available in folders within the main Video or My Video folder.

Windows comes with sample videos, and you may find them in the Videos or My Videos folder. Don't fret if the folder is empty; you can easily create your own videos.

- ✔ The folder is named My Videos in Windows 7 and Windows XP. It's named Videos in Windows Vista.

- ✔ Videos are also stored in the Videos Library in Windows 7. See Chapter 21 for more information on libraries.

Viewing a video

Windows uses the Windows Media Player program to help you view videos. To see the video play on your PC, double-click the video's icon. The Windows Media Player program starts and shows you the video.

You can also view a video by inserting a movie DVD into your PC's optical drive. The DVD also plays in the Windows Media Player, appearing on the screen just as though you were watching it on TV.

Other video viewing programs are available, including Apple's popular QuickTime. These programs, rather than Windows Media Player, may display the videos. That's okay; all the programs are similar, showing the video on the screen. Control buttons are available for play, pause, stop, and so on, just like on a real-life video player.

Getting the video into your PC

Video creeps into your PC from a video camera. It can come in live, such as from a *Webcam* (a monitor-top camera used for video conferencing), or you can import images recorded in a digital video camera.

The Webcam: The simplest digital camera you can get for your PC is the desktop video camera, also referred to as a *Webcam*. Most of these cameras are fist-size, although often smaller, and they commonly attach to the top of the monitor. A USB cable makes the connection with the PC.

Video camera: For more traditional movie making, you'll probably use some type of digital (or video) camera. The object is to transfer the video from the camera into the PC. That's done by connecting the camera to the PC with a cable or removing the media card from the camera and sticking it into a media card reader on the console. When you do, follow these steps:

1. **In the AutoPlay dialog box, choose the option Import Pictures and Videos.**

   It's the same AutoPlay dialog box you see when you attach a digital camera or add a camera's media card to the system. (See Figure 25-1, over in Chapter 25.)

2. **Type a tag for the video (optional).**

   The tag is a short, descriptive bit of text that helps you search for the videos later. Good tags are *Mary's birthday*, *Zoo trip*, and *I think this might be a UFO.*

3. **Click the Import button.**

After the videos are imported, you see them displayed in a folder window. You can then mess with them as you please: Create a movie, send them as e-mail attachments, or upload them to the Internet, for example.

   ✔ No, you cannot save or import video from a movie DVD. Those films are copyrighted, and copying them from the DVD is restricted.

   ✔ Webcams are normally used for video chat, though the software that comes with the camera lets you save snippets of video to the PC's mass storage system. It's not Hollywood, but it works.

   ✔ See Chapter 25 for information on using digital cameras and how to import pictures from the camera into the PC.

   ✔ See Chapter 21 for information on folders in Windows.

   ✔ See the next section for information on creating videos.

✔ Video files are *huge!* They're not only the most complex type of files, but they also gobble up lotsa disk space. So:

✔ If you plan to collect a lot of video files on your PC, I highly recommend that you use a hefty, high-capacity (more than 300GB) external drive to store your video files, projects, and snippets. You can also configure most intermediate-to-advanced video-editing programs to use the external drive as a video scratch pad.

Editing video

Armed with a video camera, a PC, and the right software, you can soon become your own Cecil B. DeMille or a budding Steven Spielberg. The software takes your video files — or just snatches the movies right from the video camera — and lets you weave them into a major motion picture using the power of the computer.

Well, maybe not *major* motion picture, but enough to impress your friends.

The Windows Movie Maker program is a good place to start your film career. It comes free with Windows Vista, or you can download it free from the Internet for other versions of Windows:

`http://downloads.live.com/moviemaker`

Video file formats

As with anything stored on a computer, moving images are saved to disk as *files*. And, like other media files (pictures and sound), there exists a whole host of video file formats, all depending on which program saved the video file, which type of compression is being used, and other tedious details. Generally speaking, the following types of video files are popular in the computer world:

MOV: The MOV file, used by Apple's QuickTime player, can store not only videos but also audio information. MOV is quite popular on the Internet, although you need to obtain a free copy of QuickTime to view or hear MOV files on your PC: `www.apple.com/quicktime`.

MPEG: The Motion Pictures Experts Group is a general compression format for both video and audio.

WMV: The Windows Media Video format is the most popular video format used in Windows and pretty common on the Internet as well.

Other formats exist, of course, but these are the most common. Also see Chapter 20 for information on the filename extension, which is how you identify file types in Windows.

About that "codec" thing

When you deal with media on a computer, such as audio or video stored in a file, you often encounter the word *codec*. It's a combination of two words — *compressor* and *decompressor*. A codec works with compressed information stored in a media file so that you can be entertained or enlightened.

A variety of codecs are used to encode and decode media information. The problem with the variety is that your PC doesn't come with all the codecs needed for every type of media file. So, when you go to view a certain media file, you may see a message saying that a codec is unavailable or prompting you to visit a certain Web page to download a codec. And, that's where you can get into trouble.

My best advice is to be very cautious about installing codecs. Often, the bad guys disguise a malevolent program as a codec required to view a media file — typically, pornography. Installing that false codec is detrimental to your PC.

I'm not saying that all codecs are evil. Many are good and are required in order to view certain media files. But ensure that you obtain codecs only from reliable sources, such as brand-name Web sites or from Microsoft directly.

Using Windows Movie Maker is a topic for an entire book. Still, it's not as complex as other video production software, so you should get used to using it quickly.

- ✔ Refer to Chapter 18 for information on installing programs you download from the Internet, such as Windows Movie Maker.

- ✔ When your films are ready for the world, refer to Chapter 28 on how to share your videos on the Internet.

Your PC Is a TV

As with all computer activities, to watch television on your PC, you need a combination of hardware and software.

The software is called the Windows Media Center, which (lamentably) doesn't come with every version of Windows. But that's not all bad news; keep reading.

The hardware is a PC TV tuner. It's a gizmo that pumps the television signal into the computer. The TV tuner comes as an external device, or it can dwell on an expansion card installed inside the console. The good news is that nearly every piece of TV tuner hardware comes with its own software, so if your version of Windows lacks the Windows Media Center, you're not stuck and out of luck.

✔ There's a difference between Windows Media Player and Windows Media Center. Windows Media *Player* is an audio and music program. Windows Media *Center* does what Windows Media Player does but also works with TV, FM radio, pictures, and digital video.

✔ The TV tuner requires a television signal, which is provided by whichever cable or satellite TV service you subscribe to. Using the TV tuner with your PC doesn't add to the cost of your cable or satellite subscription, and there's no need to alert your provider or alarm anyone in any way about your using a TV tuner with your computer.

✔ Yes, forget about those expensive digital video recorders (DVR) and similar TV-recording gizmos. When you buy a TV tuner, you're getting the best that those devices have to offer, plus you pay only once to have a service that others pay for monthly.

✔ Some TV tuners are HDTV capable. Consider getting one if you have HDTV or digital cable in your area.

Connecting a TV tuner

The TV tuner accepts its input from a standard coaxial video cable. External tuners connect to the PC by using the USB port. Some TV tuners may have extra jacks for plugging in a TV or accessing FM radio. The feature list of these gizmos, as well as their prices, varies widely.

✔ Installing the TV tuner is a snap, although I still recommend that you consult the documentation that came with whichever TV tuner you're using.

✔ Perform any needed software setup per the directions that came with the TV tuner. Sometimes, the software must be installed before the hardware, sometimes afterward, sometimes it doesn't matter.

✔ After doing additional setup or running a configuration program (per the documentation that came with the TV tuner), you're ready to configure Windows Media Center, as described in the next section.

Configuring Windows Media Center

After connecting your PC to a TV tuner and connecting that TV tuner to your cable or satellite TV, you're ready for the software side of configuration. You do this by running the Windows Media Center for the first time.

Windows Media Center asks you a few questions about your TV tuner and your television setup, such as which cable company you're using and your location. It does this so that information about the cable TV schedule can be downloaded into the PC. The Media Center uses the TV schedule not only as a program guide but also to assist in the recording of programs off the air.

After the Media Center is configured, you can begin watching TV on your PC.

Watching television

Feeling the urge to watch television on your computer is satisfied by simply running the Windows Media Center program: From the Start button menu, choose All Programs⇨Windows Media Center.

The Media Center sports a simple interface, which scrolls up and down for major media categories and then left to right for subcategories. The software is designed to be easily viewed on a TV set and manipulated using a television remote.

To watch television, choose the Live TV subcategory under the TV heading. Or, you can check the current broadcast schedule by choosing the Guide subcategory.

Here are some tips and suggestions to boost the power of your TV watching:

✔ Change the channel by typing a number on the keyboard. You don't need to press Enter; just type the number.

✔ Right-click the screen to see a special pop-up menu listing various options for whatever you're doing.

✔ Right-click and choose Program Info to see more information about the program you're watching.

✔ If you miss the start of the show and want to see it again, right-click the screen and choose Program Info and then, from the next menu, choose Other Showings.

✔ Moving the mouse redisplays the recording and play controls, as shown in Figure 26-1.

✔ To pause live TV, move the mouse to display the recording and play controls and click the Pause button. Click the Play button to resume, or click the Fast Forward button to catch up with real time.

Windows Media Center main menu

Full screen   What's on television

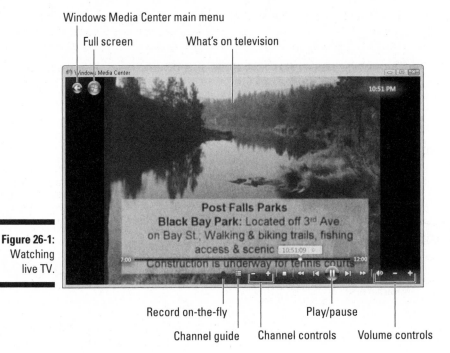

Figure 26-1:
Watching
live TV.

Record on-the-fly   Play/pause

Channel guide   Channel controls   Volume controls

Recording television

You can easily record anything you see on TV in the Windows Media Center. Recordings can be made on the fly, or you can schedule a recording.

To record on the fly, simply click the Record button (refer to Figure 26-1) while you're watching live TV. To stop recording, click the Record button again.

To schedule a recording, you can use the Guide: Choose the Guide subcategory from the TV category. Click to select a show you want to record and then click the Record button. The program listed in the guide then sports a red Record dot, which is your clue that a program has been scheduled for recording.

✔ Recorded TV is, logically, kept in the Recorded TV subcategory under TV + Movies in the Windows Media Center. See the next section.

✔ Some channels feature "restricted content." The broadcaster doesn't allow you to view (or record) the information on that channel. It isn't a parental-control issue, but rather a copyright issue with the broadcaster.

✔ You can record a series so that every time a show is broadcast, it's recorded. Click a show title in the guide to see more details, and then click the Record Series button to set things up.

✔ Recording television consumes a *ton* of storage space. Be sure to read the section "Purging recorded TV," at the end of this chapter, before it's too late!

Watching recorded TV

The Media Center organizes the TV shows you record, as well as information about upcoming recordings, in the Recorded TV subcategory, under TV. Already recorded programs are listed from left to right: Point the mouse at a recording to highlight it and see more information; click a recording to see a menu from which you can choose Play to view the recording.

To view upcoming or scheduled recordings, click the View Scheduled item at the top of the Recorded TV area. The schedule appears as a list that you can sort by date, title, series, or history.

 One outstanding benefit of watching recorded TV is that you can skip the commercials. Click the Next Chapter button to skip ahead to the next break.

Burning a DVD from recorded TV

You can create a video DVD of the shows and programs you record. It's really cinchy, as long as your PC has a recordable DVD drive. Follow these steps:

1. **Insert a DVD-R disc into your PC's DVD drive.**

   I prefer DVD-R media over DVD+R because they're more compatible with home DVD players.

2. **Close the AutoPlay dialog box, if it appears.**

   Click the X button in the upper right corner of the AutoPlay dialog box.

3. **Open the Media Center.**

4. **Choose the TV category.**

5. **Choose the Recorded TV subcategory.**

6. **Click to select the show you want to burn to disc.**

7. **Choose the Actions item from the top of the program information area.**

8. **From the list of actions, choose Burn a CD/DVD.**

9. **Click the Yes button if you see a prompt warning about media play-back being stopped.**

10. **If you're prompted to choose a lower-quality to fit the show on the media, click Yes or OK to proceed.**

11. **Choose Video DVD to create a disc that can be played like any other video. Choose Data DVD for a disc that can be viewed only by a computer.**

12. **Click the Next button.**

13. **(Optional) Name the disk.**

    The program's recorded name is preselected for you.

14. **Click the Next button.**

15. **Click the Burn DVD button.**

16. **Click Yes to confirm.**

17. **Wait while the disc is created.**

    (Optional) Click the OK button to go off and do other things with your PC while the disc is being created. Note that some discs take an awfully long time to burn.

18. **Remove the disc from the PC.**

    Burned discs are automatically ejected.

19. **Click the Burn button to create a duplicate disc, or click Done and you're finished.**

I recommend labeling the disc. I use a Sharpie and write the program name, the time, and the date I made the disc. Then I put the disc into a special disc envelope for long-term keeping.

After burning the disc, consider removing the program from the Recorded TV library. That way, you have more storage space on your PC for other information.

✔ The program may not fit on a disc. If so, the Media Center tells you so. In that case, you cannot make a DVD, but you can still view the recorded show on your PC.

✔ You can find disc envelopes at any office supply store.

✔ The DVD you create is for your own purposes only. You cannot make additional copies for friends, nor can you sell the discs you create.

✔ Also see Chapter 24 for information on creating data DVDs.

Purging recorded TV

Yes, video on your PC is one of those things that gobbles up storage space like a plague of locusts. The Windows Media Center is aware of its voracious appetite: Most programs you record stick around as long as you have room for them. So, the more you record, the less you keep.

The best way to keep a program you've recorded is to make a DVD, as described in the preceding section. Otherwise, you can manually purge older shows to make more room for future shows. The following activities assume that you're using the Media Center and have the Recorded TV area visible:

> ✔ **Remove a recorded show.** To remove a show you recorded already, click to select that show. From the menu that appears, choose Delete. Click the Yes button to confirm.

> ✔ **Remove a future recording.** To remove a show you've scheduled to record in the future, choose the View Scheduled item from the top of the Recorded TV window. Click to select the show. From the menu that appears, choose Do Not Record. The show is removed from the schedule list.

> ✔ **Remove a series.** To remove an individual episode from a series, follow the steps in the preceding paragraph. Otherwise, choose View Schedule and then click to select any episode of the series. Click the Cancel Series button and then Yes to confirm.

Unlike what NBC did to *Star Trek* in 1969, when you cancel a series, you merely direct Windows Media Center to not record the series; the series still airs on television.

Chapter 27

Music to Your Digital Ear

*T*o be a with-it denizen of the new century, you most likely want to use your PC as a hub of your musical existence. Thanks to its sophisticated audio hardware, playing music is a natural for the computer. Not only that, you can become your own deejay, create your own musical CDs, and even hear the computer talk. And, amazingly, you can talk back to the computer. It's all covered in this chapter.

Your PC Is Now Your Stereo

There's a reason why your home stereo tosses a jaundiced eye at the PC. Combined with a portable music player, the computer has essentially made the old stereo system obsolete for most people. Beyond the PC's digital audio hardware, the main culprit is the software program *Windows Media Player,* which lets you collect, play, and share your music. This section explains how it works.

Running Windows Media Player

Start the Windows Media Player by opening its program icon: Click the Start button, choose All Programs, and then click Windows Media Player.

Windows Media Player sports a simple and easy-to-use interface, as shown in Figure 27-1. Media are organized on the left. You can find your music listed under Library and get even more specific by choosing a category, such as Album or Songs.

Your music   Rip CD button appears here.   Create a music CD.

Playlists found here   Start a new playlist.

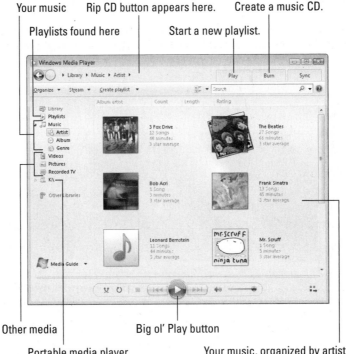

Figure 27-1:
Windows
Media
Player
library
window.

Other media

Portable media player

Big ol' Play button

Your music, organized by artist

To play a tune or listen to an album, click to select what you want to listen to and then click the big ol' Play button in the lower center of the Windows Media Player window.

✔ Windows comes preconfigured with an icon for the Windows Media Player right squat to the taskbar. In older versions of Windows, the icon is found on the Quick Launch bar.

✔ Windows Media Player isn't the only digital jukebox available for Windows. Another popular choice is Apple's iTunes (www.apple.com/itunes).

Inserting a musical CD

Windows Media Player automatically loads and plays any musical CD you insert into the PC's optical drive. The album just starts to play, displayed in the Windows Media Player window with perhaps a graphic of the album's cover art.

 To return to the Windows Media Player's library window (refer to Figure 27-1), click the Switch to Library button, found in the upper right corner of the window.

Collecting tunes

The most common way to get music into Windows Media Player is to *rip* that music from a CD you own. It's very easy and surprisingly quick. Follow these steps:

1. **Insert a musical CD into the PC's optical drive.**

   Windows Media Player automatically begins playing the CD.

   If you don't want to listen to the CD now, simply click the Play button in the window, which pauses the CD.

 2. **If necessary, click the Switch to Library button to display the Windows Media Player library view (refer to Figure 27-1).**

3. **Click the Rip CD button on the toolbar.**

   If you don't see the button, click the "show more" arrows to the right of the Organize button, and then choose the Rip CD command from the menu that's displayed.

   Windows Media Player begins copying every track from the CD, storing it on the computer. You see the progress updated in the window.

4. **Eject the disc.**

   You can repeat these steps with another disc to continue loading your musical library into the PC.

After the songs from the CD are ripped, they're available at any time in the Windows Media Player library.

Creating a playlist

Windows Media Player allows you to organize your music into *playlists*. For example, you can create your own party mix, driving music, or top hits. I listen to inspirational "brain music" when I write. It's all made by creating a playlist. Heed these directions:

1. **Click the Play tab, found in the main library window of Windows Media Player.**

   Refer to Figure 27-1 for the location of the Play tab.

   After clicking, you see a new, "Unsaved list" appear in a panel on the right side of the window.

2. **Drag the song from the music library to the pane on the right side of the window.**

3. **Repeat Step 2 to build your playlist, adding more songs.**

4. **Click the Save List toolbar button.**

5. **Type a name for the list.**

   Make it short and descriptive.

6. **Press Enter to lock in the new name.**

Completed playlists are listed under the Playlists heading in the music library. To listen to the songs collected in your playlist, select the playlist from the left side of the window and select the first song in the list. Click the Play button at the bottom of the window.

Taking your music with you

The notion of using a computer as a jukebox didn't take off until two things happened. First, on the software side, the simple CD-playing programs on the PC had to evolve into programs that could rip music from the CD and store it long-term in the computer. Second, and most important, portable music-playing devices had to evolve.

Portable music players, often called *MP3 players*, existed for some time before they truly caught on with buyers. The early models were bulky, didn't have long battery lives, and could store only a handful of tunes. With the dawn of the Apple iPod, MP3 players not only became sexy but also inter-faced well with computer-based jukebox software.

Windows Media Player works with a variety of portable music devices. The operation generally goes like this:

1. **Attach the portable MP3 player to your PC.**

   Normally, you use a USB cable.

2. **Open Windows Media Player, if necessary.**

   The AutoPlay dialog box may prompt you to open Windows Media Player when you initially attach the device, or you can manually start Windows Media Player.

   The portable gizmo appears in the library, specified as a new drive letter and icon on the left side of the Windows Media Player window (refer to Figure 27-1).

3. **Click the MP3 player's icon or drive letter in the library list.**

   The device should appear in the Sync tab panel on the right side of the window.

4. **Drag music to the Sync tab.**

   The music you drag is copied to the MP3 player.

5. **After the syncing is complete, disconnect the device.**

   You're ready for the open road!

Your portable MP3 thingy no doubt came with special software for managing music. Although these steps get you through basic music synchronizing using Windows Media Player, you might still need to use the MP3 player's extra software to help manage your music, remove tunes, or organize how the music is played.

   ✔ Ensure that your portable music doodad is properly charged. Check the batteries before you do any extensive syncing.

   ✔ *iPod* isn't a generic name applied to all MP3 players. Your PC can use an iPod, but the iPod is designed specifically to use the iTunes software.

Making your own music CDs

Creating a music CD in Windows Media Player is a snap. Pursue this procedure:

1. **Start Windows Media Player, if you haven't already done so.**

2. **Insert a CD-R into the drive.**

3. **Dismiss the AutoPlay dialog box, if it appears.**

4. **Click the Burn tab on the toolbar.**

5. **Drag individual songs or playlists to the Burn list pane.**

   The songs you place in the list pane are written, or *burned*, to the CD — and in the order you have placed them.

   Keep an eye on the "MB remaining" thermometer in the list pane. That indicator lets you know how full the disc will be; you don't want to add more music than the disc can hold.

6. **Click the Start Burn button.**

   Watch as the items are burned to the CD. The time required depends on the CD-R's burning speed (see Chapter 9) and on the number of songs you're burning to disc.

7. **Remove the disc, label it, and store it in a safe place.**

   The disc is automatically ejected when the burning is complete; you're done.

You can play the disc in any CD player or in any computer.

- ✔ See Chapter 24 for information on burning data CDs.

- ✔ Unlike with a data CD-R created in the Live File System, you cannot add more music to a CD-R after it has been burned once. (Again, see Chapter 24.)

The PC Can Talk and Listen

Don't get your hopes up. The days of talking casually to the computer are still *far* in the future. In fact, I doubt that we'll ever just bark orders at a PC; if *Star Trek* were to be redone today, I'm certain that Mr. Spock would have a computer keyboard and mouse at his workstation (along with a minimized game of *Spider Solitaire*). But I digress.

Yes, your PC can talk and listen. The following sections mull over the current state of speech on a PC.

Babbling Windows

Your computer is more than capable of speaking. An example in Windows is a program named Narrator, shown in Figure 27-2. Narrator is a tool designed to help visually impaired folk use the Windows interface. Narrator doesn't read text. In fact, it spends most of its time parroting whichever keys you press on the keyboard. That sounds nice, but after a while it just becomes irritating.

Figure 27-2:
Narrator is
of no help.

To run Narrator, from the Start menu choose All Programs➪Accessories➪
Ease of Access➪Narrator. The program starts up and immediately begins
telling you about the options available in its window. If you can tolerate that,
fine. Otherwise, click the Exit button and be done with it.

✔ A better tool in Windows for the visually impaired is the Magnifier,
which is also found in the All Programs➪Accessories➪Ease of Access
folder on the Start menu.

✔ Other programs that are available let the computer speak. They read
text much more smoothly than in Windows Narrator, and in different voices. Some programs can be found on the Internet, as described
in Chapter 18, and others may have been preinstalled on your PC or
included with its sound hardware.

Dictating to the PC

Blabbing to your PC isn't perfect, but it has come a long way from the
days when you had to spend hours (up to 20) to train the computer to
understand your voice. Man, that was tiring, not to mention the cotton-
mouth you'd get from talking for such long stretches! Things are better
today.

To get started with speech recognition in Windows, you need a microphone
or, preferably, a headset. The next stop is the Control Panel to set up the
microphone. Follow these steps:

1. **Open the Control Panel.**

2. **Click the Ease of Access heading.**

3. **Choose the link Start Speech Recognition.**

   The Setup Speech Recognition Wizard starts.

4. **Work your way through the wizard.**

Your microphone is set up, and you review some options and settings. Just keep clicking the Next button and you'll be fine.

5. **Train windows.**

Eventually, you run the speech recognition training tutorial, which teaches Windows to understand your utterances.

 When speech recognition is turned on, the Speech Recognition microphone window appears on the desktop, as shown in Figure 27-3. If you don't see the window, double-click the Speech Recognition icon in the notification area (shown in the margin). Right-clicking the Speech Recognition icon displays a handy and helpful pop-up menu of options.

Figure 27-3:
The Speech
Recognition
microphone
window.

✔ People who receive the most benefit from dictation software spend lots of time training their computers to understand them.

✔ Another popular dictation package is Dragon Naturally Speaking, at www.nuance.com.

Chapter 28

Sharing Your Life Online

· ·

In This Chapter

▶ Using Facebook

▶ Tweeting your thoughts

▶ Locating an image hosting Web site

▶ Putting your pictures on the Internet

▶ Signing up for YouTube

▶ Publishing videos

· ·

*O*nce upon a computer time, the rage was to create your own Web page. Doing so made you part of the high-tech in-crowd. You could use that Web page to tell the Internet what was going on with your life and perhaps even share some pictures. It was a technical thing, but still many people decided that they couldn't live their lives without their personal Web pages.

The days of needing your own Web page are long gone. Sure, you can still have one, but most likely all the things you planned to do with your own Web page are now possible by sharing your life online using social networking, as well as online photo- and video-sharing Web sites. How all that is done is this chapter's topic.

Social Networking

The bulk of what you would consider to be your digital life on the Internet — sharing your photos and thoughts and such — is handled by the variety of social networking sites available on the Internet. These sites allow you to share your electronic self with friends, family, and coworkers. The good news: They're free. Well, for now. This section highlights some of the stuff you can do with social networking Web sites.

Sharing your life on Facebook

The most popular social networking Web site is Facebook. It's a place where you can connect with friends, share your thoughts, send messages, post photographs and videos, play games, take quizzes, waste time, and generally keep up to date. Isn't that why everyone has a computer?

✔ The information in this section may change as Facebook occasionally changes over time.

✔ You can visit other social networking sites in addition to Facebook, such as the popular MySpace Web site, www.myspace.com, as well as the more business-oriented LinkedIn network, at www.linkedin.com.

Sign up

You start by signing up at the main Facebook page, www.facebook.com. Enter the required information, which includes an e-mail address. You have to confirm your e-mail address, which completes the sign-up process.

Find some friends

The next step is to look for people you know on Facebook. Based on your e-mail address, some friends may already be waiting to be added.

Facebook may also want to scan your e-mail account for matching e-mail addresses. It needs to know your e-mail password for this step. That's okay; nothing is being stolen. In fact, I recommend the e-mail scan to find friends because it really helps you get started.

After finding friends, you complete your profile and other settings. Don't fuss over anything; you can always come back later and choose a picture (or a new picture) and change other information about yourself.

Publish your thoughts

Most of the places you visit in Facebook let you type your thoughts using something called the *Publisher*. You see a text box saying, "What's on your mind?" or something similar. There you can type a wee bit of text or a missive or just mention what you're doing at the moment.

The stuff you publish can be viewed by all your Facebook friends. Likewise, you can see a news feed of all the comments your friends publish. It's a way to keep in touch, pontificate, or make people laugh.

You can also send your Facebook pals personal messages or write on their *Walls*. Clicking a friend's name or picture allows you to do that.

Upload a picture or video

To share photographs or videos with your Facebook pals, click the Profile heading, near the top of the Facebook window. You then see a Photos tab for your account; click it. Click the button to create a new photo album, and then start uploading pictures.

To upload the pictures, you use a Browsing-type dialog box to find the pictures on your computer. You then choose which ones to upload and click the Upload button to complete the process. Figure 28-1 illustrates how it's done.

Look for images in the My Pictures folder.   Send images to Facebook.

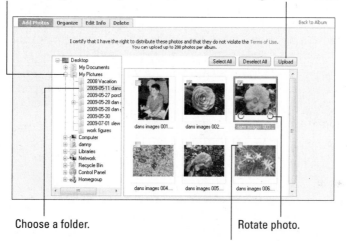

Figure 28-1:
Uploading
pictures to
Facebook.

Choose a folder.   Rotate photo.

Click to select a photo.

Uploading videos works pretty much the same way: Locate the Video tab in your Profile. (You might need to click the Plus tab to find the Video tab.) Then browse your PC for a video file to upload and share.

✔ You may have to install an ActiveX control in Internet Explorer to upload images. That's okay: Follow the directions on the screen.

✔ Uploading pictures is relatively simple using Facebook, if the images are already on your PC's storage system. See Chapter 25 for more information on digital photography.

✔ Also see the section "Share Your Photos Online," later in this chapter.

Tweeting your thoughts

Another quite popular social networking Web site is Twitter. On Twitter, you share your thoughts with others and follow their thoughts as well, where a "thought" is composed of 140 or fewer characters of text. Those little bursts of text are *tweets*.

Sign up for Twitter by visiting www.twitter.com. Configure your profile, and then I recommend using the e-mail scanning tool that Twitter provides to help you quickly locate some Twitter friends.

Twitter can be used to watch or follow others, to gather useful information or just keep tabs on your buddies. In addition to people, *things* tweet, such as weather stations, sports tickers, even robots on Mars. And, in addition to being a harmless distraction, Twitter is relied on by many people for news because various news organizations tweet as well.

Share Your Photos Online

There are a few things you need to do to share your digital images with the online universe. First you need to have the digital images to share. Second, you set up an account at a free site. Third, you post or upload your images to the site, which is a lot easier than it sounds. Finally, you let the world know how to find your images on the site, or you use the site to post your images in an e-mail message, on a blog, or elsewhere on the Internet.

Finding a free site

It's not a problem to find a free image-hosting Web site. There are dozens of them. Here are a handful I can recommend:

- **Flickr:** www.flickr.com
- **Image Shack:** http://imageshack.us
- **Photobucket:** http://photobucket.com
- **Picasa Web:** http://picasaweb.google.com/home

Each of these services lets you set up an account, create an online gallery, and post images stored on your computer to that online gallery. There's no charge, though some of the services offer specials and discounts on related products. All the sites have advertising.

You might also be able to use an online hosting service with a traditional photo developer. For example, Kodak features the Kodak Easy Share Gallery at `www.kodakgallery.com`. And, WalMart has an online photo service at `photos.walmart.com`.

Signing up for the site

To begin your online photo-sharing journey, visit one of the many free photo galleries on the Internet, such as those listed in the previous section. Most of them work similarly, though for the following steps, I use the Photobucket service as an example.

You start with a photo sharing Web site by setting up your account. I recommend doing this first, even though some of the services may let you upload an image without first creating an account. To create an account on Photobucket, follow these steps:

1. **Open your computer's Web browser.**

2. **Type the online photo sharing service's URL.**

   For Photobucket, it's `www.photobucket.com`.

3. **Click the link that says Join Now.**

   It might also say Sign Up or Create Your Account. If you choose to use Flickr or Picasa Web, you can sign in using your Yahoo! or Google account, respectively.

4. **Fill in the blanks: Type a username and then choose a password.**

   Some sites may ask for more information, such as your e-mail address, gender, or birth year. If you feel uncomfortable answering those questions, choose another service.

5. **Continue working through the steps as necessary, clicking the Next button as you go.**

   Be mindful that you don't accidentally sign up for a service you don't need: Many free hosting services offer special partner deals and options that aren't necessary to using the service. You can skip those offers if you don't want them.

6. **If prompted to create an initial album, do so.**

   After you sign up, I recommend that you immediately log out and sign up again. That way, the Web browser can more easily recall the photo sharing Web site in the future, and maybe even remember your username and password.

7. **After signing up, sign out or log out.**

8. **Immediately after logging out, go back to the main page of the image hosting service.**

9. **Bookmark the image hosting service's page: Press Ctrl+D in your Web browser.**

   Click the Add button to add the hosting service to your browser's list of bookmarks.

10. **Log in to the hosting service.**

11. **If your Web browser prompts you to remember your username and password for the site, do so; click Yes or OK.**

Now you're ready to add some images to the Web site. Keep reading in the next section.

Uploading images

The sending of an image from your computer to the Internet is known as an *upload.* Yes, it's the opposite of *download,* which is when your PC receives a file from the Internet. The steps to upload your digital pictures work similarly for most online image-hosting services:

1. **Log in to your account on the image hosting service.**

2. **If necessary, click an Upload link.**

   Not every photo-hosting service features an Upload link. Some services let you upload directly from your account's home page. The clue: When you see a Browse button, you can upload right away.

3. **If necessary, choose or create an album in which the images will be saved.**

   Some online image-hosting services, such as Picasa Web, may want you to install an upload control. Do so when prompted.

4. **Click the Browse button to locate a digital photo on your computer.**

   Use the Choose File dialog box to locate the digital photo you want. At this point, you're merely choosing a file; the sending part happens later.

5. **Go to the folder that contains the digital image.**

   Remember that the My Pictures or Pictures folder is where those images are usually kept, though you can also use the dialog box to visit a removable storage device, such as your digital camera's media card.

   As with anything dealing with images, it helps if you know where the image is saved on your PC's storage system *and* the image's filename. So, it helps to know the image's filename and the name of the folder in which the image is stored, as well as where that folder is located in your PC's disk storage system.

6. **Choose from the list the file you want to upload.**

7. **Click the Open button to select an image.**

8. **Repeat Steps 4 through 7 as necessary to choose additional images.**

   Most online image-hosting services allow you to "batch" upload images by selecting several at a time to upload.

9. **Choose an album, specify whether the images are public or private, or specify the image's size, if such choices are available.**

10. **Click the Upload or Start Upload button to send to the Internet the images you chose.**

    The procedure may take a few minutes as the images are sent and then processed by the hosting service.

11. **If prompted, add tags to your image or complete whichever additional steps might be presented.**

12. **You may need to click a Save button to save the options you set.**

13. **Enjoy your image on the Internet.**

In some cases, you can use companion software to the online photo hosting service to help manage your uploads. For example, Google's Picasa application integrates seamlessly with the Picasa Web hosting service. To upload images using that program, choose Tools⇨Upload⇨Upload to Web Albums, and you're on your way.

Sharing your images

There's no point in having images floating around the Internet if you can't brag about them and share each one with your friends, family, co-workers, and anyone else on the planet who can use the Web. The online image hosting services are set up to meet those sharing demands.

Most of the image hosting services mentioned in this chapter sport buttons that let you quickly and easily share your images with popular social networking sites such as Facebook and MySpace, blog sites like Blogger and Twitter, or any of a number of popular places that people frequent on the Internet. You also see buttons for adding links to e-mail messages.

The basic procedure involves viewing the image and then finding the Web page address, or *link,* to that image. You then select the link and press Ctrl+C to copy it. After that, open your PC's e-mail program and start a new message. Press Ctrl+V to paste the link. The image doesn't appear in your message, but the recipient can click the link to see your image in their Web browser.

Here are some specific tips for using the image-hosting sites mentioned in this chapter:

- ✔ If you're using Image Shack, after shooting an image, click the link Get Code for Email. Select the link, copy it by pressing Ctrl+C, and then paste it into a new message in your e-mail program.

- ✔ For Photobucket, click the Share link, found directly above the image you want to share. Click the tab labeled Get Link Code, and then select the check box beneath the heading Direct Link for Layout Pages. Copy the link's text, and then paste it into an e-mail message.

- ✔ When you use the Flickr image hosting site, double-click the image you want to share. Then from the right side of the window, click Share This. The second item down, Grab the Link, contains the text you should select, copy, and then paste into an e-mail message.

- ✔ In Picasa Web, click to select the image, and from the right side of the window, choose Link to This Photo. Click the mouse in the text box beneath the word *Link,* and then press Ctrl+C to copy the link. Paste the link into an e-mail message.

- ✔ These photo hosting sites may change their Web page layouts and methods from time to time. The information here is specific as this book goes to press, but may change subtly in the future.

Your Video Life

Unlike photos, videos are just too large to send in e-mail messages. Even when the videos aren't that large, it's just better to send a link to your video on the Internet than to send huge files to your friends, which can be slow and confusing.

The video-hosting service of choice seems to be YouTube, www.youtube.com. Just about anyone and everyone uploads videos to YouTube, some of them professional but many of them amateur. You too can join their ranks, as long as you heed the advice found in this section.

Creating a YouTube account

You can't post a video to YouTube until you obtain a YouTube account. That account is the repository for all your YouTube videos, the main way you share your moving pictures with others on the Internet.

It helps to already have a Google account to expedite setting up a YouTube account. Go to Google's main page, www.google.com, and click the Sign In link to get started or to connect to your Google account.

To set up your account on YouTube, visit www.youtube.com and click the Sign Up link, found near the top of the page. Fill in the blanks and follow the steps to confirm your account. You then need to identify your Google account to complete the process. After your account is set up, you can start putting videos on the Internet.

Uploading a video to YouTube

After you have a YouTube account and you're all logged in (see the preceding section), the next thing you need in order to put a video on the Internet is the video itself. You can refer to Chapter 26 for information on video and your PC. You need to get the video into a final state, ready for sharing.

After connecting to your YouTube account, locate the large Upload button. Clicking that link takes you to a page that describes the upload process and offers some tips and suggestions.

Eventually, you click the Upload Video button, which lets you browse your PC's storage system for the video you prepared.

You need to supply a title, a description, tags, and other information about the video. Be mindful of what you type because the information there is used by others to search for video on YouTube. Click the Save Changes button when you're done.

YouTube takes a few moments to process your video, and takes more time for longer videos. You might have to come back and visit your account's area on YouTube later so that you can share the link.

Sharing your videos

It's easy to share your videos with others using YouTube. Basically, you simply send your pals a Web page link to your video. Because the link consists only of text, the e-mail message doesn't take an eternity to send and receive, nor is there any worry about infected file attachments. It works like this:

1. **Visit your account on YouTube, at www.youtube.com/my_videos.**

   You may have to log in first, but eventually you see a list of all your uploaded videos displayed on the Web page.

2. **Right-click the title (link) of the video you want to share.**

3. **Choose the command Copy Shortcut from the pop-up menu.**

4. **Start a new e-mail message in your PC's e-mail program.**

5. **Press Ctrl+V to paste the YouTube video link into your e-mail message.**

YouTube videos all have a similar-looking link or URL:

```
http://www.youtube.com/watch?v=-QIQhoahbQ8
```

That's it! Clicking that link is how others can view your video on the Internet.

- ✔ Yes, the address `http://www.youtube.com/my_videos` is the same for everyone who has a YouTube account. However:

- ✔ To share your YouTube account's main page with your friends, choose your account name from the left side of the Web page. The URL format for a YouTube account looks like this:

```
http://www.youtube.com/user/account
```

where *account* is the name of your YouTube account.

- ✔ When you view a video on YouTube, you see sharing options listed on the Web page. You usually see two options: URL and Embed. Use the URL option as the direct link to the video's Web page. The Embed option is used to stick the video into a blog or another Web page.

Chapter 29

Kid-Safe Computing

· ·

In This Chapter

▶ Configuring your kid's computer account

▶ Limiting Junior's PC access

▶ Restricting games

▶ Preventing programs from running

▶ Seeing what your kids are up to

▶ Preventing online bullying

· ·

Despite its attraction to kids, a computer can be a decidedly non-kid-friendly thing. Beyond the scourge of malicious software, there are places on the Internet you definitely don't want your precious snowflake to discover. There are games that you may enjoy playing but could give a child nightmares. And, there's the issue of Too Much Computer Time. All those topics can be dealt with, first by being a responsible parent, and second by using the various kid-safe computing tools discussed in this chapter.

> ✔ The information in this chapter is specific to Windows 7, though some of it also applies to Windows Vista. The main difference comes from the innumerable User Account Control (UAC) warnings that pop up during the process in Windows Vista.

> ✔ Windows XP lacks parental controls as a feature.

An Account for Junior

To use the parental controls in Windows, and to ensure your PC's security when Junior is online, set up two accounts on the computer. You set up your own account as an administrator, and then you give the kid a Standard User account. This section explains how to do that.

✔ The Administrator account has full control over the computer. An administrator can change computer settings, install new software, and control other accounts on the computer.

✔ The Standard User account can use the computer but cannot change computer settings, install new software, or access other accounts without an Administrator account's password.

✔ The Standard User account is also known as a *Limited* account.

✔ It's those User Account Control (UAC) warnings that exercise the administrator's privileges in Windows. See Chapter 19.

✔ It doesn't matter whether the Standard User account has a password, but your Administrator account must have a password.

✔ When more than one kid is using the same computer, each should have his or her own Standard User account.

Setting up your Administrator account

Start by setting up your own account. If you already have an account on the computer, skip to the next section, "Confirming your Administrator account." Otherwise, you need to create an Administrator account on the computer. Follow these steps:

1. **Log on to the computer using an existing account or the computer's only account, if it has only one.**

2. **Open the Control Panel.**

3. **From beneath the User Accounts and Family Safety heading, choose the link Add or Remove User Accounts.**

   The Manage Accounts window appears.

4. **Click the link Create a New Account.**

5. **Type a name for the account, such as** Parent, **or use your own name.**

6. **Choose Administrator.**

7. **Click the Create Account button.**

8. **Log off the current account: From the Start button menu, choose the Log Off command from the Shutdown menu.**

   See Figure 4-2, in Chapter 4, for information about the Shutdown menu.

9. **Log in using the new account you created.**

   The account has no password, so you don't need to type one when you first log in. The account does, however, need a password:

10. **Pop up the Start button menu.**

11. **Click the mouse on your account's picture, found at the top of the Start button's menu.**

    The User Accounts window appears.

12. **Choose the link Create a Password for Your Account.**

    The Create Your Password window shows up.

13. **Type the password.**

14. **Type the password again to confirm it.**

15. **Type a password hint that isn't the same as the password.**

16. **Click the Create Password button.**

Your Administrator account is now created, and you're ready to manage the computer for your kid. Skip to the section "Adding an account for Junior"; or, when Junior already has an account on the computer, skip to the section "Configuring Junior's account."

Confirming your Administrator account

If you already have an account on the computer, ensure that it's an Administrator account:

1. **Log in to your account on your child's computer.**

2. **Pop up the Start button menu.**

3. **Click your account picture, found in the upper right area of the Start button menu.**

    You'll find yourself in the User Accounts window.

4. **Ensure that your account is administrator level; check for the word** *Administrator* **below your account name, on the right side of the window.**

5. **If your account isn't at administrator level, log in to the computer using the Administrator account to set up your kid's account.**

6. **Ensure that your account has a password; check for the words** *Password Protected,* **found below the word** *Administrator* **on the right side of the window.**

    If your account doesn't have a password, click the link Create a Password for Your Account and follow Steps 13 through 16 in the preceding section.

7. **Close the window.**

Now you need to add an account for your kid, covered in the next section, or confirm that the account is limited, covered in the section "Configuring Junior's account."

Adding an account for Junior

When your kid doesn't yet have his or her own account on the computer, you need to add one. Follow these steps:

1. **Open the Control Panel.**

2. **Click the heading User Accounts and Family Safety.**

3. **From beneath the heading User Accounts, click the link Add or Remove User Accounts.**

4. **Click the link Create a New Account.**

5. **Type the account name.**

   You might want to ask your kid which account name they want.

6. **Choose Standard User.**

7. **Click the Create Account button.**

   You don't need to slap on a password for the account, but the kids can add a password to protect their stuff later.

Repeat the steps in this section for each kid who uses the computer.

You're now done setting up the accounts. The parental controls can be applied per the directions in the later section "Parental Controls."

Configuring Junior's account

When Snowflake or Buster already has an account on the computer, follow these steps to ensure that they also have a Standard User account:

1. **Open the Control Panel.**

2. **Click the link Add or Remove User Accounts, found beneath the heading User Accounts and Family Safety.**

3. **Ensure that it says Standard User beneath Junior's account name in the window.**

   If so, you're done. If not, continue:

4. **Click Junior's account picture.**

5. **Click the link Change the Account Type.**

6. **Choose Standard User.**

7. **Click the Change Account Type button.**

8. **Close the window.**

After the account is configured, you're ready to apply the parental controls.

Parental Controls

To extend your parental fingers into the PC, and better regulate Junior's computer use, you must activate the parental controls in Windows. Here's how that's done:

1. **Log in to Windows using your account.**

2. **Open the Control Panel.**

3. **Choose the link Set Up Parental Controls for Any User, beneath the heading User Accounts and Family Safety.**

   The Parental Controls window appears, listing all accounts on the computer.

4. **Choose the account to control; click its icon.**

5. **In the User Controls window, choose On, Enforce Current Settings.**

   The User Controls window is shown in Figure 29-1. It's where you apply the various parental controls mentioned in this chapter.

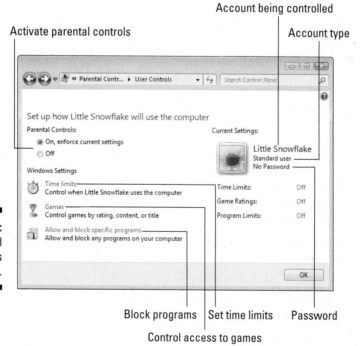

Account being controlled

Activate parental controls

Account type

Figure 29-1: Set parental controls here.

Block programs Set time limits Password

Control access to games

6. **Apply the parental controls; refer to the next few sections.**

7. **When you're done setting parental controls, click the OK button to close the User Controls window.**

Repeat the steps in this section for each kid's account on your PC.

Setting time limits

You can control when your kids can access the computer by placing time limits on their accounts. That way, they can log in and use the computer only during the hours you specify — and the computer logs them off when the time runs out.

To set time limits, open the User Controls window (see Figure 29-1) by following Steps 1 through 4 in the preceding section. Choose the link Time Limits to display the Time Restrictions window, shown in Figure 29-2.

Drag the mouse over the times you don't want Junior to access the computer. Click OK.

Time blocked

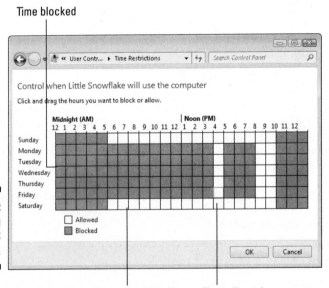

Figure 29-2:
Restricting
Junior's PC
time.

Drag mouse over hour slots to select.   Time allowed

Controlling access to games

Windows lets you combine the parental controls with the Entertainment Software Rating Board (ESRB) game rating system to control which computer games your kid can play on the PC. You can restrict access to games by the game name, its rating, or the contents of the game (violence or adult themes, for example).

To restrict access to certain games, open the User Controls window (refer to Figure 29-1) by following Steps 1 through 4 in the earlier section "Parental Controls." Click the Games link to view the Game Controls window.

In the Game Controls window, choose Yes to restrict game access. You can then choose to block the games by their ESRB ratings: Click the Set Game Ratings link. You can also choose to block specific games by clicking the Block or Allow Specific Games link.

Click OK and close the various windows when you're done putting the clamps on junior's gaming appetite.

> ✔ The ESRB defines and sets ratings for computer games similarly to the way the MPAA rates movies.
>
> ✔ Visit the ESRB Web site www.esrb.org for more information on the ratings system.

Blocking programs

In addition to blocking computer games, you can restrict your kid's access to any program that runs on your computer. For example, you can prevent them from running your computer's home finance program or other programs you'd rather have them not playing with. Or, you might want to block them from using instant messaging tools that they might be abusing.

To activate the Applications Restrictions feature, heed these steps:

1. **Open the Control Panel.**

2. **Choose the link Set Up Parental Controls for Any User, found beneath the heading User Accounts and Family Safety.**

3. **Choose the icon for account to restrict.**

4. **Click the link Allow and Block Specific Programs.**

   The Applications Restrictions window appears.

5. **Choose the second (bottom) option, *User* Can Only Use the Programs I Allow.**

   Soon, a list is populated, detailing all programs found on your computer.

6. **Place a check mark by the programs you want Junior to run.**

   Only those programs can be run by that user.

   Yes, the program names are technical and mysterious! When you don't recognize a program name, don't put a check mark in its box.

7. **Click the OK button.**

Beyond restricting program access, you don't need to worry about your sweetums getting into your account and looking at your stuff. First, your account has a password, right? Second, all accounts in Windows are separate from each other. When your child has a Standard User account, they cannot peek into your account's folders or access your own computer data, e-mail, or other private information without knowing your account's password.

PC Parenting

Here are my parental rules for kids who use computers:

✔ Know your kids. Talk with them. Be their parent.

✔ Exercise your license to drop in on them and see what they're doing on the computer.

✔ Use the parental controls provided in Windows, as covered in this chapter.

Spying on your kids

Before jumping into your James Bond suit and beginning the art of snooping around Junior's PC, talk with your child. Ask what's up or whether anything is bothering them. It may be nothing, but as a parent, you should know your own child, so use your best judgment when you suspect that something is amiss.

When mood swings and unusual behavior dictate, you can check up on your kid's account to see what they've been up to. You need to log in under their account and review two things: their recent Web pages visited and their document history.

The Web history: To review the Web history, open your child's Web browser and press Ctrl+H in Internet Explorer. Open the various dates and Web sites listed on the History tab (on the left side of the browser window). If the sites look suspicious, click their links to visit them. You'll know in a few minutes whether you have cause for concern.

Recent documents: Examine documents your child has opened recently by visiting the Start menu and opening the Recent Documents menu next to Recently Opened Programs. (Refer to Figure 23-1, in Chapter 23, to find out where to look.) In Windows Vista, the recent documents are found on the Recent Items list on the right side of the Start button menu.

What kind of recent documents are you looking for? You won't know until you open them yourself.

If you find anything unsavory, your next step is to discuss your discovery with your child. Remind them that their activities aren't allowed by you as a parent. Then cite your reasons and concerns.

- ✔ I don't recommend buying PC snooping software. If the situation with your child is so great that you feel this type of software is necessary, you already have a big problem on your hands. Sit down and discuss the situation with your child immediately.

- ✔ Your child can cover their tracks, especially when they're already computer savvy. In fact, if you notice that the Web browser history seems surprisingly empty for the amount of time Buster spends on the PC, something is probably going on.

- ✔ Talk with your kids, not at them.

Dealing with a cyberbully

Count among the many downsides of glorious technology the anonymous, nasty, and persistent creep commonly called a *cyberbully*. Like his (or her) schoolyard namesake, they can make life online a living hell for you, your child, and your entire family.

Unlike the bully you might remember from childhood, a cyberbully has the sneaky advantage of stealthy anonymity on the Internet. This person is found in chat rooms, instant messaging programs, and even cellphone text messages — places your technically adept child probably clings to for social interaction.

Beyond intimidation, the cyberbully can use personal attacks, such as making private information public, creating false images using photo-editing techniques, faking messages from other friends, and generally misrepresenting your child's behavior. Such attacks have devastating emotional effects, especially on vulnerable children.

For good advice on cyberbullying, visit the Web site www.cyberbulling.org. You'll find information there on how to deal with a cyberbully as well as tips on how you and your family can avoid becoming one of their victims.

✔ The best way to avoid having personal or embarrassing information float around the Internet is not to put it on the Internet in the first place. Teaching your children about modesty and self-respect goes a long way.

✔ Many areas have laws against cyberbullying. Check with the police if you or your children become a victim.

✔ Cyberbullying may also violate the terms of the Internet service provider (ISP) contract. Contact your ISP if you feel victimized.

✔ It helps to document cyberbullying episodes: Print Web pages, and note when the attacks occur.

✔ Adults can also be victims of cyberbullying, though the terms that are used are *cyberharassment* and *cyberstalking*.

Part VI
The Part of Tens

The 5th Wave   By Rich Tennant

"Oh, jeez! I hate when you fish out toasted chips with a butter knife!"

In this part . . .

My grandmother told me that "things happen in threes." Maybe. I would counter Grandma with "Things *always* happen, it's just easy to name three things when given the chance." What's far more difficult is to move up from three to ten. Though anyone can name three state capitals, three famous bald guys, or three things not to step in, it's more difficult to repeat the task with ten items.

Rest easy: I'm not asking you to come up with lists full of ten items. Instead, I've done that job for you: I've created some handy lists of tens, helpful information for any computer user. And I've put those lists in this part of the book, the Part of Tens.

Chapter 30

Ten PC Commandments

*T*ake it from me: I've been there, I've done that. I've survived the worst of using a computer and have lived to write about it. Let me share my experiences with you by passing along a chunk of digital wisdom. I may not have descended from Mt. Sinai, and I certainly look nothing like Charlton Heston, but here are my Ten PC Commandments.

1. Thou Shalt Not Fear Thy PC

The computer isn't out to get you. It won't explode suddenly. It harbors no sinister intelligence. Honestly, it's really rather dumb.

Knowledge is the key to overcoming fear.

II. Thou Shalt Save Thy Work

Whenever you're creating something blazingly original, use the Save command *at once!* In fact, use the Save command even when you make something stupid that you don't even want to save. You're not going to run out of room on the PC's storage system by saving stuff you don't need, so why not save for the sake of it?

You never know when your computer will meander off to watch NASCAR or chat with the wireless router across the street while you're hoping to finish the last few paragraphs of that report. Save your work as often as possible. Save when you get up from your computer. Save when you answer the phone. *Save! Save! Save!*

III. Thou Shalt Back Up Thy Files

Nothing beats having that just-in-case copy of your stuff. The computer itself can run a backup program to make that safety copy, or you can duplicate your files yourself. Either way, that secondary, backup copy can save your skin someday.

See Chapter 22 for information on Backup.

IV. That Shalt Not Open or Delete Things Unknownst

Here's the rule, written in modern English: *Delete only those files or folders you created yourself.*

Unlike computer hardware, where sticky labels with red letters read Do Not Open, unknown computer files have no warning labels. There should be! Windows is brimming with unusual and unknown files. Don't mess with 'em. Don't delete them. Don't move them. Don't rename them. And, especially, don't open them to see what they are. Sometimes, opening an unknown icon can lead to trouble.

V. Thou Shalt Not Be a Sucker

The Bad Guys are successful in spreading their evil, malicious software on the Internet because people let down their guard. Don't be a sucker for *human engineering*. Basically, here's a list of don'ts for you to adhere to:

- **Don't reply to any spam e-mail.** Doing so brings you even more spam. A popular trick is for spammers to include some text that says "Reply to this message if you do not want to receive any further messages." Don't! Replying to spam signals the spammers that they have a "live one" and you then receive even more spam. Never, ever, reply to spam!

- **Don't open unknown or unexpected e-mail attachments.** Seriously, you're not missing anything if you don't open them. Yet that's how human engineering works: The e-mail fools you into believing that opening the attachment is important. It's not.

- **Never open any program file attachment.** These attachments end with the filename extensions exe, com, or vbs. See Chapter 20 for more information on filename extensions and how to display them in Windows.

VI. Thou Shalt Use Antivirus Software, Yea Verily, and Keepeth It Up-to-Date

I highly recommend that you use antivirus software on your PC. Keep that software up-to-date. See Chapter 19 for more computer security advice.

VII. Thou Shalt Upgrade Wisely

New hardware and software come out all the time. The new stuff is generally better and faster, and it's important to some people to be the First On The Block to have a new hardware gizmo or software upgrade. You don't have to be that person.

- Upgrade your software only if you truly need the new features it offers, if you need to have that version to be compatible with your coworkers, or if the new version fixes problems and bugs that you're experiencing.

- Buy hardware that's compatible with your PC. Especially when you have an older computer, confirm that the new hardware will work with your system.

VIII. Thou Shalt Compute at a Proper Posture

Using a computer can be a pain. Literally. You must observe proper posture and sitting position while you operate a PC. By doing so, you can avoid back strain and the risk of repetitive stress injury (RSI). Here are some suggestions:

Get an ergonomic keyboard: Even if your wrists are as limber as a politician's spine, you might consider an *ergonomic* keyboard. That type is specially designed at an angle to relieve the stress of typing for long — or short — periods.

Use a wrist pad: Wrist pads elevate your wrists so that you type in a proper position, with your palms *above* the keyboard, not resting below the spacebar.

Adjust your chair: Sit at the computer with your elbows level with your wrists.

Adjust your monitor: Your head should not tilt down or up when you view the computer screen. It should be straight ahead, which doesn't help your wrists as much as it helps your neck.

IX. Thou Shalt Keepeth Windows Up-to-Date

Microsoft keeps Windows continually fresh and updated. The updates fix problems, but they also address vulnerabilities that the Bad Guys exploit. In my book (which you're reading now), that's a good thing, but it's effective only when you use the Windows Update service on a regular basis. See Chapter 23.

There's a difference between *updating* Windows, which I recommend, and *upgrading* Windows, which I don't recommend.

X. Thou Shalt Properly Shut Down Windows

When you're done with Windows, shut it down. Choose the Shut Down command from the Start button menu. The PC automatically turns itself off.

Refer to Chapter 4 for detailed PC shutdown instructions.

Chapter 31

Ten Tips from a PC Guru

1 don't consider myself a computer expert or genius or guru, though many have called me those nasty names. I'm just a guy who understands how computers work. Or, better than that, I understand how computer people think and I can translate it into English for you. Given that, here are some tips and suggestions so that you and your PC can go on your merry way.

Remember That You're in Charge

You bought the computer. You clean up after its messes. You feed it optical discs when it asks for them. You press the Any key (which is the Enter key). You control the computer — simple as that.

Think of the computer as an infant. You must treat it the same way, with respect and caring attention. Don't feel that the computer is bossing you around any more than you feel that a baby is bossing you around during its 3 a.m. feedings. They're both helpless creatures, subject to your every whim. Be gentle, but be in charge.

Mind Who "Helps" You

Nothing beats getting computer help when you need it. Most computer nerds love to help beginners. Sometimes, they help you at no cost, though you shouldn't abuse a good relationship by becoming a pest.

When you can't find help, use the support you paid for: from your manufacturer, computer dealer, software developers, and Internet service provider.

Above all, keep in mind that not everyone who tries to help you truly knows what they're doing. My advice is to avoid friends or (especially) relatives who offer to "fix" your PC when you haven't asked them to. That leads to big trouble.

- ✔ Treat your PC like your wallet. You wouldn't hand it over to anyone, right?

- ✔ You may like your smart nephew Victor, but don't let him near your computer. Don't let the grandkids or out-of-town relatives "play" on the Internet while they come to visit. You'll thank me later.

Give Yourself Time to Learn

Things take time. No one sits down at a computer and instantly knows everything, especially with new software. True, the boss may have given you only a day to learn how to work some new program. Such a task is unrealistic and unfair (and you can literally point to this sentence for support).

It takes about a week to become comfortable with an application. It takes longer to really figure out how it works, even if you get a good book on the topic. Honestly, I don't think that anyone out there knows *everything* about a major software product. So, don't set the bar so high that you can't leap over it.

Create Separate Accounts

When there are two of you, make two accounts on the computer. That way, you can keep your stuff separate. The issue isn't secrecy; it's just organization. It's better to have one account for each person who uses the computer than to have two or more people share — and mess up — the only account.

The same thought applies to e-mail: Get yourself separate e-mail accounts, one for you and one for your partner or one for everyone who uses the computer. That way, you receive only your mail and you don't miss anything because someone else has read or deleted it.

You can use the information from Chapter 29 to set up multiple accounts in Windows.

Use a UPS

The uninterruptible power supply (UPS) is a boon to computing anywhere in the world where the power is less than reliable. Plug your console into the UPS. Plug your monitor into the UPS. If the UPS has extra battery-backed-up sockets, plug your external hard drive into one.

Chapter 4 has information on using a UPS as well as using a power strip.

Consider Some Hardware Upgrades

Now that the computer is a consumer commodity, people don't take the time to research their purchases beforehand. The result is often that you buy less computer than you truly need. To remedy the situation, a hardware upgrade is in order.

The first thing to consider upgrading is computer memory. Unless your PC is already packed with RAM (and my guess is that it isn't), you can add more memory at a relatively low cost and see a massive increase in performance.

The second thing to consider is getting a second hard drive, such as an external hard drive for making backups. You can add a second internal hard drive to most PCs, which gives you more storage. Or, you can replace your PC's main hard drive with a higher-capacity, faster model.

A third issue to look into is getting a headset for online communications as well as for computer games. A *headset* resembles a pair of headphones but with the addition of a microphone. I recommend that you avoid the cheaper headsets; the more expensive versions are much nicer to wear and better reproduce sound.

✔ Your computer dealer can upgrade PC memory, or you can do it yourself. I recommend Crucial for online memory purchases: www.crucial.com. The Web site even scans your computer to determine which memory upgrades you need. But:

✔ Upgrading PC memory can be a scary thing! You might consider having someone else do it for you.

✔ See Chapter 7 for information on adding external storage to your PC.

✔ Replacing the PC's main hard drive adds years to your computer's life, but the process of copying over the original hard drive's contents —

referred to as *cloning* — can be very, very technical. My advice: Have someone else do it.

✔ Try to get a headset with a volume adjuster and mute button built in.

Avoid Crying "Wolf" in E-Mail

People new to PCs and fresh on e-mail somehow feel emboldened that they're personally responsible for the health, safety, and entertainment of everyone else they know on the Internet. Let me be honest: If you're just starting out, be aware that those of us already on the Internet have read that joke. We have seen the funny pictures. We know the stories. And, everyone has already sent us that e-mail saying that if you send it to seven people you know, somehow Bill Gates will write you a check for $4,000.

Please don't be part of the problem. Telling others about viruses and *real* threats is one thing, but spreading Internet hoaxes is something else. Before you send out a blanket e-mail to everyone you know, confirm that you're sending the truth. Visit a few Web sites, such as `www.truthorfiction.com` or `www.vmyths.com`. If the message you're spreading is true, please include a few Web page links to verify it.

Thanks for being part of the solution and not part of the problem!

Don't Reinstall Windows

A myth floating around tech-support sites says that the solution to all your ills is to reinstall Windows. Some suspect that tech-support people even claim that it's common for most Windows users to reinstall at least once a year. That's rubbish.

You *never* need to reinstall Windows. All problems are fixable. It's just that the tech-support people are urged by their bottom-line-watching overlords to get you off the line quickly. Therefore, they resort to a drastic solution rather than try to discover what the true problem is. If you press them, they *will* tell you what's wrong and how to fix it.

✔ In all my years of using a computer, I have never reinstalled Windows or had to reformat my hard drive. It's not even a good idea just to refresh the bits on the hard drive or whatever other nonsense they dish up. There just isn't a need to reinstall Windows, ever. Period.

✔ Refer to my books *Troubleshooting Your PC For Dummies* as well as *Troubleshooting & Maintaining Your PC All-In-One For Dummies* (both from Wiley) for all the various solutions you can try instead of reformatting your hard drive or reinstalling Windows.

Shun the Hype

The computer industry is rife with hype. Magazines and Web sites tout this or that solution, crow about new trends, and preannounce standards that supposedly will make everything you have obsolete. Ignore all of it!

My gauge for hype is whether the thing that's hyped is shipping as a standard part of a PC. I check the ads. If they're shipping the item, I write about it. Otherwise, it's a myth and may not happen. Avoid being lured by the hype.

Remember Not to Take This Computer Stuff Too Seriously

Hey, simmer down. Computers aren't part of life. They're nothing more than mineral deposits and petroleum products. Close your eyes and take a few deep breaths. Imagine that you're lying on a soft, sandy beach in the South Pacific. Having just dined on an exotic salad, you close your eyes as the surf lulls you into a well-deserved afternoon nap.

Next, you're getting your feet rubbed as you sip champagne and feel the bubbles explode atop your tongue. Soothing music plays as everyone who's ever said a bad thing about you in your life tosses $100 bills at you.

Now, slowly open your eyes. It's just a dumb computer. Really. Don't take it too seriously.

Index

• X •

• Y •

• Z •